Richard Stanley

ROSE GEORGE is the author of *The Big Necessity* and *A Life Removed*. She has written for *The New York Times*, *Slate*, *The Guardian*, and *Scientific American*, among many other publications. She lives in Yorkshire, England.

ALSO BY ROSE GEORGE

The Big Necessity:
The Unmentionable World of Human Waste
and Why It Matters

Praise for *Ninety Percent of Everything*

"Fabulous." —*Time*

"A fascinating account." —*The Seattle Times*

"A remarkable work of embedded reportage—hair-raising, witty, compassionate. . . . An ethnographic travelogue that is as fascinating as it is troublingly insightful." —*The Guardian* (UK)

"Deeply researched and compelling . . . Plenty of books promise to reveal the secrets of little-known worlds but few actually deliver. This is one that does." —*The Telegraph* (UK)

"A marvel of information, insight, and intelligence laced with humor, humanity, and high spirits." —*The Times* (UK)

"A very important book . . . George really does ask the right questions. She has sussed out the 'frontier' nature of so much of shipping, and the limited laws which prevail on the high seas, with ships flying strange flags and registered in exotic places. . . . She is an outsider, but has succeeded in getting inside shipping's skin and penetrating the thick carapace with which the industry likes to protect itself." —*Lloyd's List*

"Heart-stopping, mind-boggling . . . A superb book, well-written and bravely researched at sea." —*Energy Metro Desk*

"Worth comparing to John McPhee's *Looking for a Ship* . . . Offers a fascinating look at an anonymous industry affecting our daily lives, and gives a personal face to those working in that industry." —*The Daily News* (Galveston)

"Consistently illuminating in-depth analysis . . . An eye-opening maritime exposé." —*Kirkus Reviews*

"Rose George beautifully captures the surprising nuances of this little-known world: beauty and privation, pathos and greed, tragedy and hilarity. Her strong, spare, gleaming prose steams along, powered by curiosity, compassion, outrage. As a writer, a reporter, and a human being, George is—stand by for nautical term—First Rate."
—Mary Roach, author of *Gulp: Adventures on the Alimentary Canal*

"For a modern seafaring adventure, there couldn't be a better guide than Rose George. Her intelligence, curiosity, and compassion shine through on every page to reveal a fascinating world that no one knows about, though it is fundamental to our economy and way of life." —Chris Anderson, curator, TED Conference

"The two greatest stories are supposed to be 'A man goes on a journey' and 'A stranger comes to town.' In this enthralling, literally wide-ranging book, Rose George tells both: She goes on a voyage that few other journalists have accomplished, and she unveils the unknown seafarers who bring us all the world's goods. Her sympathetic, deeply reported, and unexpectedly poignant account reveals the private, prickly, brave tribe on which much of our daily lives, and most of the world's interlinked economies, depend."
—Maryn McKenna, author of *Superbug: The Fatal Menace of MRSA*

"To the classic incredible journeys—*Moby Dick, Two Years Before the Mast*—Rose George adds another, her voyage round the world aboard a container ship, revealing what happens before the big bang of merchandise explodes from the high seas into civilization via cargo containers holding thousands of sneakers, millions of plastic bags, and trillions of other products."

—Curtis C. Ebbesmeyer, coauthor of
Flotsametrics and the Floating World

"The best books make you think about our world in a new way, and *Ninety Percent of Everything* is definitely one of those books. In this smart, lucid, and often beautiful investigation of the little-known world of freight shipping, Rose George finds new ways to illuminate our impact on the planet and explore that restless sense of motion that so often defines who we are."

—Deborah Blum,
author of *The Poisoner's Handbook:
Murder and the Birth of Forensic
Medicine in Jazz Age New York*

"Rose George, with her precise and beautiful clarity of prose, has now fired a brilliant star-shell over the wine-dark sea and the ships that pass in its night, illuminating the details of the invisible ocean industry that is, and always will be, essential to all of us."

—Simon Winchester, author of *Atlantic:
Great Sea Battles, Heroic Discoveries, Titanic Storms,
and a Vast Ocean of a Million Stories*

NINETY PERCENT

OF

EVERYTHING

Inside Shipping, the Invisible Industry

That Puts Clothes on Your Back,

Gas in Your Car,

and Food on Your Plate

ROSE GEORGE

Picador

A Metropolitan Book
Henry Holt and Company
New York

A different version of part of this book was published in Slate in 2010.

www.picadorusa.com
www.twitter.com/picadorusa • www.facebook.com/picadorusa
picadorbookroom.tumblr.com

Picador® is a U.S. registered trademark and is used by Henry Holt and Company under license from Pan Books Limited.

For book club information, please visit www.facebook.com/picadorbookclub or e-mail marketing@picadorusa.com.

Designed by Meryl Sussman Levavi

The Library of Congress has cataloged the Henry Holt edition as follows:

George, Rose, 1969–
    Ninety percent of everything : inside shipping, the invisible industry that puts clothes on your back, gas in your car, and food on your plate / Rose George.— First edition.
        p. cm.
    Includes bibliographical references and index.
    ISBN 978-0-8050-9263-9 (hardcover)
    ISBN 978-0-8050-9604-0 (e-book)
    1. Shipping—History.   2. Freight and freightage—History.   I. Title.
    HE571.G465 2013
    388'.044—dc23   2013000293

Picador Paperback ISBN 978-1-250-05829-4

Picador books may be purchased for educational, business, or promotional use. For information on bulk purchases, please contact Macmillan Corporate and Premium Sales Department at 1-800-221-7945, extension 5442, or write specialmarkets@macmillan.com.

First published in the United States by Metropolitan Books,
an imprint of Henry Holt and Company.

First Picador Edition: September 2014

10   9   8   7   6 . 5   4   3   2   1

For Emma Louise Page

I'm not a great admirer of the sea. There's too much of it from my point of view.

—MAURICE OLIVER, lighthouse keeper

CONTENTS

NINETY PERCENT

OF

EVERYTHING

Maersk Kendal, *three football pitches long*

(ROSE GEORGE)

INTRODUCTION

FRIDAY. NO SENSIBLE SAILOR GOES TO SEA ON THE DAY OF THE Crucifixion or the journey will be followed by ill-will and malice. So here I am on a Friday in June, looking up at a giant ship that will carry me from this southern English port of Felixstowe to Singapore, for five weeks and 9,288 nautical miles through the pillars of Hercules, pirate waters, and weather. I stop at the bottom of the ship's gangway, waiting for an escort and stilled and awed by the immensity of this thing, much of her the color of a summer-day sky, so blue; her bottom is painted dull red, her name—*Maersk Kendal*—written large on her side.

There is such busyness around me. Everything in a modern container port is enormous, overwhelming, crushing. *Kendal*, of course, but also the thundering trucks, the giant boxes in many colors, the massive gantry cranes that straddle the quay, reaching up ten stories and over to ships that stretch three football pitches in length. There are hardly any humans to be seen. When the journalist Henry Mayhew visited London's docks in 1849, he found "decayed and bankrupt master butchers, master bakers, publicans, grocers, old soldiers, old sailors, Polish refugees, broken-down gentlemen, discharged lawyers' clerks, suspended Government clerks, almsmen, pensioners, servants, thieves." They have long since gone. This is a Terminator terminal, a place where humans are hidden in crane or truck cabs, where everything is clamorous machines.

It took me three train journeys to reach Felixstowe from my northern English home. On one train, where no seats were to be had, I swayed in the vestibule with two men wearing the uniform of a rail freight company. I'm about to leave on a freighter, I said, but a ship. They looked bewildered. A ship? they said. "Why on earth do you want to go to sea?"

Why on earth.

I am an islander who has never been maritime. I don't sail or dive. I swim, although not in terrifying oceans. But standing here in the noise and industry, looking up almost two hundred feet— higher than Niagara Falls—to the top of *Kendal*, I feel the giddiness of a Christmas morning child. Some of this is the rush of escape, for which I had reasons. Some is the pull of the sea. And some comes from the knowledge that I am about to embark to a place and space that is usually off-limits and hidden. The public is not allowed on a ship like this, nor even on the dock. There are no ordinary citizens to witness the workings of an industry that is one of the most fundamental to their daily existence. These ships and boxes belong to a business that feeds, clothes, warms, and supplies us. They have fueled if not created globalization. They are the reason behind your cheap T-shirt and reasonably priced television. But who looks behind a television now and sees the ship that brought it? Who cares about the men who steered your breakfast cereal through winter storms? How ironic that the more ships have grown in size and consequence, the less space they take up in our imagination.

The Maritime Foundation, a charity that promotes seafarer matters, recently made a video called *Unreported Ocean*. It asked the residents of Southampton, a port city in England, how many goods are transported by sea. The answers were varied but uniformly wrong. They all had the interrogative upswing of the unsure.

"Thirty-five percent?"

"Not a lot?"

The answer is, nearly everything. Sometimes on trains I play a numbers game. A woman listening to headphones: 8. A man reading a book: 15. The child in the stroller: at least 4 including the stroller. The game is to reckon how many of our clothes and possessions and food products have been transported by ship. The beads around the woman's neck; the man's iPhone and Japanese-made headphones. Her Sri Lanka–made skirt and blouse; his printed-in-China book. I can always go wider, deeper, and in any direction. The fabric of the seats. The rolling stock. The fuel powering the train. The conductor's uniform; the coffee in my cup; the fruit in my bag. Definitely the fruit, so frequently shipped in refrigerated containers that it has been given its own temperature. Two degrees Celsius is "chill" but 13 degrees is "banana."

Trade carried by sea has grown fourfold since 1970 and is still growing. In 2011, the 360 commercial ports of the United States took in international goods worth $1.73 trillion, or eighty times the value of all U.S. trade in 1960. There are more than one hundred thousand ships at sea carrying all the solids, liquids, and gases that we need to live. Only six thousand are container vessels like *Kendal*, but they make up for this small proportion by their dizzying capacity. The biggest container ship can carry fifteen thousand boxes. It can hold 746 million bananas, one for every European on one ship. If the containers of Maersk alone were lined up, they would stretch eleven thousand miles or nearly halfway around the planet. If they were stacked instead, they would be fifteen hundred miles high,

7,530 Eiffel Towers. If *Kendal* discharged her containers onto trucks, the line of traffic would be forty miles long.

Trade has always traveled and the world has always traded. Ours, though, is the era of extreme interdependence. Hardly any nation is now self-sufficient. In 2011, a quarter of the United Kingdom's gas came by sea. The United States relies on ships to bring in two-thirds of its oil supplies. Every day, thirty-eight million tons of crude oil sets off by sea somewhere, although you may not notice it. As in Los Angeles, New York, and other port cities, London has moved its working docks out of the city, away from residents. Ships are bigger now and need deeper harbors, so they call at Newark or Tilbury or Felixstowe, not Liverpool or South Street. Security concerns have hidden ports further, behind barbed wire and badge wearing and KEEP OUT signs. To reach this quayside in Felixstowe, I had to pass through several gatekeepers and passport controllers, and past radiation-detecting gates often triggered by naturally radioactive cargo such as cat litter and broccoli.

It is harder to wander into the world of shipping, now, so people don't. The chief of the British navy—who is known as the First Sea Lord, although the army chief is not a Land Lord—says we suffer from "sea blindness" now. We travel by cheap flights, not ocean liners. The sea is a distance to be flown over, a downward backdrop between takeoff and landing, a blue expanse that soothes on the moving flight map as the plane jerks over it. It is for leisure and beaches and fish and chips, not for use or work. Perhaps we believe that everything travels by air, or magically and instantaneously like information (which is actually anchored by cables on the seabed), not by hefty ships that travel more slowly than senior citizens drive.

You could trace the flight of the ocean from our consciousness in the pages of great newspapers. Fifty years ago, the shipping news was news. Cargo departures were reported daily. Now the most necessary business on the planet has mostly been shunted into the pages of specialized trade papers such as *Lloyd's List* and the *Journal of Commerce*, fine publications but out of the reach of most, when an annual subscription to *Lloyd's List* costs more than $2,000 a year. In 1965, shipping was so central to daily life in London that when Winston Churchill's funeral barge left Tower Pier to travel up the Thames, it embarked in front of dock cranes that dipped their jibs, movingly, with respect. The cranes are gone now or immobile, garden furniture for wharves that house costly apartments or indifferent restaurants.

Humans have sent goods by water for four thousand years. In the fifteenth century BC, Queen Hatshepsut of Egypt sent a fleet to the Land of Punt and brought back panther skins and ebony, frankincense and dancing pygmies. Perhaps Hatshepsut counts as the first shipping tycoon, before the Romans, Phoenicians, and Greeks took over (she was certainly the only Egyptian queen who preferred to be called king). Shipping history is full of such treats and treasures. Cardamom, silk, ginger, and gold, ivory and saffron. The Routes of Spice, Tea, and Salt, of Amber and Incense. There were trade winds, sailor towns and sails, chaos and color. Now there are freight routes, turnarounds, and boxes, and the cool mechanics of modern industry, but there is still intrigue and fortune. Maersk ships travel regular routes named Boomerang and Yo Yo (from Australia and Yokohama), or the Bossa Nova and Samba around South America. There are wealthy tycoons still, Norse, Greek, and Danish, belonging to family companies who maintain a level of privacy that makes a Swiss banker seem verbose. Publicly listed shipping companies are still a minority. Even shipping people admit that their industry is clubby, insular, difficult. In this business, it is considered normal that the official Greek shipowners' association refuses to say how many members it has, because it can.

Maersk is different. It must be, because it is letting me onto a working ship, usually barred to ordinary citizens. Even Maersk officers are no longer permitted to take family members to sea because of concerns about safety from pirates. But Maersk is known for risks, at least in the places where its name is known at all, which is in shipping and Denmark. I find Maersk fascinating. It is the Coca-Cola of freight with none of the fame. Its parent company A. P. Møller–Maersk is Denmark's largest company, its sales equal to 20 percent of Denmark's GDP; its ships use more oil than the entire nation. I like the fact that Maersk is not a household name outside the pages of *Lloyd's List*; that it has an online store selling Maersk-branded T-shirts and cookie tins called Stargate, after the company symbol of a seven-point star, white on a background of Maersk Blue, a distinct color that can be created from a Pantone recipe. The star has seven points, goes an employee joke, because they work seven days a week. I like that Maersk is a first name. It's like a massive global corporation named Derek. For much of recent history the company was run by Arnold Maersk Mc-Kinney Møller, son of the founder, a pleasingly eccentric patriarch who worked until he died in 2012 at age ninety-eight. Mr. Møller was known for his firm control of his firm; for walking up five flights of stairs to his office, although when he reached ninety-four he allowed his driver to carry his briefcase; for being one of only three commoners to receive Denmark's Order of the Elephant; and for driving around Copenhagen in a modest car although he was one of the two richest people in Denmark. The other inherited Lego.

Reuters, in a profile of Maersk, describes it as "active primarily in the marine transportation sector." Behind that "primarily" are multitudes. Founded in 1904 with one ship named *Svendborg*, Maersk—through its subsidiary Maersk Line—now operates the largest container shipping company in the world, with a fleet of six hundred vessels. It also has the vast and dizzying interests of a global corporation. It is active in 130 countries and has 117,000 employees. It is looking for and drilling for oil and gas in Denmark,

Angola, Brazil, Greenland, Qatar, Algeria, Norway, Iraq, the United States, and Kazakhstan. If you have visited Denmark, you have probably shopped in a Maersk-owned supermarket. You can save in a Maersk-owned bank. The list of its companies and subsidiaries is twelve pages long, double columns. Its revenues in 2011 were $60.2 billion, only slightly less than Microsoft's. Microsoft provides the software that runs computers; Maersk brings us the computers. One is infamous. Somehow the other is mostly invisible.

This is remarkable, given the size of its ambition. Maersk is known for its experiments with economies of scale. Its E class ship (according to an internal classification system) *Emma Maersk*, built in 2005, excited the industry partly because she could carry at least fifteen thousand containers. Triple-E class ships, expected in 2014, will carry eighteen thousand and be able to fit a full-sized American football field, an ice-hockey arena, and a basketball court in their holds, if they care to. *Emma* was envied by naval architects and engineers, but her arrival in Felixstowe in December 2006 also caught the public imagination. With her 150 tons of New Zealand lamb and 138,000 tins of cat food, she carried 12,800 MP-3 players, 33,000 cocktail shakers, and 2 million Christmas decorations; she became SS *Santa*, come to call.

SS *Santa* demonstrated more than industrial hubris. She also proved how little an ordinary citizen understands about shipping. For two weeks afterward, Felixstowe received calls from people wanting to know if she was still in port. She had come and gone in twenty-four hours. I have met well-meaning men—and too few women—in boardrooms across London and New York who complain about this ignorance. They want a more visible image for an industry that in the UK alone employs 634,900 people, contributes £8.45 billion in taxes, and generates 2 percent of the national economy, more than restaurants, takeaway food, and civil engineering combined, and only just behind the construction industry.

They despair that shipping draws attention only with drama and disaster: a cruise ship sinking, or an oil spill and blackened birds. They would like people to know the names of the *Wec Vermeer*, arrived from Leixões and heading for Rotterdam, or the *Zim Genoa*, due in from Ashdod, not just *Exxon Valdez* and *Titanic*. They provide statistics showing that the dark days of oil spills are over. Between 1972 and 1981, there were 223 spills. Over the last decade there were 63. Each year, a shipping publicist told me, "More oil is poured down the drain by mechanics changing their engine oil than is spilled by the world's fleet of oil tankers."

Yet the invisibility is useful, too. There are few industries as defiantly opaque as shipping. Even offshore bankers have not developed a system as intricately elusive as the flag of convenience, under which ships can fly the flag of a state that has nothing to do with its owner, cargo, crew, or route. Look at the backside of boats and you will see home ports of Panama City and Monrovia, not Le Havre or Hamburg, but neither crew nor ship will have ever been to Liberia or Mongolia, a landlocked country that nonetheless has a shipping fleet. For the International Chamber of Shipping, which thinks "flags of convenience" too pejorative a term (it prefers the sanitized "open registries"), there is "nothing inherently wrong" with this system. A former U.S. Coast Guard commander preferred to call it "managed anarchy."

Danish-owned *Kendal* has also flagged out, but to the national registry of the United Kingdom. On her monkey deck she flies the Red Ensign, the British maritime Union flag. This makes her a rarity. After the Second World War, the great powers in shipping were Britain and the United States. They had ships and supplied men to sail them. In 1961 the United Kingdom had 142,462 working seafarers. The United States owned 1,268 ships. Now British seafarers number around 24,000. There are fewer than one hundred oceangoing U.S.-flagged ships. Only 1 percent of trade at U.S. ports travels on an American-flagged ship, and the U.S. fleet has declined by 82 percent since 1951. Who in western

Europe or America now knows a working seafarer? At a nautical seminar held on a tall ship—a proper old sailing vessel—in Glasgow, a tanker captain told a story that got laughs, but it was sad. When online forms offer him drop-down options to describe his career, he selects "shipping" and is then given a choice. DHL or Fedex?

Two men have descended from *Kendal* to fetch me. They look Asian and exhausted, so they are typical crew. The benefits of flagging out vary according to registry, but there will always be lower taxes, more lenient labor laws, no requirement to pay expensive American or British crews who are protected by unions and legislation. Now the citizens of rich countries own ships—Greece has the most, then Japan and Germany—but they are sailed by the cheap labor of Filipinos, Bangladeshis, Chinese, Indonesians. They are the ones who clean your cruise cabin and work in the engine room, who bring your gas, your soybeans, your perfumes and medicine.

Seafaring can be a good life. And it can go wrong with the speed of a wave. On paper, the seas are tightly controlled. The Dutch scholar Grotius's 1609 concept of *mare liberum* still mostly holds: a free sea that belongs to no state but in which each state has some rights. The United Nations Convention on the Law of the Sea (UNCLOS) is known as the umbrella convention. Its 320 articles, excluding annexes, aim to create "a legal order for the seas and oceans which will facilitate international communication, and will promote the peaceful uses of the seas and oceans, the equitable and efficient utilization of their resources, the conservation of their living resources, and the study, protection and preservation of the marine environment." Nations that have ratified the convention (the United States has not, not liking its deep-sea mining stipulations) have a right to a twelve-mile boundary from their coastline and also to a two-hundred-mile "exclusive economic zone." Beyond that is the high sea. The International Maritime Organization, a

UN agency, has passed dozens of regulations and amendments since the 1940s to regulate ships, crews, and safety, more than most other UN agencies. The International Labour Organization looks out for seafarers' rights. For boundary disputes there is an International Tribunal on Maritime Law.

But the sea dissolves paper. In practice, the ocean is the world's wildest place, because of both its fearsome natural danger and how easy it is out there to slip from the boundaries of law and civilization that seem so firm ashore. TV crime dramas now frequently use ports as a visual shorthand for places of criminal, suspicious activity. I don't know why they don't just go out to sea. If something goes wrong in international waters, there is no police force or union official to assist. Imagine you have a problem while on a ship. Who do you complain to, when you are employed by a Manila manning agency on a ship owned by an American, flagged by Panama, managed by a Cypriot, in international waters?

Imagine you are a nineteen-year-old South African woman named Akhona Geveza, fresh out of maritime college, the first in your family to reach higher education, the household earner and hope. In January 2010, you go to sea as a deck cadet—an apprentice navigator—on a good ship run by a good company, the *Safmarine Kariba*. Six months later, your shipmate reports to the captain that you have been raped by the Ukrainian first officer. He summons you and the officer to his cabin the next day, as if an alleged rape is a regular human resources matter. But you don't turn up, because you are already dead in the sea off Croatia. The Croatian police subsequently concluded Akhona had committed suicide. She had been in a relationship that was "consensual but rough." An internal inquiry by Safmarine also concluded suicide and found no evidence of harassment or abuse. And that, according to sea law, was all that could be demanded.

Reporters from South Africa's *Sunday Times* then interviewed other cadets from the same maritime school. They found two had been made pregnant by senior officers, two male cadets raped, and a widespread atmosphere of intimidation. A female cadet said embarking on a ship was like being dropped in the middle of a game park. "When we arrived," another said, "we were told that the captain is our god; he can marry you, baptize you, and even bury you without anybody's permission. We were told that the sea is no-man's-land and that what happens at sea stays at sea."

Other workers and migrants have hard lives. But they have phone lines and Internet access, unlike seafarers. They have union representatives, a police force, all the safety nets of society. Even in space, astronauts are always connected to mission control. Only 12 percent of ship crew have freely available Internet access at sea. Two-thirds have no access at all. Cell phones don't work either. Lawyers who fight for seafarers' rights describe their clients as moving targets who work in no-man's-lands. They describe an industry that is global but also uniquely mobile, and difficult to govern, police, or rule. They are careful to say that most owners are scrupulous, but for the unscrupulous ones there is no better place to be than at sea. For the International Transport Workers' Federation (ITF), a global union with 600,000 seafarer members, the maritime and fishing industries "continue to allow astonishing abuses of human rights of those working in the sector. . . . Seafarers and fishers are routinely made to work in conditions that would not be acceptable in civilized society." If that sounds like typically combative union rhetoric, ITF will point to, for a start, the $30 million they recovered in 2010 of wages unpaid to seafarers who had earned them, and the year before was the same. The blankness of that blue sea on our maps applies to the people who work on it, too. Buy your fair-trade coffee beans by all means, but don't assume fair-trade principles govern the conditions of the men who fetch it to you. You would be mistaken.

In 1904, the great Norwegian-American seafarer unionist Andrew Furuseth—known as Lincoln of the Sea for his cheekbones and achievements—was threatened with prison for violating an injunction during a strike. "You can throw me in jail," he responded, "but you can't give me narrower quarters than, as a seaman, I've always lived in; or a coarser food than I've always eaten, or make me lonelier than I've always been." More than a century on, seafarers still regularly joke that their job is like being in prison with a salary. That is not accurate. When the academic Erol Kahveci surveyed British prison literature while researching conditions at sea, he found that "the provision of leisure, recreation, religious service and communication facilities are better in U.K. prisons than . . . on many ships our respondents worked aboard."

The International Maritime Organization once published a brochure about shipping entitled "A Safe and Friendly Business." Shipping has certainly become safer, but not always friendlier to humans or the planet. This safe and friendly business emits as many greenhouses gases as airplanes but is only just being regulated, decades after gas became lead-free and short-haul flights an ethical issue. In this safe and friendly business, at the moment I embark, 544 seafarers are being held hostage by Somali pirates. I try to translate that into other transport industries; 544 bus drivers, or 544 cabdrivers, or nearly two jumbo jets of passengers, mutilated and tortured for years. When thirty-three Chilean miners were trapped underground for sixty-nine days in 2010, there was a media frenzy. Fifteen hundred journalists went to Chile and, even now, the BBC news website maintains a special page on their drama, long after its conclusion. The twenty-four men on MV *Iceberg* held captive for a thousand days were given no special page and nothing much more than silence and disregard.

The men from *Kendal* are ready to go. They advise me to hold the gangway rail tightly: One hand for you, Miss, and one for the ship. I have traveled plenty and strangely on land: to Saddam Hussein's birthday party in Tikrit, to Bhutanese football matches blessed by

Buddhist monks, down sewers and through vast slums in great cities. I look at the gangway, leading up four stories of height, my portal to thirty-nine days at sea, six ports, two oceans, five seas, and the most compellingly foreign environment I'm ever likely to encounter. Lead on, able seamen. I will follow.

Boxes
(ROSE GEORGE)

1

EMBARKATION

Formalization and Filipinos

Kendal LOOKS ENORMOUS, BUT SHE IS A MIDSIZED SHIP. HER DECK is only three football fields long when the biggest decks now stretch for four. I find her beautiful, although sailors of tall ships and trim yachts will scoff at this. A container ship? So ugly and boxy. Those practical lines, that unsubtle stern slumped like a fat diner's backside on a restaurant chair. They feel superior with their wooden masts and sails and windy romance. Cruise ship fans dote on the flanks—pockmarked with cabins—of their floating holiday camps, with all that gleaming, preening white. Give me instead this working ship laden with her multicolored box stacks, waiting passively at the dock while industry is done to her.

The men who work here think there is nothing exceptional about what will happen next, which is a transformation. Once the loading is done, the ropes unlashed, and the gangway withdrawn, *Kendal* will become an astonishing, remarkable thing: thousands of tons of thousands of types of cargo, floating on miles deep of nothing but water, traveling safely to the other side of the world, just as she does every two months, reliable as a yo-yo or a boomerang. *Kendal*'s job is to travel to Felixstowe, Bremerhaven, and Rotterdam; to call at Le Havre in France then go down the Suez Canal to Salalah, Oman; on to Colombo, Sri Lanka, then into the Straits of Malacca to stop at Port Klang in Malaysia, then Singapore before the final destination of Laem Chabang, Thailand, where she will turn around and come back. The World Shipping Council, attempting to amaze, informs visitors to its website that a container ship travels the equivalent of three-quarters of the way to the moon and back in one year. The council doesn't need to do that: an ordinary voyage on an ordinary ship is extraordinary enough.

At the top of the gangway, two more escorts await, one Asian and one not; one cheerful and one not. The grump is Igor, second officer, deck, and misery is his default setting because he was supposed to go home weeks earlier and now he exudes frustration in his face like sweat. He has been detailed to show me to my quarters. Some container lines carry passengers. Paying guests on working ships can bring revenue, and the experience can be sold as cruising without the crowds. But no commercial ships passing through the Indian Ocean take passengers anymore because of piracy risks. So I am here as a supernumerary (dictionary definition: "not wanted or needed; redundant," or "not belonging to a regular staff but engaged for work"). I will be the last outsider allowed on Maersk ships through the Gulf of Aden until further notice.

The people of *Kendal* live and work and play in its accommodation house, a cream superstructure placed toward the rear of the ship, a direction that I should now call "aft." The building rises ten stories up to the bridge, the navigational center of the ship, which stretches T-like over the breadth of the containers, or "boxes," in industry language, for superior visibility. I step inside the steel lip of a heavy metal door, into upper deck, the lowest level of the accommodation house but so named because of the decks below it, down to the engine room and cargo holds. Samuel Johnson wrote that "being in a ship is like being in a jail, with the chance of being drowned," and although Maersk is known for running good ships, the interior decor is the prison side of comfort: plain walls, institutionally dimpled rubber floors, clinical lighting. A ship is both workplace and home but workplace aesthetics have won.

The decks rise up through the alphabet. Senior officers live higher up; non-officers below. My cabin is on D deck, port side, in the officer levels but not at the heights of F deck, where the captain lives, beneath the bridge. The quarters are spacious because they usually house visiting officers: a dayroom, bedroom, and en suite bathroom. There is a computer, a printer, a DVD player, and TV; a hi-fi system, a compact shower room, and a biological sewage toilet. The furnishing is business-functional; the color scheme is beige and dark blue. It is better and bigger than many hotel rooms I have stayed in, and it floats.

Igor departs with a mutter that I will be summoned by the captain at some point, so I read a letter left by the Floating Society of Christian Endeavour thanking the cabin's resident for his or her part in bringing cargo to this country, then I pass the time before dinner by looking out of the porthole. The view is busy. Every port between Felixstowe and Singapore requires boxes to be loaded and others to be discharged. The blankness of the boxes is entrancing, although this is an unpopular, weird opinion among people who work with them, who think they are boring, opaque, blank. Stuff carrying stuff.

At her most laden, *Kendal* carries 6,188 boring TEUs, or twenty-foot-equivalent unit containers. TEU is a mundane name for something that changed the world, but so is the "Internet." I watch a crane lifting a TEU into the air, its cables dancing the box across onto the ship, thudding it into place in front of my porthole, then retracting with serpentine loops. The movement would be balletic if it weren't for the thuds. My view now is a gray box, its corrugated iron ridges slightly scuffed and rusted, its exterior branded with "*MAERSK*." Other boxes are stamped with "Evergreen," "Hapag-Lloyd," "CMA CGM," "Hanjin": household names at sea, in freight yards, and in maritime offices but nowhere else. Yet similar boxes and the same brands surround modern life. They lie in stacks in rail freight yards as you pass on a train. Attached to a truck they slow your passage on a highway. You buy hair products from market stalls set up in those familiar corrugated steel walls, or you sleep in a boutique hotel created from them. I have seen boxes dumped by African roadsides several days' drive from the nearest city, splashes of red among green jungle, displaced deposits of commerce. They are everywhere if you care to look, if you look harder.

This box is probably empty. Britain is postindustrial and has little to export. "Waste and hot air," one laconic port official said, when I asked him what our exports consist of. He could have included weapons, too, and scrap metal, exported to Turks who have invested in recycling plants to process it, unlike the British who call it waste, wastefully. But that would be it. The geographic boundary of the Suez Canal is also a gateway to plenty: beyond it *Kendal* will begin to collect what the East has made for the West, gathering up goods all the way to Thailand before turning around and bringing the bounty home. This is the pendulum of the supply chain and it swings with its own curious logic. Shipping is so cheap that it makes more financial sense for Scottish cod to be sent ten thousand miles to China to be filleted, then sent back to Scottish shops and restaurants, than to pay Scottish filleters. A Scottish newspaper called this practice "madness," but actually it's just shipping.

Dinner is at six on A deck. There are two eating rooms, one for crew and the other for officers, who are also part of the crew but who are not known as crew. This never makes much sense, along with why there are three words for going backward (astern, making sternway, aft). Ship life is a foreign country and I must learn the language. The crew mess is homely, with a large cauldron of rice that is always full and a microwave with two settings: Instant Ramen for one and Instant Ramen for two.

My seat is in the officers' saloon. Next door the crew eat off

Formica, but here the tables have blue cloths and lacy paper doilies, already well used and grubby. I am directed to a seat next to the porthole, underneath a portrait of the Queen. Apparently she is standard decoration on British-flagged ships, although discomfiting to anyone who has traveled to countries—Iraq, for example—where the number of official portraits reflects the level of fear required in the population. But there she is, and I am too unsure of my place to argue about my place. Men drift in and take food from the buffet on the sideboard. No one speaks. My neighbor is a silent man who eats by holding his bowl close to his mouth in a way that is improper for Westerners but not for Easterners. Later I learn that his name is Chan, that is the third engineer and from Burma, and that ashore Burmese may be rare and exotic but they are common in shipping. They make up one of the modern labor pools, in the language of economists, as if rich shipowners take their rods and fish for able seamen, oilmen, bo'suns among the men of Bangladesh, the Philippines, eastern Europe. Opposite me is the third officer, a lanky young blond man, then Igor, still grumpy. The silence is intimidating but I try to make conversation with the third officer, from nerves.

"What's your name?"

I think he says, "Maris."

"Oh. Like the sea? What a good name."

"No. Not like the sea. Marius."

He looks at me with fatigued disdain and returns to fueling, fast and silently. With further effort I learn that he is Romanian. Igor is Moldavian. The captain is a chilly South African. The chief engineer is a Briton named Derek, from Plymouth or nearby, with the rounded vowels of Devon. Mike, another Romanian, is the second engineer; a languid Indian named Vinton is chief officer; and the man whose seat I have taken is Li, fourth engineer, Chinese. Eight places, five nationalities. A normal ship. At the table behind are two British cadets, apprentice engineers. Maersk takes on cadets to qualify for lower taxes from the British government, so here are lads from Newcastle and the Western Isles of Scotland, traditional maritime places that still send their young to sea. The cadets don't talk much either. At the end of this sad, silent meal, I wonder what I've done, signing up for weeks of this gloom with a big ocean outside to jump into.

I sleep through our departure. For someone used to land, the movement of the ship turns it into a giant crib, though one with engine noise. I wake in German Bight, something that sounds like a tree disease but is a parcel of sea past Dover. For most people it exists only in the BBC's *Shipping Forecast*, a nightly broadcast of weather and worse in South Utsire, Dogger, Rockall, Hebrides, of storms rising and boats falling, dispensed in tones so soothing you feel lulled by other people's danger and a sharp, guilty delight at being safe abed.

No ship can protect itself against the sea. When the cruise ship *Costa Concordia* was holed in 2012 by a rock off Italy and toppled, a headline read, BIG SHIPS STILL SINK, as if this were news. *Kendal*, despite the dimensions of her hull and engine—a Doosan-Wartsila the size of a house—is still a chunk of metal floating on an element that can withdraw its support at any time; that can list us, wind us, or hole us; swamp and sink us. So we are as prepared as possible, with lifesaving equipment for thirty-four persons and safety certificates from the American Bureau of Shipping, one of the leading classification societies, as the setters of ship safety standards are known. There is a comforting number of interests concerned in this ship and its safety: line them up and they would stretch from *Kendal*'s smoothly curving bow to her squat backside. An incomplete list includes shipbuilders, owners, financiers, charterers, classification societies, regulators national and international, insurers for its hull, cargo, and war risks, and so on. Even with all those interests and oversight, every minute at sea is a minute in which danger has been avoided. Every minute trouble is expected, from other ships, from unseen obstacles, from something sailors call "weather" but which is more malign, more elemental than the weather we have ashore.

The English Channel, for example. A domestic sea, a stretch of water so unthreatening that swimming across it has become commonplace. In 2010, in this domestic sea, the yacht *Ouzo* disappeared, probably swamped by a passing P&O ferry named *Pride of Bilbao*, and its crew of three young men were found in the sea, correctly dressed in life jackets but dead. The Channel was called the sea of sore heads and sore hearts by sailors who knew they should fear it, who were not fooled by its size or proximity to two reassuringly safe, civilized countries. The Narrow Sea, as it is also known, is one of the world's busiest shipping lanes. It contains small boats, fishing trawlers, yachts, container vessels, bulk cargo freighters carrying grain, coal, anything. There are slow-moving tankers and ferries that cross fast and furiously as if with God-given right to take priority. Those are the surface perils. The charts reveal sea places called Garden City, Fairy Bank, the Black Deeps, but also firing ranges and wrecks. They show the Sunk Traffic Separation Scheme, which is not a thoroughfare of disaster but a policing of a sea highway near a place called Sunk. Not being a sailor, I didn't know the sea had highways. My land maps show the smallest lane, but the sea is blank blue, serving only to contrast to land. Nothing to see, fly over it, move along.

Somewhere in German Bight, I go for morning coffee with the crew in their Ramen room. There was no chance of missing them: eating and drinking times on *Kendal* are strictly kept. Breakfast at 7:00 a.m., morning break at 10:00–10:30, lunch at 12:00, dinner at 6:00 p.m. They are usually well attended: eating punctures boredom. Some sailors still call the morning break the "smoke-o," although there is no smoking inside the accommodation house and hopefully nowhere near any containers containing flammable liquids.

There are twenty men and one woman—Pinky, the cook—

employed on *Kendal*, a manning ratio that would baffle anyone working on a military ship, where thousands can live. I'm surprised to find a woman on board when only 2 percent of seafarers are female, but I'm glad to see her, too. The officers are mixed, but the crew are all Filipino. This is to be expected: Filipinos make up more than a third of all crews worldwide. A quarter of a million of them are at sea. They are popular, a Filipino seafarer once told me, because "We are cheap and speak good English." They are the new Malays, who were the new lascars—Asian seafarers widely employed up to the Second World War—and they will probably be replaced by the next wave of cheaper, English-speaking crews.

Introductions: the bo'sun is Elvis. He rules the realm of manual labor in which all the crew work: a marine factory foreman. Beneath him is Julius Jefferson, a muscled Able Seaman (AB) named for the U.S. president; Ordinary Seaman Dilbert; an electrician named Pedro; and Denis the painter, whose job is to chip rust, then paint, chip rust, then paint. There is Pinky in her chef's whites and her galley helpmeet and steward, Francis. There are Joselito and Axel, ordinary seamen or ratings, who do grunt work. Finally, a stocky AB who introduces himself as Archie. Actually, it's Archimedes. "Archimedes for long, Archie for short."

They look tired. The officers drive and navigate the ship, but these men care for it, with labor that is manual and exhausting: constantly climbing the stacks to check on six thousand boxes, hosing the decks of salt and oil, fixing, repairing, tending, welding, heaving. Even their work clothes look worn out, because the men leave their boiler suits hanging at the accommodation house entrance, with boots attached. The suits are so heavy they keep their shape, and they look like ghosts hanging there, faces turned despondently to the wall.

Still, the crew is as friendly as dinner last night was frosty. They have a ready humor that you'd expect from nationals of the Philippines, where the country's two long occupations by Spain and the United States are often described as "four hundred years in the convent and fifty in Hollywood." Besides, a new face is something new. Some have been at sea for months with hardly an hour ashore, but that is what they want. Unlike the senior officers, they don't belong to the ship but to a one-off contract. Pedro and Archimedes could be on *Kendal* for six months, moving boxes, then hauling cornmeal from Iowa or chemicals to Hamburg. Many months at sea puts off the uncertainty involved in getting a new contract. (Not just uncertainty. Some Manila manning agencies require job seekers to work for months unpaid before deigning to give them a contract.)

Pinky has been on board for six months now. Francis was once on a ship for ten months. Once, Pinky got home to the Philippines after six months and three and a half weeks later they called her back. She had to go, although she has a small son. Needs must. All the crew have children, even boyish Francis. One says, "The first time I was home for my son's birthday was when he was seven." Missing births is as common as missing birthdays. It is the price you pay for the money you earn. Both Pedro and his wife work overseas, like ten million other Filipinos. He is everywhere and she is in Hong Kong, a domestic servant. Their children are with grandparents, and Pedro and his wife have missed all their growing up. A special government body—the Commission on Filipinos Overseas—looks out for migrant workers like Pedro and prepares an annual stock estimate of the size of the diaspora, treating its workers as grain or nails. The stock is divided by country, and at the bottom of the list, below Vanuatu, are the stateless: seabased workers. The rush to seafaring began in the Philippines in 1974, with encouragement from President Ferdinand Marcos. By now, there are ninety maritime academies pushing out forty thousand seafarers a year. In 2011 they sent home $4.3 billion in remittances.

Pinky's boy is with her parents, and it is for his sake that she is living with twenty men for months on end, cooking to the best of her abilities, which were formed by a short cooking course in European food and which are variable. On the windowsill in the galley, she keeps the seeds from peppers. "They are for my big garden.

If I plant enough peppers, I won't have to go to sea." All the crew are here for the money. They say this with no embarrassment or preamble. They call their job "dollar for homesick." A senior government bureaucrat in Manila can earn $300 a month; the minimum seafarer wage required by the International Labour Organization is $555. If these men worked instead in British or American hospitals, they would be paid British rates. At sea, they work under British law but on Filipino rates. Even so, an AB, a lowly rank, gets $1,000 a month on *Kendal*, excluding overtime. Also, on shore, you have to buy jobs and the bribes can be $5,000. They have calculated carefully: so many years buys so big a house. Fifteen, usually, or ten if you are lucky. More buys a shop; more puts all your children through decent schools, colleges, and universities.

The calculations are not always accurate. Julius has been at sea for seventeen years now and is still here. "But the years go so fast. Every time I come on board I think I will stop. But then I can't escape." He grew up by the sea and has a degree in marine transportation. He was sold on the romance of the sea at first. "I thought it was nice, you can see the rest of the world, China, Japan. Every kind of people." Now he wouldn't recommend life at sea to anyone. "Because I know what it's like."

A seafarer joke: I travel the world but it all looks like my engine room (or bridge, or gangway). When ships carried general cargo— a cornucopia of everything, in bales and barrels and piles—and dockers unloaded all by hand, there was more time ashore. There was rest and recuperation. In *The Box*, a history of the container, the economist Marc Levinson describes a 1954 voyage on a typical cargo ship, SS *Warrior*. It carried 74,903 cases, 71,726 cartons, 24,036 bags, 10,671 boxes, 2,880 bundles, 2,877 packages, 2,634 pieces, 1,538 drums, 888 cans, 815 barrels, 53 wheeled vehicles, 21 crates, 10 transporters, 5 reels, and 1,525 undetermined items. A total of 194,582 pieces, all of which had to be loaded and unloaded by hand. The total weight came to just over five thousand tons of cargo and would have taken weeks to move. *Kendal* can unload and load several thousand boxes in less than twenty-four hours.

The next day brings formalization, when newcomers are introduced to the ship in depth. Third Officer Marius is in charge. He gathers me and the two cadets, a small brood, and we set off from the ship's office on A deck, past the noticeboard that indicates who is on- or off-duty. Ashore options—"in" or "out"—don't apply here, where "out" means overboard. First, the interior attractions: a karaoke machine in the crew lounge; a dartboard and Wii machine in the officers'. A library on D deck is equipped with cheap DVDs, books, and two computers for gaming only. *Kendal* is only four years old, but it provides for no Internet browsing and no Skype. Internet access is neither freely available nor private. Crew members send their e-mails to the captain once a day and he sends them on and transmits replies. The last time I had so little Internet freedom was in 1995.

Here are the outdoor facilities: a basketball hoop on the poop deck near the stern, where the decks seem too slippery to play safely and the low railings an invitation to lose balls in the ocean. Behind the accommodation house is a swimming pool, empty, and a set of shabby chairs next to a barbecue made from an oil drum and lashed to a railing for stability. It is an unlikely setting for merriment, right beneath a huge wall of refrigerated containers— for fish, medicine, and bananas—that hum insistently, constantly, antisocially. I ask if the barbecue is ever used. "Oh god, no," says Marius. "It's even worse than dinner. Everyone standing there with long faces and the sound of the generators and all you can see are containers. Horrible."

We move to upper deck. Here there is a gym, with rowing and treadmill machines, with weights that the buff Julius looks like he uses, although his heavy manual work is probably exercise enough. There is a well-used laundry with one machine marked BOILER-SUITS

ONLY for men who work among the oil, rust, salt, and spray of the deck. Up on A deck is the noticeboard where all personal electrical items must be listed for customs purposes, and the bond store, the ship's convenience store. For sale are soft drinks, water, and chocolate, and useful sundries like toothpaste and shaving cream.

Alcohol was banned two years ago on Maersk ships. Its employees are forbidden to drink at sea or ashore and can be breathalyzed. There are sensible reasons behind the prohibition. Driving a ship requires as much sobriety as driving a car, and alcohol has been linked to accidents ranging from sailors drowning off gangways in port to smashing a ship into Southend Pier. But it is an unpopular rule, thought to be babying, insulting. It has deadened life on the ship. People used to wind down after a watch with a beer. Now they retreat to their cabins with a DVD and laptop. This is a familiar modern lament about antisocial machines, but in the intimate, incessant environment of a ship the effects are magnified.

Now the safety features: large orange lifeboats, hard and enclosed at the moment, and immersion suits for escaping in open waters or on an open life raft. I am allotted to the starboard lifeboat, which is equipped with water bottles and emergency rations branded Seven Seas, Compact for Life, 2,500 calories a packet. Inside, the lifeboat looks like a military cargo plane, with harnesses and numbered places on the hard benches. It carries flares, a sea anchor, and oars to be used when beaching so that the surf doesn't crush the boat or turn it over. There is no toilet, only two red buckets and a hatch that opens. The boat looks both safe and terrifying. If needed, it would either swing its way down to the water suspended on cables, a descent described to me as "sickening," or drop inadvertently from a height that would break teeth.

Throughout the formalization, the talkative Scottish cadet keeps up a running commentary of gags and opinions. I wonder at his career choice: all the noise and color of his personality trapped in an engine room. He has an opinion on that, too. "I won't stay on

containers. Boring. I want to go on rig supply ships." The ships
that shuttle supplies to offshore oil rigs are known to have better
food, better pay, all in all a better life. Their crews have home time.
This boy doesn't understand why I have chosen to come to sea.
"Because shipping is so fundamental and crucial and no one knows
about it," I say.

"But it's boring."

I look at these two boys and wonder how long they will last.
They have only been at sea for months. There are decades to go.
When I ask Marius how long he has been at sea on this contract, he
knows to the hour.

Things need to happen in Rotterdam. This is where we take on
supplies for the whole trip, so Pinky is looking through her books
with a slightly frantic air. She is a good bookkeeper although she
once misplaced a decimal point so that *Kendal* wasn't carrying one
thousand eggs but ten thousand. Pinky of the ten thousand eggs. A
fitness instructor is also coming aboard for four days to educate the
crew about fitness and nutrition, because of the obvious logic that
healthier crews are better crews. Shit, says Marius, who is thin as a
beanstalk, I'd better figure out where the gym is. A new third officer will also arrive, and Marius will be promoted, although Igor
still hasn't managed to leave. His contract is now several weeks
expired. I hear complaints about shore staff who understand nothing of the seafarers' life, who don't realize that an extra week after
six months at sea feels like a month.

They also don't understand that time moves differently here.
We set our own, for a start. Already Marius's thick Romanian has
come over the PA announcing a "retardation of the clocks" by an
hour. The alerts are required because sometimes the shift in time
is commanded by the captain, not Greenwich. It confuses humans
and computer clocks but it is done out of kindness. Executed properly, this time manipulation avoids the worst of jet lag, no brutal

loss or gain of hours by a bewildered body, just a gentle push from a voice on the tannoy.

The port of Rotterdam is forty miles long. It is the largest port in Europe, partly because it is used for transshipment, whereby big ships decant goods into smaller ones that can then cross the Channel and don't need deepwater ports, which are few and expensive. There seems nothing poetic about Rotterdam, but someone has tried to leaven the ferocious necessity of its industry by naming its quays after great rivers: Amazon, Yangtze (and also Petrol and Chemical). Shipping can be poetic despite itself. There is the singing of its winds, for one: the katabatics that roll down off Scottish glens to knock over unsuspecting boats in the lochs, or the chocolate gale, a northwest wind of the West Indies and Spanish Main. On mechanized, inhuman docks, people in hard hats look at a ship, estimate how many boxes are going on it, and say, "a thousand moves." They talk of containers left in yards building up "dwell time" (and charge for it). In maritime offices in London, Hong Kong, and New York, they talk of "wet law," applying to grounding and casualties and such, and its "dry tail," the follow-up negotiations with charterers and insurers. They discuss the jungle-sounding "bareboat charter" (leasing of a ship without paying for maintenance or administration) or the gaiety of a "charter party" (a leasing arrangement). There is the elegance of seafarer certificates, shortened to "tickets," so that a captain has a deep-sea "ticket," for example, not coastal, and he is foreign-going, not home-trade. At Rotterdam, there is also an area I think is called Bootleg, which sounds charming, except it is Botlek, known by the crew for its duty-free store. This is only five miles from the ship and saves them 100 euros on a taxi ride into town, because it will provide transport if you promise to spend enough. That won't be difficult: the prices are far higher than their dutied equivalents. I am puzzled that the Filipino crew buy Nintendos here when they are cheaper in Asia. But they do, and with glee. "For my son." "For my daughter. I missed her birthday." They plug their absence with electrical items.

At dinner, there is a surprise. A new captain. The South African has left. His chilliness makes sense now: he was four days from the end of a two-month tour at sea, and guests were not a priority. My hindsight is kinder to him, to his attempts at warmth, such as when I asked about shipboard rules for supernumeraries, and he said, "Don't fiddle with the anchor." Now he is gone and here is his "back-to-back," his partner-captain, who has been two months at home and will now be two months in command while the other is ashore. He comes to the door of the dining room while I struggle with another indifferent Pinky salad and introduces himself. "Call me Glenn." He is a skinny, friendly man from North Shields, a town known for coal mines, seafarers, and poverty. He is clean-shaven, gray-haired, and ascetic to look at, but his accent has the warm tones of the north of England and so does his manner. Don't worry about formalities, he says. Enjoy your dinner. More importantly, enjoy my ship. And I think I will now.

The view from the bridge
(ROSE GEORGE)

2

ABOARD

Blue Eyes and His Boxes

Two tribes run a ship. Deck or engine room; navigators or mechanics; water or oil. You pick one or the other and rarely cross lines. Once I step onto *Kendal*'s bridge, I know my allegiance is deck. All those windows and all that sea. And a sofa, a kettle, and, if I am lucky, decent cookies, not just the SkyFlakes biscuits that Filipinos tell me are their only food back home in bad weather. Typhoon crackers. The bridge provides a view, always, to port or sea, or weather, and binoculars to borrow, charts to read, and VHF radio crackles to be puzzled over by my unaccustomed ears.

The bridge of a modern ship is a shock on first encounter. Although this place is still known as the wheelhouse, the wheel at the helm is not wooden and impressive, but mundane plastic, the kind that would suit a video arcade game. Nearly all else is automated. A bank of screens contains radar, ECDIS—an electronic chart system—and AIS, an automatic identification system that transmits the ship's name, speed and heading, and other details to other ships, port authorities, and well-equipped pirates. There is radio, a gyrocompass and magnetic compass, a tachometer and echo sounder. There are no voice pipes or telegraphs, as *Titanic* had, and barely any brass, but so many beeps and screens that I wonder if ships will soon be able to drive themselves. Pedro or Julius, washing the exterior bridge windows in a raging storm or trying to hose down the decks with a hose, might disagree.

Captain Glenn is often to be found on the bridge. He is here for port approaches and departures but also whenever he can escape paperwork, which is not as often as he would like, now that the role of ship's purser has ceased to exist and all the administration falls on the captain and senior officers. He can be on his computer for four to eight hours a day now. Glenn is the most senior captain in Maersk's container fleet. In older times, he would have been known as commodore and saluted by the raising of flags on courteous passing ships. His talk turns often to earlier times, because he has done enough years to have plenty and because in his four decades, life at sea has changed dramatically. His first ship was a tramp steamer, a freelance vessel that picks up trade where it can, not a liner with a scheduled route like *Kendal*. A taxi, not a bus. It was iron, had derricks on deck to heft cargo about, and was held together by rivets. Rivets! Not like this Korean-made welded ship, only four years old. Still, Captain Glenn is not entirely nostalgic and always loves the ship he commands. He says of *Kendal*, "Isn't she beautiful?" and salutes her every day with a stroke or a tap, a formal and ritual greeting. He is scornful of a modern trend in maritime journalism—notably led by *Lloyd's List*—to call ships "it." What nonsense. His ship is a she. Why? She just is.

If Captain Glenn stands on the bridge facing forward to sea, the old life is behind him and the new one in front. Behind him are the national flags a ship raises when she calls at port, each kept in a wooden cubbyhole on a shelf that stretches halfway across the wheelhouse. You never know when you might need to be nice to Nauru. There is the chart table and drawers filled with 169 charts drawn up by the UK's Hydrographic Office, a chart-making entity nostalgically known as the Admiralty. Other nations produce charts—Russia and Japan, for example—but the Admiralty's are known to be better.

In front of him the captain sees sea, but mostly he sees boxes. Orange, blue, gray, red. If the captain leaves the wheelhouse to stand on the port or starboard wings—the bridge's two terraces—he will see boxes fore and aft. That is if he sees them at all. For him they are blank, boring. "I am indifferent to them. They're just boxes, you've got to admit." He thinks they have destroyed the soul of a ship and of shipping. This is an old lament, too. In the middle of the shift from sail to steam, Joseph Conrad complained that "the loading of ships was once a matter or skill, judgment, and knowledge." With the modern steamship, cargo was "dumped into her through six hatchways, with clatter and hurry and racket and heat, in a cloud of steam and a mess of coal-dust."

After Rotterdam, I begin to spend hours on the bridge, hanging out, though I choose my hours carefully, avoiding one officer and happy to bother others. It is easy to plan ahead: at sea you always wake up to a different sunrise but the watches don't change. So that *Kendal* can operate for twenty-four hours a day, each of the three officers has two four-hour watches. The captain is not included: his watch is constant. The 4–8 morning and afternoon watch is given to the chief officer, the captain's second-in-command. Vinton's is one of the plates covered in plastic wrap that sits on the table during dinner for later consumption. The second officer gets the 12–4 a.m. and p.m., and the third the 8–12, so that the most junior is in charge at times when senior officers are likely to be awake.

The duty officers are always hospitable, because company is distraction (an AB is often on watch to steer the helm, but it's the same AB as yesterday and the day before that). There are things to be done on duty, but not enough to fully fill four hours of time.

The tasks include plotting courses, checking the magnetic gyro, monitoring changes of weather and running conditions, keeping an eye on vessels in the vicinity. This list is laminated and pinned to the bridge console, but it can be summed up by "keep a good lookout." Good watch officers need to master the gadgets, but they must never neglect the human element. They need sea eyes. Often, the captain points out lights that I have not seen or ships that emerge from the blue horizon only when he indicates them, handing me binoculars while managing to keep to himself his disbelief at my ineptitude. Darkness vision is also important: this is why F deck, where the captain and the chief engineer live and work, is lit at night with red lights only, in the way of a submarine, so that the eyes of senior officers can adjust to the darkness of the bridge more quickly in an emergency. The investigation that decided the yacht *Ouzo* had been swamped by a P&O ferry attached some blame to the watch officer's photochromic lenses, which handicapped his night vision. To prevent outdoor light pollution, the chart room, which needs to be illuminated, is blocked off with heavy curtains at night. Even with this care, anyone coming into the wheelhouse in darkness will have impaired vision for ten to fifteen minutes, a significant handicap in a crisis. Ships have sunk in less.

The captain is aware of this, and the threat governs the ship. An affable nature does not mean a lack of discipline. Bridge rules are as follows. Strict uniform is not required. Boiler suits are allowed, as are sandals, but with socks, so that a watch officer might look like a seafarer from the ankles up and a priest below them. An officer on watch may sit down, but he must never fall asleep. Every eleven minutes, the "deadman alarm" sounds and must be switched off, to encourage wakefulness. I come to learn which notices come from the captain and which are the company's instructions. Maersk communications don't include phrases such as "Slovenliness will not be tolerated." Every Sunday, the captain's cabin inspections are feared with good reason, for he runs fingers along lintels for dust and expects military standards of cleanliness on this civilian ship, and clean mouths, too (the Scottish cadet soon learns to speak more sweetly after the captain's interventions).

A happy ship is the result of careful balance that the captain has worked hard to construct. He served under unapproachable masters in the 1960s, when they were meant to stay distant and godlike. He is still the master, but he mixes authority with friendliness. "Some masters work the crew too hard. They might run a tight ship but it's not a happy ship. There's got to be a living side, a human side." *Kendal* is a floating warehouse, a means of transport, an office, but also a home. In reality, the captain's position puts him in social isolation, when only the chief engineer is of almost equivalent rank. Sometimes he chooses isolation, too. When he comes aboard, he shuts himself away for a day or two, just as captains did in Conrad's day, taking "a long dive into their stateroom, only to emerge a few days later with a more or less serene brow." Captain Glenn tries the same decompression at home, although it is more difficult there, and even after weeks he can wake at night panicked by the quiet, convinced the engines have broken down.

I begin to interview the captain daily, 11:00 a.m. shipsharp, for several reasons. He has the best coffee on board and a coffeemaker in which to brew it properly. His spacious, comfortable quarters—bedroom, dayroom, and office—are high and starboard, and so the least vibrating on *Kendal*. Mine are not, which is why in my cabin there are bits of paper stuffed behind picture frames, under the television, and plugging the hinges. I assumed they were connected to the Smuggling Precautions form I had signed, confirming that the cabin had been searched for contraband, and that a previous conscientious occupant had filled possible cavities. That didn't explain the paper under the TV, but the first night did, because everything in my quarters vibrated beyond tolerance and through sleep. After nights of leaping out of bed and stuffing more paper into the bathroom door hinge, into parts of the bulkhead, and beneath anything with a space under it, the serenity of the captain's dayroom was a relief. Yes, says Second Engineer Mike, when I complain at breakfast one morning, my bones still juddering. Portside cabins are the worst. He has one, too. Sometimes he can't use his computer because the mouse is dancing. Some engineers mutter about Korean-built superstructures that vibrate more than a good old British-built ship would have. Cruise ships modify their structures to prevent this from happening to passengers. Working seafarers must live with it.

The biggest pull of the captain was his forty-two years in the merchant navy. This means he has been at sea probably as long as the Glaswegian officer on his first ship who dampened the arrogance of the young Glenn by saying, "Sonny, I've been at sea since Moby Dick was a sardine." It also means that he decided to join the merchant navy just as it began to change beyond recognition. He had grown up as the box and globalization had grown up, and he had watched a world of general cargo, thieving stevedores, and hard work—properly leavened by leisure and pleasure—become one of paperwork, foreigners, relentless schedules, stress, and fatigue.

In 1968, he needed a career. For boys in North Shields, that meant the mine or the sea. Ships were his mother's idea. "She said, what a wonderful world it would be to be a captain, to see the world." She thought it would always be a secure job because people would always need ships. A local man in South Shields, over the River Tyne, had been teaching him the cornet. In his house the man had models of wooden sailing ships from his time as a merchant seafarer, and he told stories. To the son of a miner, they sounded like freshness and adventure, the opposite of imprisonment in the earth. Even so, Glenn applied to maritime college to be an engineer until he realized his mistake: Who knew what an engineer did, except an engineer? Everyone knew then what a ship's captain did. But that has changed, too. Now when Glenn tells strangers he is a ship's captain, they have no idea that means operating the largest man-made moving objects on the planet.

The captain was average at college, better at what he loved, inadequate at what he didn't. Astronomy was easy but navigation took him years, until he applied himself, pennies dropped, and he understood it all beautifully, enough to supply three calculations in his exams when only one was asked for. He still loves navigation as much as he loves *Kendal*, and he made the right choice to scorn the engine room. He realizes this every time he socializes ashore with more than one engineer. "All they talk about is engines." And if he talked about navigation and charts and stars? "They'll be saying, 'Who does he think he is, Henry the Navigator or something?' "

The captain mentions Henry the Navigator frequently. I don't think it is because of a powerful love for a fifteenth-century Portuguese prince who sponsored great voyages of exploration to the Cape of Good Hope and India: Glenn doesn't like to read about the sea when he is at sea, and even less so when he is ashore. It's just a tic he has, along with his often expressed conviction that the merchant navy are treated like the scum of the earth. Captain Glenn the Navigator commands a ship guided by gadgetry but he still loves to move through the sea using what it and the sky can tell him. "I get great satisfaction just steaming on an ocean passage and plotting the position and the heavenly bodies," as he calls the sun, moon, and stars. "The biggest kick is when you haven't seen land for days on end and you don't have a satellite navigator and then, right on the money, where you say there should be land or a terrestrial feature, there it is. Henry the Navigator."

Captain Glenn is an odd mixture of end-of-career weariness and fierce attachment to tradition. The rules of watchkeeping: pay attention to the gadgets, but use your eyes most. If you see a target on the radar, turn to your binoculars. You would be surprised how many don't bother looking out of the window. He can quote shipping's rules of the road—anticollision regulations known as

ColRegs—by memory, along with the principle of the sextant. He knows his knots. As a cadet, he took constant compass bearings on a ramshackle general cargo ship owned by the long-gone Scottish shipping firm Ben Line, which named some of its ships after mountains and others after whisky.

On an online forum, I find postings from cadets who write fondly of "Ol' Blue Eyes," as they call Captain Glenn, who was kind to them and taught them well. They reminisce about his attachment to the sextant, and his attachment to their understanding it. He is the same now, despairing that his officers can't use *Kendal*'s sextant, Chinese-made and still kept in a box on the bridge, just in case. If all the technology breaks, there will always be the sun or moon or stars and the horizon with which to calculate their position. "It's a lovely bit of knowledge," he says, and explains with delight about mirrors and reflected light and why it is possible to measure 120 degrees on a curve that shows only 60. It is a long and intricate lesson, and by the end of it I hope that, if we sink, I'm in the captain's lifeboat and he has his sextant.

Sometime toward the end of the 1960s, when the captain was a young cadet, he saw his first boxes. They were being carried by an American ship that was departing Hong Kong as he was arriving. "I was out on the poop deck and some of the crew said, Look! That's a container. That's a thing of the future." He didn't pay much attention because cadets didn't pay much attention to things like the creation of globalization. "We were too busy blinking learning stuff." But he listened to the crew, who kept talking about these strange metal things. They said, "That'll never take off." They said, "How are they going to get a truck in that? How will they get steel and timber into it?"

But it did take off. There are at least twenty million containers crossing the world now, quiet blank boxes, thanks to a U.S. businessman named Malcom McLean who thought people who moved freight would find it easier if they could shift everything in a box, rather than the confusion of general cargo, of barrels and boxes and piles, of each company having its own system. Standardization was not a new concept in transportation. Ancient Romans tried it when they shipped liquids in amphorae, and in the nineteenth century coal was transported in wooden boxes on canal barges. McLean's spark was to call on an engineer, Keith Tantlinger, to create a design that could be seamlessly stacked and locked in place, using twist-locks. This new box could fit trains, trucks, cranes, and ships alike. The "intermodality" made perfect commercial sense, and labor unions hated it. Dockers in particular were furious. McLean claimed his box system reduced labor by two-thirds, cutting dockers' workload, salary, and power. This labor force could be powerfully obstructive when it chose, often instigating strikes that became national. In a 1950 survey assessing the popularity of thirty professions among the British public, dockers came twenty-ninth.

For a while they held up the march of the box, as did geography and physics. Ships that carried many boxes would have to be bigger, with deeper draughts. New ports had to be built: New York's maritime wharves—too shallow, too narrow—became useless, and the massive Greater Port of New York–New Jersey was constructed instead. But the rewards of containerization were too great for the dockers to defeat change. Before containers, transport costs ate up to 25 percent of the value of whatever was being shipped. With the extreme efficiencies that intermodality brought, costs were reduced to a pittance. A sweater can now travel three thousand miles for 2.5 cents; it costs 1 cent to send a can of beer. Shipping a container can cost next to nothing, an invaluable advantage in hard economic times, when there is more supply than demand.

In his junior officer days, the captain was in favor of boxes. They looked like a simpler life. "No more general cargo, all the work involved, no more gear, cranes, derricks, nothing. I thought, this has got to be easier." His first cellular container ship—one specially built for boxes rather having to fit them in and among derricks and holds—carried 110 containers. Then there were more and more, and he learned that the boxes gave the gift of speed but they also sucked away his time. You couldn't get any sleep when port hours were so rushed and hurried. Before boxes, he wondered if he had time to go ashore for dinner. Now he wonders if he has time to get a newspaper.

He doesn't wonder about the contents of the boxes. They are things full of things, to be moved according to schedule. He doesn't know what's inside them and he doesn't care. I know he drives a Harley-Davidson at home, so I needle him. What if there were a box full of Harleys? "Then there's one full of Harleys. I'm used to the fact that there's no way to get to see them anyway." It would take him days to read the full manifest of all the cargo on *Kendal*, and anyway, there isn't one on board. A modern container ship is crewed by people who have no idea what they are carrying.

Kendal's crew know only the contents of the refrigerated boxes and the flammable or toxic goods, so that they can put out fires if necessary. We are carrying paint, lacquer, enamel, stain, shellac solutions, varnish, and polish. Somewhere there is liquid flavoring, which is highly flammable and may cause vapors that explode if they meet air. Elsewhere there is some octahydro-tetramethyl-napthalenyl-ethanone, a chemical that can be used in air fresheners or to reduce odor in permed hair. There are 1,828 kilograms of carbamate pesticide, a substance highly toxic to humans, and 180,000 kilograms of metal powder, self-heating. This, I read, "may react violently with water"—on a ship at sea, in containers that are weatherproof, not waterproof. Marius guesses at other contents. He sees the listing for "BMW airbags, batteries wet, filled with acid" and says that means we are carrying cars to the markets of the East. Not that he cares much. "When the navy call us in the Gulf of Aden and ask us what type of ship we are, we say 'container.' 'What's in the containers?' 'No idea.'"

One of the crew tells me he can overcome the blankness of the boxes, although that's not how he phrases it. He can break a container seal and reseal it convincingly, although I suspect his intent would be for monetary, not intellectual, gain. This skill is more common than it should be. The U.S. Government Accountability Office (GAO) reported on a U.S. Customs and Border Patrol study that "existing container seals provided inadequate security against physical intrusion." Criminals who don't know how to reseal a seal could do an adequate workaround by taking the door off.

Much of modern security rests on theater and assumption. That applies to airport lines, questionable laws about liquids, and the supposed safety of twenty million containers containing who knows what. Who does know? Only 1 to 3 percent of containers in Europe are physically inspected. Worldwide, the rate is thought to be between 2 and 10 percent. U.S. ports receive seventeen million containers a year and physically inspect 5 percent of them. Container manifests rely on the legal term "said to contain." Security people will assure you that intelligence and clever analysis can fill in the rest of the percentages, that they can spot smuggled goods, people, or weapons. I wonder. When *MSC Napoli* grounded off a Devon beach in January 2007, its burst boxes of motorbikes, shampoo, and diapers attracted looters and treasure hunters. It was also a rare opportunity to compare what was declared on container manifests with actual contents. In 20 percent of the containers, the contents and weights were wrong. The difference was sometimes as much as three tons. When a ship must be carefully stabilized with weight and ballast, enough of those differences can overturn it.

All sorts of criminals like ships. Counterfeiters ship $200 billion worth of fake goods in them, or more than the GDP of 150 countries. People traffickers regularly send their desperate clients off in boxes. In 2006, Seattle police arrested forty traffickers for procuring foreign women to work in brothels. Some had paid $50,000 to travel in shipping containers. Drug barons love boxes.

In one report, the GAO was blunt: "U.S. initiatives relating to cargo container security have been limited and generally ineffective for the international counter narcotics effort." In 2012, the Stockholm International Peace Research Institute (SIPRI) published data from its Vessel Maritime Incident Database. This showed that container ships were six times more likely to be involved in destabilizing military and narcotics-related transfers than their share of the world market fleet would suggest.

In 1939, Albert Einstein wrote a letter to President Franklin Delano Roosevelt about the feasibility of setting off a uranium chain reaction. He didn't think of dropping his new bomb by air, but by ship. "A single bomb of this type, carried by boat and exploded in a port, might very well destroy the whole port together with some of the surrounding territory." Einstein was wrong and *Enola Gay* was right, but the "bomb in a box" theory still concerns plenty of U.S. security analysts. The fashionable threat is not cocaine but Al-Qaeda, and has been ever since Osama bin Laden said that "if [the U.S.] economy is finished, they will become too busy to enslave oppressed people. It is very important to concentrate on hitting the U.S. economy with every available means." Bin Laden was not a bin Laden—a powerful, business-minded family that uses shipping for its construction empire—for nothing.

In 2004, Al-Qaeda reportedly recruited a maritime expert. U.S. security sources revealed in 2010 that the organization had been working out how best to blow up oil tankers. Though why bother with intercontinental missiles or explosives, the urban planning academic Stephen Cohen writes, when you can just ship everything you need in parts and assemble it at the required destination? "Containers . . . are the poor man's missiles: you no longer have to be a big powerful government to create catastrophe." In 2003, ABC News shipped depleted uranium from Jakarta to Los Angeles in an attempt to expose the weaknesses in port barriers. The stunt didn't go down well at the Department of Homeland Security, whose declared mission is to "stop dangerous things and dangerous people from entering the country," even if those dangerous things are sent by people from a national news channel. "Can a reporter rob a bank to prove that bank security is weak?" said a spokesman, complaining that as he understood things, you don't break laws to break news. In fact, shipping uranium is legal, as long as you declare it. ABC didn't and no one checked.

Connecting the sea to terrorism has become popular in security studies. Al-Qaeda certainly understands ships: not only because it rammed USS *Cole* with a boat, but because it is thought to own or charter a small fleet. North Korea has its own flag, a fleet of 242 vessels, and the ability to make maritime mischief. *Lloyd's List* reported in 2012 that 120 vessels had reported GPS malfunctions in seas near North Korea, in an article entitled "Pyongyang Death Jam" that suspected the work of a North Korean signals jammer. I wouldn't bother with shipping a dirty bomb: a GPS jammer can be bought in the UK for one hundred dollars (though they are banned in the United States) and can cause mayhem. When the UK's General Lighthouse Authorities experimented in 2010 with what happens to ships whose signals are jammed, the data showed that the experiment vessel was traveling overland. Captain Glenn would be pleased that *Lloyd's List* recommended reliance on traditional navigational equipment as well as technology. The antiterrorist sextant.

A senior government official was asked in 2002 about the threat of maritime terrorism. "This industry is a shadowy underworld," he said. "After 9/11 we suddenly realized how little we understood about commercial shipping. You can't swing a dead cat in the shipping business without hitting somebody with phony papers." But phony papers aren't always the problem. In 2010, Nigerian security forces discovered 240 tons of rockets, mortar shells, and small arms ammunition in thirteen containers that had been shipped on the German-owned, French-operated, Marshall Islands–flagged *Everest* from Bandar Abbas in Iran, despite UN sanctions that prohibit Iran from selling arms. The contraband was hidden behind marble slabs and fiberglass. The manifest showed that the recipient was "to order." In short, writes Hugh Griffiths in SIPRI's report, "the ship's owners, operators and officers had no knowledge or reason for suspicion regarding the container." The defense of ship operator CMA-CGM was telling: the containers had been loaded and sealed by an Iranian company that was not on any list of prohibited traders. They had done nothing wrong.

In response to such uncertainty, the Customs and Border Protection Agency is charged with implementing a "layered security strategy" to protect terrorism reaching the United States by water. It wants to lower a portcullis around its borders and turn the whole ocean into a manageable moat. With various initiatives like the Safe Port Act, the Secure Freight Initiative, and the Container Security Initiative, suspect containers are supposed to be identified with intelligence and screening. Nations buy the screening equipment in return for their containers getting faster entry into the United States; U.S. customs officers are deployed to foreign ports to oversee the process.

Under this layered security scheme, the perfect U.S.-bound container behaves like this: first the foreign factory that packs it will have joined the Customs-Trade Partnership against Terrorism and been previously vetted. A safe pair of packing hands. Importers and carriers provide information to U.S. Customs, which uses an automated tracking system to identify high-risk containers. The box is shipped to a foreign port that has signed up to the Container Security Initiative, where foreign officials working harmoniously with U.S. Customs identify and scan containers using "non-intrusive inspection equipment and radiation portal monitors," in the words of the GAO. While the box is sailing safely onward, updates on its progress are electronically transmitted to the United States. If further doubt remains about the level of risk it poses, upon arrival the container is screened with more nonintrusive inspection equipment and detained or set free to furnish an American home or fuel an American car.

It is a beautiful vision of a safer global supply chain. For now, it is still only a vision. According to the Implementing Recommendations of the 9/11 Commission Act, enforced in 2007, a system to scan 100 percent of all U.S.-bound cargo must be in place by July 2012. Six foreign ports signed on to the 100 percent requirement, but by February 2012 five had dropped out. The process was too expensive and too difficult, said Salalah, Southampton, Busan, Hong Kong, and Puerto Cortes, leaving only Qasim port in Pakistan. In reality, scanning every single U.S.-bound container is an outlandish idea: customs officials attempting to scan all U.S.-bound containers leaving one Hong Kong terminal managed only 5 percent. It is more outlandish than a proposal by a company named Inscentinel to use sniffer bees to detect drugs and explosives. The authors of a study commissioned by the EU thought the 100-percent target akin to a trade barrier and undiplomatically said so. Many customs and security experts think it unworkable. The technology to do the scanning isn't yet good enough; the blockages would choke ports. The new scanning and radiation equipment required, the report's authors wrote, would cost the EU alone €10 billion and could cost world trade $17 billion. Trade is movement. Trade is sacred. In 2012, the Department of Homeland Security quietly pushed the 100-percent deadline to 2014 and counting.

There is a message from the office. The office is in Europe but the message is written in the lovely phrases of subcontinental English. It begs the captain to get "earlier gangs for your good vessel," and it instructs *Kendal* to be at the pilot station—the pickup point for the port pilot—at 16:30, earlier than predicted. Schedules can slip in shipping when ports are clogged and berthing space precious.

The speed is adjusted accordingly and we are on time to pick up the pilot for Le Havre. Le Havre is a harbor whose name means *harbor*. It lies on one of shipping's superhighways, because all Europe's stuff arrives across these waters; or all its empty boxes are sent Asiaward for more. If these shipping channels were highways they would be potholed. Instead they have shallows and quirks. For this reason, a local pilot is required, on the assumption that even the officers on a regular loop like this one can't learn the intricacies of all the foreign ports they call at. Once, while looking at charts, I asked Marius what some funny-colored patches of blue were. A different blue. He didn't know that they were lagoons. He shrugged. "If I don't have to sail through it, I'm not interested."

Some captains resent pilots. Failed seafarers, they say, who couldn't hack it at sea. Or seafarers who escaped, more likely, and who delight in talking of their better pay and hours to these men trapped on a ship for months, and of how they can go home every day. Perhaps this pilot-officer rivalry is required, just as ship life needs tribes or hierarchies to provide boundaries in limited space and endless time. So there is oil and water here, too, though the rivalry is not vicious as it was in the days of black gangs, when the coal stokers called sailors kulaks or drones and the sailors called them moles or bats. "Bad weather," writes Theodora Fitzgibbon in *A Taste of the Sea*, "was 'those kulaks are at it again,' for whenever the ship rolled it was the fault of the bridge." One day the Scottish cadet invites me to do an engineering shift and visit the bow thruster, going down "as far as you can go and it's dark and spooky." I decline, as anyone who has watched the *Poseidon Adventure* would, and he says, "You deck people do nothing! Nothing!"

There are officers, then crew. There are Europeans against Asians and Russians against Ukrainians. There are probably Filipinos from one island against Filipinos from another. There are seafarers and then there is everyone else. Anthropologists put seafarers into a "high-contrast folk group," along with firefighters, loggers, and miners, where what binds the group is shared danger ill understood by others. The Scythian philosopher Anacharsis was once asked whether there were more people alive or dead. He couldn't answer, said Anacharsis, because he didn't know where to place seamen. "Seamen," concluded the seventeenth-century clergyman John Flavel, who quotes this remark, "are, as it were, a third sort of persons, to be numbered neither with the living nor the dead; their lives hanging continually in suspense before them."

This was true when Flavel wrote his book. It has not yet become untrue. Seafarer fatalities are still ten times those of land-based occupations. Men fall off gangways or are crushed between the ship and the quay. They are thrown by swells against steel machinery. They suffocate. In 2007, the crew of the emergency response vessel *Viking Islay*, twenty-five miles off the northern English coast in the Amethyst gas field, heard clanking from the anchor. Some cabins abutted the anchor locker, where the chain was stored, and one night it disturbed their sleep. The following morning, Robert Ebertowski, a forty-year-old Polish AB, and Bob O'Brien, a fifty-nine-year-old Scot, went to see what was happening. The crew heard Ebertowski say on the radio, "I'm going to put a clip on this," then silence. Seaman Findlay MacFadyean followed, wearing protective gear as he should, but he was a big man and couldn't get into the anchor locker, so he took it off. Within a few seconds, there were three dead men on a ship of twelve. The chamber had rusted and the oxygen had been sucked from the air. The men had all suffocated immediately, or in the time it takes to say eight words.

Worldwide, four times more people die in ferry accidents than in airplanes—mundane, commuting ferries like *Dona Paz*, a Filipino passenger vessel that collided with a tanker in 1987. Many people—4,375—died. It still counts as the worst peacetime disaster in Filipino history. In the same year, the *Herald of Free Enterprise*, a cross-Channel ferry, sank just outside Zeebrugge, drowning 193 people. The bow doors on the *Herald of Free Enterprise* were supposed to have been closed by an assistant bo'sun, who was asleep on his bunk when Harbor Stations were called and all things were to be readied for departure, like making sure the sea was on the outside of the ship. For years afterward, "he left the bow doors open" was a metaphor for general or colossal incompetence. But still I disembark a cross-Channel ferry and realize that I didn't listen to safety announcements, and I didn't know where the life jackets were or which muster station to go to. If the ship went under or tipped, and the darkness made a mockery of its layout so the bar was over my head and the doors didn't work upside down, I would have had nothing to protect me but my assumption that I would survive. But I wouldn't, probably, and if I did it would be through luck and upper arm strength: the majority of survivors on the *Herald of Free Enterprise* were the younger and fitter of passengers, who could haul themselves through windows.

The sea drowns the solid outlines and protection of modern technology and society. To go peaceably to sea, you need pretense. You are buoyant on assumptions and water, even though the water is miles deep, downward, but you can't see the distance like you can from a plane, so it is not there. (When the Dutch cargo ship *Soekaboemi* was sunk in 1942, a young British radio officer sitting in one of its lifeboats asked a Dutch crewman where the nearest land was. "Two miles away," said the crewman. "Straight down.")

Such dark thoughts swirl around the seemingly mundane activity of getting a ship safely into harbor. But it is not mundane. I like to listen to port approaches, because getting this enormous ship into a safe harbor is acted out aurally: Starboard 10, please, Captain. Starboard 10, Pilot. Thank you, Captain. Thank you, Pilot. Everything is repeated for certainty. They are safety echoes. And as has happened thousands of times before, *Kendal* is nudged into her berth by two tugs with their noses pushed into her side; their strength a match, proportionately, for ours, their azimuth propellers engineered to turn on a dime; marine donkeys, gritty and underappreciated. I once traveled on a tug up the Thames, escorting HMS *St. Albans* into Canary Wharf, and watched with amusement as spectators gathered to gaze at the glamour of a gray warship and her white-uniformed sailors, ignoring the astonishing nimble mass of horsepower behind her that was the tug.

Slowly, noisily, but safely, the good vessel slows, slides, and stops. We have found safe haven in a port named for it.

Junior Officer Marius
(ROSE GEORGE)

3

HARBOR

Another Day in Paradise

Port hours are busy hours. Cargo must be watched, because the crew must do dockers' jobs now, caring for containers and watching out. Things aren't as tricky as they used to be, when cargo was loose and undefended by steel uniformity. The captain remembers all sorts of waywardness in all sorts of ports. There were stevedores who were all kinds of thieves. "And we were little cadets: how were we supposed to stop them? These huge, grown men? We just said 'no, no, no.'" But the stevedores—dockers who work in ship holds—still deliberately dropped the cases of whisky they were carrying, punched holes in the cases, and poured the whisky directly into tin mugs they had brought for the purpose. In the Far East, they didn't bother with tin mugs: they just took the bottles. London dockers demanded an "embarrassment tax" for having to load toilet pans. It was a penny a pan. They got it.

The captain remembers sweet revenge in Penang, when the cargo being discharged looked like chocolate bars but was laxatives. Of course the stevedores helped themselves, and the crew

consequences, until they went down in the hold and
clean up all the crap. "The stevedores used to pee and do
all sorts of things down the cargo hold. Now we've got internal
systems, but then—you've got no idea." He describes a scupper, a
waste pipe on older ships that emerged from the side. In ports, the
scupper's contents could fall directly on the docks, so they used
"shitboards," chutes rigged from planks that redirected the offend-
ing material into the water. It didn't always work, if the shitboard
wasn't properly in line. Sometimes it used to land on the quay and
the dockers would go crazy and the crew would have some hilarity.
I have seen pictures of on-ship sanitation that were a little better: a
restroom in an engine room that is only a toilet with a curtain
round it. On ships that the Second World War merchant seaman
Frank Laskier sailed on, you expected little and were given less. In
his autobiography—in which Laskier barely disguises himself as
"Jack"—he writes of a "sailors' Gethsemane" that he worked on,
where the lavatory was a doorless cubicle in the engine room; the
sanitation itself was a simple drain flushed with a hose pipe if there
was water, not flushed if not. "The smell was terrific and it was the
condiment to every meal Jack had on board. The flies were murderous."

There are no stevedores in *Kendal*'s cargo holds; instead the
dockworkers lounge outside smoking cigarettes, standing up
every so often to manipulate the twist-locks that pin down the
containers in their stacks. Maersk locks are branded with the
seven-point star. It is not the job of dockers to safeguard either
the cargo or the metal boxes, so one ship's officer or another is
usually running around looking harried, searching for dents and
damage, holding a camera for evidentiary purposes. The captain
is not to be seen, because port time for him means a stream of
visitors to his office: the ship's agent, who looks after the ship's
affairs while she is docked; the chandlers who supply it; the customs people who inspect it; and the various busybodies who find
something to ask, who have some forms to fill out, who exhaust

him with questions. To cheer a captain in port, you just need to arrive without a clipboard.

Telling sea stories is known as swinging the lantern, and the captain's memories of trips ashore swing a wide arc. He supplies every story I expect and hope for: being arrested and shot at in West Africa; throwing soap bars at maidens in the northern Philippines so they would dive down to fetch them under the gaze of dazed English lads; encountering banana spiders and footlong millipedes. He has tales of bar life and sailor towns, probably, but he doesn't share those beyond agreeing that there was wine, women, and song, drink and knives. He would not agree that sailors are the "devil in harbor," as they were known by shore people who only ever saw sailors when they were relaxing, mostly alcoholically. The first-ever advice columnist, an eighteenth-century bookseller named John Dunton, recommended that a woman fearing lonely spinsterhood get down to the docks and find a sex-starved sailor.

These days, Captain Glenn goes ashore only when strongly persuaded by the chief engineer. The pressure is applied most insistently at Pattaya, the notorious Thai resort near Laem Chabang. The captain sometimes cedes to the persuasion not because it is Pattaya but because it is the final port on the loop, and he can relax a little. But the sight of all those old Caucasian men with young Thai girls disgusts him. He doesn't know how the men have the gall to do it, and he doesn't want to be mistaken for one of them, so he goes ashore only every other trip, if that. The crew may do as they please, though he feels obliged to tell cadets to be careful. I am surprised he has the chance to do this fatherly stuff with them, when the cadets are usually sprinting down the gangway as soon as we berth. They are nineteen years old: wouldn't you? Once, the captain had to report seven of his crew in one day for making a freedom bid when they leaped off the gangway in Hong Kong while the ship was still a yard from the dock, a maneuver that looked simple but risked a nasty squashing death by a ship surging on swells against the quay. For that, they were "logged" in the ship's daily log. That seems like tame discipline, but the powers of a modern captain are limited, when all crew is controlled by offices in Singapore, Cyprus, or Manila. The captain used to be able to fire troublemakers or anyone who disturbed the harmony of the ship. He had a trip where one sailor got a spike in his arm, and another pulled a sailor out of his bunk by fingers stuck up the man's nostrils. Glenn told the aggressor that his goose was cooked and sacked him. He sounds wistful about this autonomy, long gone.

Hardly anyone can manage to get ashore in daylight hours. But Marius has somehow found some time between his morning and evening shift. Marius is a junior officer, but he has been at sea for years and seen hundreds of ports. He has spent two weeks in a force 11 storm in the Bering Sea, watching his ship roll to a degree that sent all objects flying. He wasn't seasick. That is, he may have been, but it was overpowered by not being able to sleep. The strongest storm is force 12, when winds blow at more than sixty-five nautical miles per hour, the air is filled with spray, and visibility is seriously affected. On the Beaufort scale, a force 11 storm is thought to produce seas thirty-seven feet high. This kind of force is what Charles Dickens encountered when he sailed to America.

> And so [the ship] goes on, staggering, heaving, wrestling, leaping, diving, jumping, pitching, throbbing, rolling, and rocking; and going through all these movements, sometimes by turns, and sometimes together; until one feels disposed to roar for mercy.

He calls the attention of a passing steward, who tells him this is but "rather a heavy sea on, sir, and a headwind." A headwind? That sounds benign.

> Imagine a human face upon the vessel's prow, with fifteen thousand Sampsons in one bent upon driving her back, and hitting her precisely between the eyes whenever she attempts to advance an inch.

Marius has survived two weeks in an Arctic storm, but he has never been nearer to France than the deck of a ship berthed in one of its ports. He asks shyly if he can come with me, and we head with little foreknowledge to a main square for coffee. This is usual for seafarers: they can't Google for maps or tourist information without the Internet and are reliant on old brochures and word of mouth as guides to the new places they encounter. When we called at Bremerhaven, the chief engineer went off to find some culture and at dinner reported that "it was freezing and everywhere was shut." Still, he had wandered around for hours, in a cold Sunday town, because it was not the ship, and the people he saw were not his shipmates.

It is not force 11 or fifteen thousand Samsons, but a gale is blowing and tables and chairs are tipping and toppling. Marius looks about him. Is this what France is like? I see what he is seeing: a desolate square of concrete surrounded by brutal concrete buildings, flat and squat. No, Marius. It's what a town obliterated by Second World War bombs looks like. I try to describe Paris, its narrow shuttered windows and cast-iron balconies, its elegance and softness. I try to describe what France looks like, but it isn't possible in the face of this concrete and the gale. Instead, we explore. Marius wants to see some Second World War beach fortifications, so off we walk, a mile along the beach, then up a road, then into some bushes. There is no sign of fortifications on the beach. Maybe they are on the other side of the hill. The bushes are dense, and every so often they reveal a lone man staring out to sea. Marius doesn't ask me again if this is what France looks like, but I think he is thinking it. Finally I understand where we are when I see a poster for a gay disco. Quick march, Marius. I didn't mean to take a seafarer cruising. So we shop for supplies: coffee and green tea, kilos of fruit, yogurts. Perishables are likely to run out no matter how good Pinky's calculations. The ship's fruit is already forlorn. Also these will be the last shops for a while, and Pinky hasn't yet understood what "vegetarian" means. She still offers fish as an option, or bean soup "with a little meat. Only a little." It is best to stock up.

We leave Le Havre in evening light. Unusually, the port of Le Havre is attached to its town, so our exit route passes the beach and windsurfers profiting from the gale nipping past. See how many we can run down, says someone on the bridge. The windsurfers survive us, and by breakfast we are off Ushant. The Bay of Biscay defeated Charles Darwin on *Beagle*, who wondered how on earth he would survive the dreadful seasickness. *Kendal* has passed through with ease.

At the end of breakfast, Mike says, Have a good day.

Marius says, Another day in paradise.

Mike says, SSDD, as the Filipinos say. Same shit, different day.

Actually, it is different today. There is a new passenger. A pigeon arrived during Igor's watch the night before, and it now sits, feathers puffed from cold or nerves, on the starboard window ledge of the wheelhouse. It has a ring on its leg, so it must be a racing pigeon, and I tell Marius about the pigeons of the Second World War who won medals for taking messages to important places. He says, "I'm going to stick a sticker on him to say he was on the *Maersk Kendal* and he cheated. He didn't fly, he sailed." The pigeon is an excitement. Really. Even the captain pays the pigeon attention. "We're forty miles out so it can't go anywhere. It might get a scent around Lisbon or Gibraltar and try its luck." He is not hopeful. Already it has a tray of water to drink from and a bowl of bread. Later it will be given dried rice, split peas, dried foodstuffs in a variety that means affection. The pigeon also has a name on a leg lag: 4097430 BELG 2009. In less than twenty-four hours it has become the ship's mascot, and as such, it has a long line of antecedents, at least according to *Ships' Cats*, a particular favorite on my shipping bookshelves. Cats suit ships, despite the water. They are self-contained creatures, and find places to hide in. And they eat rats. Every modern ship has rat guards—plastic collars on the mooring ropes—more to prevent rats from climbing off the ship than on it, a disturbing thought. Cockroaches also cause trouble. They come on board, but there is no food in the walls of the bridge house, so they keep exploring until they find some. For this reason Francis is kept busy cleaning crumbs, and food in cabins is discouraged.

Cats also soothe a lonely life: there are plenty of pictures of ships' cats snoozing in tiny hammocks fashioned by lonely sailors, even in wartime. Able Seaman Simon, ship's cat on HMS *Amethyst*, managed to catch five rats a day even after being wounded in 1949 by shells from Chinese communists on the Yangtze River. He was given the Dickin Medal—awarded to courageous animals—and became a British celebrity. The U.S. Coast Guard preferred dogs. A mongrel puppy adopted in 1938 by the crew of the Coast Guard cutter *Campbell* retired with honors after the war, rank chief petty officer (K9C), dog. One wartime cat was named U-Boat.

Cats were banned by the Royal Navy in 1975, for health and hygiene reasons. They ate rats, but they were also dirty. But unexpected animal passengers still give shipping some sought-after positive press. In 2011, the crew of *Skagen Maersk* found that a crab-eating macaque had jumped aboard in Malaysia. A crew member saw the stowaway searching for food near the mess, and the chief engineer paused from running a ship to build a humane trap. Sinbad—of course—now lives in Wales Ape and Monkey Sanctuary along with a Japanese snow monkey called Julie, found wandering the streets of Antwerp. It might not have been a happy ending, a Maersk source tells me. "The older seafarers said they would just have thrown him overboard. But the younger crew turned him into a pet." It's sad that crews bond over a pigeon or a monkey. But what else do they have to bond over?

Kendal seems like a harmonious ship, but that is due to the captain and happenstance. Nearly two-thirds of ships have more than one nationality on board, but 38 percent have several. This is not new: ships have always made up numbers in their ports of call. Spanish ships sailed with Greeks, English, Norwegians, Portuguese. Lascars were numerous enough to have their own sailors' homes in foreign ports. Because navies liked to steal crew from merchant ships, merchant crews were restocked from passing ports:

Portuguese, Greek, Norse, Maltese. That was happenstance globalization. Today's multinational crews are selected by planners in shore offices in Manila, Mumbai, Singapore. Rumors abound about their choices. They put Ukrainians and Russians together because they will stand each other off, like magnets, and the force field in between will be harmony. Filipinos drink and sometimes fight but they are hard workers and cheap. The Chinese are also cheap, and adequate seafarers, but their English is poor. Indians are good officers but getting to be expensive. Pakistanis cause problems these days in security-sensitive U.S. ports, so that one manning company simply sacked its Pakistani staff. American hostility to seafarers is now regularly cited as a reason the job has worsened. American ports have been difficult ever since the implementation of the 2004 International Ship and Port Facility Security Code (ISPS). Although international maritime law specifies that seafarers should be freely allowed some time ashore, the practice is much different. A survey of 230 seafarer unions and 700,000 seafarers found that more than half had been denied shore leave, particularly in the United States. A survey by the Filipino AMOSUP union found that 70 percent of its members had been forbidden to go ashore, even though seafarers are far more likely to be victims of crime or terrorism than to perpetrate it.

It is a skill, this mingling and melding of the world's peoples. For the most part, it works. "We have found many seafarers who actually prefer mixed nationality crews," writes the maritime academic Tony Lane. "After all, a single nationality crew will inevitably be some sort of microcosm of the society from which it is drawn, and might therefore carry within it the conflicts of that society."

Kendal's officers know what their nationalities mean in the present and the future. The captain says often that he is being used to train his replacements, because British officers are good, but they cost too much. Romanians and Ukrainians are cheaper and also well trained by the excellent maritime academies in Constanta and Odessa. But they are more expensive than Filipinos and Chinese and have already had pay cuts. All the Europeans are gloomy and apprehensive, and with reason. In 2009, *Lloyd's List* reported that Maersk had sent a memo headed "Zero Recruitment in Europe." The columnist was scathing. "Famously, there are already more blue whales than there are British seafarers on British ships. The difference is that people are taking conservation measures to save the whale."

All workforces have waves and changing of guards. There were lascars and now there are Filipinos. But the diminishment of British and American merchant navies is unprecedented. There is regular fretting about recruitment in the pages of the shipping press. Some British seafarers plan to retire early or move into shore jobs. The captain doesn't want to do that. He can be cold about his job—it is moving giant boxes, and that is that—but the force of his anger about his changed industry conveys something other than coldness. Before the oil crisis in 1973, there were British crews, British labor laws. "After that they took the companies offshore. They offered us contracts with thirty percent lower wages, take it or leave it." The captain won't tell me how much he earns, but it is enough for his house to have been extended, for his neighbors to envy him, and for his car to have become a nice Mercedes. Also, British seafarers pay no income tax. On a good ship with a good company, the seafaring life has obvious attractions. The captain of a Liquefied Natural Gas (LNG) tanker controls a multimillion-dollar asset and earns accordingly: one told me that he earns $100,000 tax free for six months a year at sea.

Captain Glenn's grievances are not just about shrinking British job opportunities. He loves the sea still. Often he comes over to me when I am gazing at the water, just to join in. His complaints are about an industry he once loved and now can't bring himself to. The crew: twenty men to run a ship this size? "The only things they can cut down are manpower, wages, and victualing." Fatigue is inevitable. Chris the cadet was up until 2:00 a.m. the other night doing refueling, and the next fuel barge arrived at 4:00 a.m. Marius had three hours' sleep last night, four the night before, and three the night before that. Through Suez or Panama, there is no sleep. It is too risky; there is too much to watch out for. The captain can be awake for thirty-six hours. Staying awake for twenty-four hours increases the chances of being involved in an accident by seven times. Until 2012, international standards allowed seafarers to work a ninety-eight-hour week. Even then, a study by the Marine Accident Investigation Branch looking into the role of fatigue in sixteen hundred accidents found seafarers actually falsifying papers to show they had worked only ninety-eight hours when actually they had worked more. The new Maritime Labour Convention—known as the Seafarers' Bill of Rights—has reduced that to seventy-two, which is still twice the maximum recommended in the EU Working Time Directive. A 2006 study found that one in four seafarers had fallen asleep while on watch. Their level of fatigue is as dangerous as drinking seven times the legal limit of alcohol. Sixty percent of shipping accidents are due to human error. When the *Exxon Valdez* struck Alaska's Bligh Reef in 1989, spilling eleven million gallons of crude oil, an investigation found that the watch officer had been mostly awake for eighteen hours before his shift.

The captain knows this, but what can he do? He also knows, as do maritime academics, that fatigue can be alleviated by a quiet environment and good nutrition, but victualing is a cost that can be more easily cut than fuel or insurance. *Kendal*'s officers, confronted by Pinky's offerings on the sideboard buffet, often reminisce about when they had lobster and fresh seafood. Instead, here is a frankfurter stuffed with Cheez Whiz, or a lambchop speckled with sesame seeds, like little maggots. "This is nothing," says Marius. "I've been on ships where you have to stand staring at the food for minutes, wondering what it is." You can tell how good the food is by how long the crew spends eating it. The average on *Kendal* is six and a half minutes. Pinky is in a thankless position: the ship's cook has been the subject of seafarer humor for centuries. In 1942, a young seaman named Arthur Montaigne was interviewed on a New York radio station. It was the year of the worst losses of ships on the Atlantic, and Montaigne had just returned from there. The interviewer asked him whether he had ever had a chance to be a hero.

Yes, once I saved the whole crew of the *Tuscorora*.

You did? How?

I shot the cook.

Not long ago, Maersk's container fleet was free to fix its own food budget. Captains were trusted to be careful. Now the money per head is seven dollars a day, and the food goes from adequate to worse. The captain once took photographs of the food they were being served—soup so watery you could see the china pattern—and sent them to the office. He sends regular dispatches about the food, and something is done—for a week or so Pinky doesn't serve french fries as the foundation of quite so many meals—but it never lasts.

I think the captain probably sends dispatches about many things, protected by his senior position and his approaching retirement. Paper towels, for example. Flimsy scraps of tissue with solid, powerful significance. Earlier that year, the company had sent out a memo: napkins were no longer to be used by container ships like *Kendal*. The container line business of Maersk is its least profitable. Until further notice, the officers and crew of the container fleet are expected to use paper towels to dab their lips and mop their crumbs, and this would save the company $50,000 a year. This sends the captain into a rage. He would never allow paper towels at the dinner table at home. "We're supposed to be officers and gentlemen. We're professionals. And they're treating us like third-class citizens." Maersk tug crews have napkins; Maersk shore staff have napkins: he has checked. Not the merchant navy, scum of the earth.

These feelings have nothing to do with the ship. "When people see my ship, I want to say, what did you think? It's like I want to show off my girlfriend. She's smooth as anything and she looks the business. She's pretty." He is never this passionate unless he is talking about his Harley-Davidsons or the importance of shaving daily with straight razors, of which he has two on board. Straight razors on a moving ship, and never a nick or cut. That's my captain.

His last ship was a G class, only 292 meters long to *Kendal*'s 300; 32 meters wide to *Kendal*'s 40. It had a sloping stern "like an old man-of-war." He liked the G, but he loves the K class more. In the corner of his dayroom is a framed photograph of *Kendal*'s godmother. I am flummoxed. Ships have godmothers? What for? "It's a Danish thing. I'd never heard of it until I came to Maersk. We used to have a woman to break a bottle of champagne, but not a godmother." On the first new ship that he took out from the yard— the privilege of a senior captain—the office e-mailed a reminder to send the godmother a Christmas card. It is singular, this softness in the middle of a giant company like Maersk, and it is strategic: Tesco is a customer, and *Kendal*'s godmother is the Korean wife of a Tesco executive, a Frenchman. Madame takes her duties seriously. There are pictures of her at the naming ceremony in the Korean shipyard that built *Kendal*, and she has given the ship two small effigies of Korean gods for luck. They sit on the corner table between the captain's two sofas, quietly protecting the ship.

There are no naming ceremonies now; they cost too much and shipping is suffering. In 2008, shipping entered its worst recession for decades. Recession happens now and then: there was one after the 1973 oil crisis and another in the early 1980s. When times are good, ships are built; then something flattens the market, freight rates drop, and there are too many ships and not enough business. In 2005, time charters—rental rates for average tankers—were $75,000 a day. Very Large Crude Carriers (VLCCs) could cost $450,000 per day. Times were excessively good. New shipyards appearing everywhere, countless new shiny ships. Three years later, day rates had dropped to $7,000 or worse. Sometimes owners were effectively paying the oil companies to shift their cargo. Talk to anyone in shipping about this period and they will at some point use the word "cliff" or "precipice." People were going bust. Seafarers were being abandoned on ships that were suddenly cheaper to scrap and stuck on board for months while they waited for wages that were never paid.

That was one result of recession. The other was that ships needed to be parked. Before *Kendal*, I visited six Maersk ships tied together in the middle of Loch Striven near Glasgow. Barnes Wallis had tested his Dambusters bouncing bombs here. There are still bounced bombs on the bottom of the loch, and in 2009 for nearly a year the ships were stranded in the middle. Storing them there was a sensible option economically: Maersk had done a deal with Clydeport, which owns the loch, for long-term parking, which was vastly cheaper than £4,000 daily berth fees in port. But it was a scientifically risky enterprise. No one knew then what would happen to ships that were laid up for so long. There is more knowledge now, gained from long-term parking of pirated ships anchored off Somalia. Several have sunk, though whether through failure or for insurance purposes is unclear. Some have steamed into Mombasa or Djibouti followed by sharks attracted to the crustaceans and sea life that had moved to this new, strange artificial reef and liked it enough to stay.

On Striven, the engineers had been inventive. All the engine parts were wrapped in plastic wrap, the kind that you buy in your local shop and that the engineer had actually bought in the local shop in Rothesay, along with other supplies such as fresh water, which boosted local trade and placated locals who complained of "rust buckets" coming to spoil their pristine, stunning loch. They were not rust buckets. Five of the six were Maersk B class ships, according to the company's internal classifying system, and only four years old. They were special, because they had been built for speed, with sleeker lines than other container ships, less cargo space, engine and accommodation decks in the middle rather than aft, as *Kendal* had. Marius once traveled with a B class through the Straits of Malacca at 32 knots, and other ships were hailing them on the radio saying, "What is that, a jet engine?"

The B class were intended to do a shuttle route from China to the United States, but as soon as they were launched, the price of fuel escalated. They would have cost $35,000 a day to run, and they were the first to lay up, like a company's new hires. But in a way, nothing is ever new in shipping. Pirates come and go; fortunes come and go along with tycoons; and so do grand ships and ideas. Tea clippers were the B class ships of their time and were made unemployable by engines. The U.S. shipping company Sea-Land Service, Inc.—now owned by Maersk—had tried to introduce speedier vessels in the 1970s with SL-7 ships. They had a top speed of 33 knots, but their fuel bills wiped out any advantage. They were soon sold to the U.S. Navy, which has more money or braver accountants.

There will be no stops for seven days now. Sea time will cover 5,167 nautical miles and will last through the Bay of Biscay, down the edge of western Europe, around Gibraltar, through the Pillars of Hercules, along the Mediterranean, past Malta, between Libya and Greece, past Egypt and through Suez, through the Red Sea, through pirate waters, into the Gulf of Aden, and around the corner past Yemen to Salalah, a lyrically named port in Oman.

Before I came aboard, people asked me how I would fill my days. They also asked me whether I would be safe. By now, I have stopped locking my cabin door when I go out and leave it wide open like everyone else. And filling days is easy. They move along, fast. First breakfast and a walk on deck. I am supposed to report to the bridge when I go outside and to wear a hard hat. But as the time goes on my clothing gets less safety conscious. My heavy-toed boots—required for deck activity, according to my leaflet of ship instructions—become trainers or sandals as the weather gets more southern. The hard hat is soon discarded. I have seen jogging corridors on ships, but there is no running on *Kendal*'s deck. The mileage—four loops to a mile—can be walked only, and the boredom of it is leavened only by changing directions. One morning forward, the next aft.

I wonder at the eccentricities of maritime English. It can't be easy for a non-English-speaker to understand "making sternway" for "going backward." Maritime colleges try to teach a dialect known as Maritime English. This dispenses with inessential grammar, so that "Are there fenders on the berth?" becomes "Are fenders on berth?" There is also Seaspeak, which requires users to identify what they're going to say before they say it, hence: "Question. Are fenders on berth?" Both dialects sound intriguing, but hardly any seafarer uses them. When you're screaming down a radio on a ship rolling 45 degrees each way, any English will do—broken, pidgin, Filipino. I hope this is when I learn that my unspeaking Burmese table neighbor is the ship's safety officer. His English is poor, but he has to evacuate a sinking ship if need be.

There are miscomprehensions. I tell the captain one morning during sea time that I have been for my morning constitutional. He looks aghast. "A what?"

"A morning walk."

"If you say 'constitutional' on a ship it means you're going for a crap."

I often head for the fo'c'sle. It has become my terrace and my garden. Unescorted, I am free to lean over the bulbous bow and watch it move water. This doesn't feel like a hazardous activity, but it is. A swell could tip me with ease. Who would know? Francis sailed on a ship where a crew member was killed when he was thrown across the fo'c'sle by a wave. The bridge can't see the fo'c'sle because of the containers in its line of sight. I have no radio. The crew on deck are too busy. There is usually the whining sound of a drill somewhere as someone chips off the rusted paint to replace it with new. The seamen are in the narrow corridors between containers or have their head down splicing ropes. They have no time to look out to sea and no cause to. A small head in the water would not be seen. Nothing can be heard over the engine and the waves.

The ship needs constant care, an 80,000-ton toddler. It is perpetually assaulted by salt, wind, and other corrosive weather. Shore staff expect the crew to repeatedly blast off the salt with pressure hoses of freshwater, let the ship dry, then repaint it. But when can they do that? Only in port or at anchor, and there is never time to let the paint dry. "So we paint over the salt," the captain says. "And the shore staff say, 'You've painted over the salt!' But there is no other way." Another captain once told me that his ship had departed freshly painted, and he had been asked to scatter the ashes of a fellow captain who wanted to be dispersed at sea. The ceremony was done on the poop deck, the ashes were sent out into the wind, and the wind blew them back again onto the fresh paint. The crew had to chip it all off and scatter the painted ashes. That's not quite as bad as a tale I read in *Flotsametrics*, by the oceanographer Curtis Ebbesmeyer, who flushed the ashes of an oceanographic colleague down the toilet when her friends had drunk too much to sail into the bay and leave her in the waters of Puget Sound, as she had asked. "With heads bowed and hands crossed, we launched Keiko on her journey." To Seattle's West Point sewage treatment plant.

Off Portugal, on a Sunday. After lunch the usual four had remained: Marius, me, Mike, and the captain. The talking ones. The conversation turned to entertainment. The captain remembered an organization in his early days that provided the crew with films. "Back then there were wooden hatches, and the accommodation was amidships. So the officers would project the film out of the officers' saloon onto the canvas that covered the wooden hatches and all the crew would sit on the next hatch and watch the film. That was the monthly entertainment." On Mike's first ship, he traveled from Constanta to Victoria, Brazil. Thirty days each way, no stops. They had no generous film-providing association. No TV, no books, only a backgammon set. By the end, the winner had over four hundred matches on his score.

There are no film screenings for the crew now. Why would I watch a film in the saloon, says Marius, genuinely mystified, when I can watch it in my cabin? Instead, they watch DVDs in isolation, "and then we watch them again." Efforts are still made to fill onboard time with something other than work but the relaxation now is solitary, sad. The captain always travels with a guitar, though I never hear him play. He reads books: nonfiction, but never sea stories. Conrad? No chance. Everyone else retreats to laptops.

I unearth the unused backgammon set in the officers' saloon and begin to play Marius daily, while he maintains throughout a deliberately distracting commentary that conveys his level of fatigue better than any academic survey could. If he has energy to spare, he manages a thoroughly irritating monologue. Exhaustion keeps it to a minimum.

The Filipinos play computer games and sing. It is common to climb the accommodation house stairs to the faint caterwauling of a Journey song in a Tagalog accent. Perhaps other entertainment happens behind cabin doors. In a paper entitled "The Filipino Seafarer: A Life between Sacrifice and Shopping," the Norwegian academic Gunnar Lamvik revealed the alarming practice among Filipino seafarers of slicing open their penis with a razor and implanting ball bearings or coffee beans. The implants are called *bolitas*, and the logic behind them is flexible. They keep wives from straying by enhancing their sexual pleasure, and they are useful to attract Brazilian prostitutes. This "secret weapon of the Filipinos," wrote Lamvik, has something to do with the fact that "the Filipinos are so small, and the Brazilian women are so big." Lamvik is told that nearly every Filipino seaman is equipped with *bolitas*. I don't intend to verify that, not even verbally.

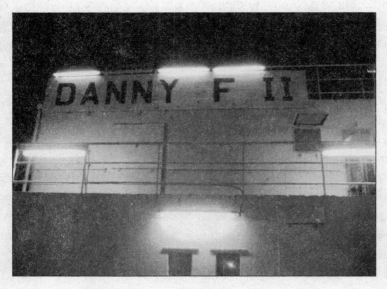

A no-frills ship, an ordinary journey, no trouble expected
(NICOLÀS ACHARD)

4

OPEN SEA

Calves Can Swim

Loss: Propelled merchant ships of not less than 100 gross tons which have ceased to exist—International Maritime Organization

SHIPWRECK. IT SEEMS SUCH AN OLD WORD THAT CONTAINS OLD worlds, of wood and dashing surf; of wreckers who wait with malign patience on beaches; of incidents definitely past. It seems as far away from *Kendal*, this serene ship, as gaslights and horse carriages. It is not far away, though. Two thousand seafarers die at sea every year. In 2006, the International Union of Marine Insurance declared it a catastrophic year for "hull claims," for compensation of lost ships. The next year was four times worse. Even now, even with all our efforts and intentions and instruments, more than two ships are lost every week.

Christmas 2009. The time was late afternoon, the skies were dark, and *Danny F II*, a livestock carrier arriving from Uruguay, was a few miles off Lebanon on her way to a port call in Tripoli. carried 10,224 sheep, 17,932 cows, and 83 men. The sheep and were being taken to the Middle East to become meat. *Danny F II* was a modern-day Noah's Ark going about her business.

Danny F II had not always been a livestock carrier. She bega

1975 as *Don Carlos*, a car transporter. Then she was spruce, well kept, the sheer cliff sides of her flanks that are the sign of car carriers—high sides keep fragile cargo securely enclosed—painted bright green. Her hull was red so that despite her size she was almost jaunty. Before she was twenty, *Don Carlos* became *Danny F II*, when she was sold to a Singapore company and named after who knows who. In a way it doesn't matter how her new name arose, only that it was changed: name changing is considered bad luck at sea. Sometimes superstitions come true. A year after that, *Danny F II* was sold again, to Rachid Fare Enterprises, a livestock transporter. Her paint changed and so did her flag, once again. In thirty-four years, she had flown the flags of Sweden, Singapore, Liberia, Saint Vincent and the Grenadines. Now she was painted wholly white and looked grubbier, less tended. The rust was more obvious against the white paint. The air of her had changed.

By 2009, *Danny F II* was operated by Falcon Point International, a Cairo-based company. She now flew the flag of Panama, the largest maritime registry in the world, and her crew was mixed: a British captain and electrotechnical engineer, an Australian stockman, Uruguayans, Pakistanis, Filipinos, Lebanese. The captain was John Malcolm Milloy, a well-respected and jovial Scot from Campbeltown in Argyll. The electrotechnical engineer was another Scot, fifty-year-old Alan Atkinson. He was a quiet man, says his identical twin brother, Martin. Alan had been working at sea for twenty-seven years, and when he came ashore, he liked to build model ships from kits or play golf. The twins were unmarried and preferred to hang out together. Martin was a firefighter, and they each thought that he had the far more dangerous job.

Alan hadn't really wanted to sail on *Danny F II*. He had started his career on supply vessels, then BP tankers, both of which are known for having the best conditions at sea. The Scottish cadet on *Kendal* talks of working on supply vessels with childlike dreaminess, as if he is a crop sprayer who wants to fly space shuttles. But Alan Atkinson's eyesight had deteriorated; he failed a medical exam and so was no longer accepted for work on tankers or supply. Ferries and livestock transporters had less exacting standards, so he applied to Stena Lines, his first choice, and to *Danny F II*, his second. The offer from *Danny F II* came first and he accepted it. The next day Stena wrote too with an offer, but he didn't think it was right to go back on his word. He would go to sea on the livestock carrier, to work in a sector of shipping that he knew nothing about. Possibly he was seduced by the friendly e-mail sent by Falcon Point's head of shipping, Captain Richard Thomas. "I must say," wrote Thomas, "you will find the livestock trade extremely interesting. Best job I ever had at sea and I have been on all sorts of ships in my time."

On October 26, 2009, Martin Atkinson took his twin to Glasgow airport to catch a flight to Beirut. He presumes that is where Alan was picking up the ship, but he didn't ask and Alan didn't say. *Danny F II* did a regular run between South America and the Middle East, usually from Montevideo to Beirut or Tartous in Syria or Sokhna in Egypt. Six people were listed on the manifest as passengers, including a thirty-five-year-old Uruguayan, Nicolás Achard, but their status was a fiction. Nicolás is a veterinarian and that is the job he was hired to do. He thinks that listing him and two other Uruguayans as passengers meant they didn't have to go through health and safety training. Some crew couldn't swim, including nineteen-year-old Guillermo, another Uruguayan. Some were veterans, such as the popular captain, and the head stockman, Gary Beckett, an Australian who had been going to sea for years. They were both big friendly men, serious on the job but fond of a joke. Baker once managed to convince the captain's wife that koalas were fish.

Snapshots from previous trips show onboard life that looked fine, even fun. There were barbecues on the open deck, and European-looking men in shorts and short-sleeved shirts mingling with smaller, wiry older men in kurta pajamas. That is more group socializing than I ever see on *Kendal*. There are shots of the ship on a glittering, benign blue sea, and another of a wall map showing *Danny F II*'s route marked with dots of Blu-Tac. A no-frills ship, an ordinary journey, no trouble expected. "I am sure," wrote Captain Thomas to Alan Atkinson, "that you will thoroughly enjoy yourself."

I wonder. Animal welfare organizations dislike livestock carriers profoundly, and with reason. (So do Somali pirates: they have captured, then released a few livestock carriers without asking for ransom. Too much hassle.) They criticize the overcrowded conditions, lack of food and water, inadequate bedding for the beasts. They point to countless reports of swine, sheep, or cattle being crushed on their journey and think that shipping frozen meat would be more humane. The Australian Royal Society for the Protection of Animals says that 40,000 cattle and sheep die being transported from Australia every year. It keeps a casualty list: 1,683 sheep and 6 cattle died during a 2006 sea voyage on *Al Messilah* because of heat and failure to eat. Six thousand sheep were stranded at sea for three months in 2003 when their Saudi Arabian importer rejected them. When another buyer could not be found, the sheep were bought by the Australian government and given free to Eritrea. In 2002, 6,119 sheep died in high temperatures on four ships. One, *Al Shuwaikh*, was then allowed to load more sheep, and 2,304 of those died, too. Live meat traders, as livestock transporters are known, dismiss such statistics. "What these loony lefties fail to understand," wrote a contributor in *Meat Trade News Daily*, "is the fact that the animals are better off on the vessels running with food and water, than they are in the drought-stricken outback of Australia."

Alan phoned his parents now and then from the ship's satellite phone, but he never expressed any grave concerns. There was dirty water in the taps. There were cockroaches, but that was to be expected with so many animals. Otherwise he didn't complain. Probably he didn't want to worry them. They were elderly and knew nothing of life at sea beyond what he told them. As children do, Alan edited, although the conditions must have been hard for a man used to the sleeker environments of tankers and supply ships. Nicolás Achard describes conditions as "horrible." He was working mostly with the animals, whose pens were on decks below sea level. Although she had passed the safety inspections required by Panama, the flag state, *Danny F II*, by many accounts, was rusting, old, decrepit. The decks were in such a bad state that regularly the floor would cave in and the leg of a heifer would appear from the deck above, an inch from Nicolás's head. He was used to working in the open with animals on Uruguayan ranches; he didn't much like this confined, cramped, noisy, smelly ship, but he needed the money.

The journey from Montevideo to Lebanon took three weeks with no land calls. On December 16, the crew watched *Titanic* together. The following day, they prepared the ship for port. After so many days at sea, the animals had made a colossal mess. Nicolás remembers that they stopped about thirteen miles off Tripoli. He isn't sure about the sequence of events, but thinks that a storm came, and that the captain thought this was a good opportunity to clean up. It seems an odd decision from such an experienced captain. Perhaps they were already cleaning when the storm came.

The usual cleaning method is to tip the ship slightly and hose the muck into the sea. But all weight on ships, whether ballast water, cargo, or animals, must be carefully distributed to maintain stability. Some of the weight on *Danny F II* was animal feed, stored on the lower decks, but after three weeks the volume had depleted. For Nicolás, this meant that the ship was by now unavoidably unstable. When the ship tilted slightly to let the water and dirt off into the sea, the balance was skewed. Not only that, but the animals moved, too, destabilizing it further. The cows weighed an average of 350 kg each and the sheep 50 kg: that makes up a lot of weight to suddenly shift. Perhaps the discharge of the manure, the movement of the animals, and the waves all came together to overcome the ship. On deck 2, working with a couple of colleagues, Nicolás began to hear "weird sounds." It was livestock on the decks above falling over. With his crew mates, he headed up to deck 6, above the waterline. There they could see that the ship was tilting far more than it should be, as if it were drunk. More crew gathered and worried together. Then everything got worse very quickly.

Nicolás went up to deck 13 and found a life jacket. The boat was listing too much for them to launch the enclosed lifeboats that *Danny F II* carried: one side of the ship was too near the water, the other too high and too tilted. He looked for life rafts—self-inflating dinghies that can be tossed into the sea by hand—but found none nearby, and they could all see that the ship was sinking quickly. Ahmad Harb, a Lebanese crew member, remembered that the captain sounded the alarm. "He knew that the ship was gone and we were already in the disaster stage." Harb was still on a deck beneath the waterline. The captain announced that everyone should make their way up to open decks, but it was too difficult. The angle of the ship made walking up the stairs "like walking up a wall." Harb was stunned by the speed and extent of the disaster. "We could not believe what was happening; we believed in our ship." The weather was bad, but the weather had been bad before. "We had survived much worse conditions. It is a mighty ship." Shocked, trapped, he began to recite his prayers.

On deck 13, the Uruguayans knew they had to jump. They were in work clothes—overalls, heavy boots—and Nicolás told the nonswimmer Guillermo to remove his boots. They would only weigh him down. They all "fell into the sea," a ten-foot descent. "Then we just sat and watched the thing disappear." Nicolás describes *Danny F II* as sinking "like the *Titanic*," but that took almost three hours. *Danny F II* disappeared in twenty minutes, and became the thirty-seventh ship to sink that year.

In the water, Nicolás saw that someone had managed to chuck a life raft into the sea and that it was about one hundred yards away, so he swam for it, front crawl. But he found swimming unexpectedly difficult. There were huge waves, and later he learned that when you are wearing a life jacket it is easier to swim on your back. There were cattle in the water. Pounding waves, darkness, people screaming, howling and thrashing beasts everywhere: it sounds like a section of hell that Dante forgot to include. Nicolás saw a Pakistani crewmate holding on to the tail of a heifer as a flotation device. Ahmad Harb saw this, too. He found it as astonishing as the fact that calves can swim. "A person should know that what is destined to happen will happen," he said. "If a person is to live, he will live, and the reason could be a calf." The Pakistani man lived, reaching shore at Akkar with his cow-shaped life belt.

After about half an hour in the water, Nicolás reached a life raft. He was in a pitiful state by now. He had ingested oil and "all the other crap" a sinking ship vomits up as it founders. There was oil on his skin, in his throat. The raft he found was full of frozen water, but it had flares, so he threw one up, then another that fell back into the dinghy and almost punctured it. He spent an hour on the raft, alone. He heard screaming from another dinghy a hundred yards away, which had twenty men in it, including a Uruguayan friend, Rubén. Rubén called to him. Nico, Nico, come! He wanted the extra space in Nicolás's raft, but it was full of icy water and a deadweight and Nicolás couldn't shift it. After a while he saw a half-dead Filipino man float past and pulled him in. All the while, they could hear people screaming, and the dinghy was being thrown around by the storm waves: up ten feet, up and up, and then bang, it would fall again "into the whole of the sea and you couldn't see anything."

Nicolás is sure that Alan Atkinson made it into a raft. He remembers seeing him. There were many on board, but they had spent enough time together to know who was who. After three hours the first rescue ship arrived. Nicolás and the Filipino waved and screamed, but everyone was screaming, and their gestures were hidden by the huge waves. Another ship arrived, possibly a car carrier. Nicolás calls it "a gigantic boat." He says, "The gigantic boat went into the area of the sinking to save people. The only problem was that it was so big, instead of rescuing them it ran over them. Then it went away."

After eight hours, Nicolás and his companion were rescued by an Italian naval vessel that flew a UN flag. Others were picked up by Lebanese naval vessels. A Royal Navy helicopter had also arrived from Cyprus to assist. The Italians gave their guests immediate medical attention, hot baths, thermal clothing, and food, then sent them by helicopter to Tripoli. There, the ship's managers paid for hotel, but most survivors had arrived with no possessions beyond rubber boots given to them by their Italian rescuers. Luckily the Uruguayan ambassador provided his citizens with clothes, enough for them to donate some to their Pakistani and Filipino shipmates, whose embassies gave them nothing. Only on the last day of their time ashore did Falcon Point International, the owners, provide a ir of trousers, socks, and shoes for each survivor. Forty-three men returned from the foundering of *Danny F II*. Alan Atkinson, Gary Beckett, and Captain John Milloy did not.

There are tales and rumors about the sinking of *Danny F II*. Ahmad Harb said that when the ship started tilting, Gary Beckett "stood in the middle of the ship and lit a cigarette. I looked at him, but he just waved with his hand saying that he doesn't care anymore, he wanted to go down with the ship." As for Captain Milloy, Nicolás Achard has a secondhand story from the Filipino second mate. The second had approached the captain and offered him a life jacket but Captain Milloy refused. He said, "No, I am staying here until the end." Ahmad Harb thought he was injured. "I heard the captain calling Mayday. He recited the complete distress call and said that we are thirteen miles away from Tripoli port. This is where the captain went into silence, his voice disappeared, and I think that he got hurt."

In a poignant video tribute to his father, Owen Milloy called his dad "amazing" because he saved so many lives. He showed a box of mementos: photos, certificates, memories. He held up the watch that his dad wore "for about fifteen years," which was found when his body was recovered, the day after the sinking. They had to cut it off him, said Owen, but he was glad to have it.

He sounded so proud of his dad. The ship's captain, going own with his ship. It seems such an old-fashioned heroism, one that belongs in the nineteenth century with shipwrecks and flogging, until something happens that proves we still expect our captains to be heroes. In 2011, Italian cruise-ship captain Francesco Schettino was widely and violently vilified for leaving the cruise ship *Costa Concordia* when there were still hundreds of passengers aboard. Not only had he not stayed on his ship, let alone gone down with it, but he had fled with indecent haste (and done so by "falling into a lifeboat"). Perfidious captains are remembered. When the cruise liner *Oceanos* foundered off South Africa in 1991, its captain, Yiannis Avranas, was among the first to depart the sinking ship. Afterward, he was not apologetic. "When I give the order to abandon ship, it doesn't matter what time I leave. If some people want to stay, they can stay." Two hundred and twenty-five passengers were left on board after the lifeboats had been launched. Their rescue was coordinated not by a crew member, but by the ship's entertainer. When Moss Hills, having managed to call the coast guard from the bridge, was asked to identify his position, he replied, "I'm not a rank. I'm a guitarist." This is a curious thing about ships: when something goes wrong, every staff member must become a safety expert, even if usually they varnish nails or dance twice nightly in a show.

On December 18, 2009, the police came to the Atkinson house in Ayrshire. They told Alan's parents—Fergus, eighty-five, and Rebecca, eighty-one—that the ship was in trouble and a search and rescue operation was taking place. That was twenty-four hours after the ship had gone down. They assured Martin that everyone was on life rafts. This was the worst thing that could have been said to his mother, because she hoped for months afterward that it was true. At the Milloy house nearby, the family—two sons and the captain's wife—had been told the same thing. That night, Owen said, it was hard to sleep. "I just kept tossing and turning, thinking, what if, is he dead, is he alive? He could be in a boat somewhere, a lifeboat. It was painful." The next day there were news reports. Some said his dad was dead; some said he simply hadn't been found yet. Owen didn't know what to believe. "I thought, This is horrible. Getting told before the police have heard anything? It's fricking disgraceful." It wasn't until later that day that confirmation came. Captain John Milloy was found dead.

For three days after the police visit, the Atkinsons were given updates by the Foreign and Commonwealth Office (FCO) and Falcon Point International, the ship's owner. The information was always the same: the sea conditions were terrible. It was difficult. The animals in the water were making it even harder to see survivors in storm conditions. But the search and rescue operation was still going on.

Later, the shipping agent's representative came to the funeral of Captain Milloy. On the way back he visited the Atkinsons. He said bodies were turning up in Turkey, in Syria, up and down the coast. He wanted DNA. That's easy, said Martin, the identical twin, who was willing to donate. He told this to the FCO again and again, but nothing happened until February 2010, when he gave a blood sample at his doctor's and the Turkish authorities rejected it because "it wasn't in the right format." By then the bodies washing up had increased threefold. A week or so earlier, Ethiopian Airlines flight 409, flying to Addis Ababa from Beirut, had crashed into the sea after takeoff, twelve miles south of the airport. Ninety passengers and crew died. More bodies washing ashore, more confusion. I read the press reports about the crash and learn two things: that the wife of the French ambassador to Lebanon died, and that the Lebanese transport minister immediately began an investigation. Why didn't he do that for *Danny F II*? Because he couldn't. It sank in international waters. Its flag linked the tragedy to Panama, even though the ship carried Lebanese crew. This was a shock for Martin. He was used to the possibility of fatalities in his firefighting job, where loss of life was followed by an immediate investigation. He expected the same would happen for his brother, but he was wrong. Legally, Alan worked on a small part of Panama, floating in no-man's-sea. If Panama didn't want to release the results of its investigation, there was nothing Martin could do about it and nowhere he could go to protest.

In the early 1920s, American cruise lines were faced with a difficulty. They wanted to serve alcohol on their ships, but it was the time of Prohibition. Their ships flew a U.S. flag, and according to maritime law they were governed by the United States no matter where they sailed. They were, as ships have been for centuries, a floating chunk of the nation-state, even in the *mare liberum* of the high seas. Historically, a nation has issued flags, kept a register of its ships, and offered sovereign protection and oversight. This deal has always been flexible: ships often ran up a different flag if they found themselves in the wrong place during an inconvenient war. So the Prohibition-wary American cruise lines decided to turn their ships into Panamanian vessels.

After the Second World War, Greeks and Italians bought the ships that had been built for war and were now surplus and realized they could avoid taxes, crew salary standards, and draining union requirements by flagging their ships "out." The "out" was Panama and then Liberia, a West African state with strong U.S. links, which used the U.S. dollar as currency, considered itself Little America, and did what the United States bid. American business interests were behind Liberia's new flag registry because they thought Panama too corrupt, however convenient. Honduras and Costa Rica followed, and then the rest of the world. Why not? For a nation, an open registry brings welcome income and can require little work. Now 68 percent of ships fly a flag that does not belong to the country their owner is from or resident in. Those American then Panamanian cruise ships began a practice that has changed international shipping as dramatically as the box.

The people who run open registries detest the term "flag of convenience," a phrase coined by the International Transport Federation in 1948, along with an ongoing campaign against the practice. But there is no doubt that convenience is something an open registry offers in abundance. If you flag your ship out, you will be able to register in any nation you please despite not being a citizen: you can do this quickly and easily, sometimes within twenty-four hours and by e-mail; you can choose your crew from anywhere, pay lower taxes, and enjoy fewer labor restrictions or pesky union diktats. All these things are the accepted advantages of a flag of convenience, and they add up to an unbeatably good deal for shipowners in a competitive industry. In 2011, the U.S. Department of Transport compared running a foreign- and U.S.-flagged ship and found it costs 2.7 times more to run an American-registered ship. Because American crew are mandatory, staffing costs are 5.3 times higher. Flagging out can save millions. It is a brave or rich shipowner who resists.

The UN Law of the Sea attempts to control the practice of flagging out by requiring that a ship have a "genuine link" with its flag nation, a company premises in the flag state, perhaps. Debates have raged for years over what this might consist of. It does not consist of the flag registry actually being located in the state that owns the flag. Liberia may have a Liberia International Shipping Corporate Registry soccer team based in Monrovia (it changed its name from Barcelona FC in 1990), but the registry itself is run from the United States in Vienna, Virginia. Kiribati, a tiny Pacific island that set up a registry in 2010, chose the Singapore-based Sovereign Ventures as administrator, despite the company's previous hosting of Cambodia's flag registry, which had ships found to have trafficked cocaine and weapons and people.

Port state control is supposed to be another regulatory brake on open registries. Various port authorities now issue a White List of flags judged to be responsible and a Black List of ones that are not. The Paris Memorandum of Understanding, an association of European port authorities, includes Liberia and Panama on its latest White List, as it has done for years. In the depths of the Black List, as you'd expect, swim North Korea, Libya, Sierra Leone, and Montenegro. The principle behind these lists is sound: port authorities have the power to detain unsafe ships in their ports. They home in on ships flagged to Black List countries, regularly detaining the rust buckets and unsafe ones, so that it becomes more trouble than it's worth—and too expensive, with detention fees and lost income—to flag to poor or unstable states. Academics call this a "race to the middle," whereby the pressures of repeated detentions push bad flags to get better. This happened in the Marshall Islands, a lax and dodgy registry when it began, but now respectable and respected.

Anyway, open registry spokespeople say the distinction between good and bad registries is mistaken. They point out that many state-run flags—not defined as flags of convenience—have poorer standards than open registries on the White List. Liberia's general counsel, Brad Berman, wrote that Liberia, despite its desperate development statistics and GDP, "mandates that its registry is more than a small office manned by a clerk and a pet dog trained to carry registry documents to the local post office." Liberia is certainly no longer in the dark time of the war criminal and former president Charles Taylor, who diverted flag registry income for his personal use, namely to fund rebels in neighboring Sierra Leone. (That is, rebels like Issa Sesay, who I met inadvertently one evening in the Rwandan prison where he is serving a fifty-year sentence, and we had a polite conversation about his chicken supper before I realized I was talking to a man whose troops had amputated the arms and legs of babies. Then I hoped the chicken choked him.)

Most shipowners operate decent ships that are safe and pay their crews a decent wage. But if you are unscrupulous, there is no better place to hide than behind a flag. The ITF calls flags of convenience a "corporate veil." The *Economist*, a supporter of free markets and so surely a supporter of this freest market of all, calls them "cat's cradles of ownership structures." I call them a back door, easy to slip through if necessary.

This ease was best exposed by the oil tanker *Erika*, which broke up off the coast of Brittany in 1999, polluting 250 miles of French coastline. The tanker had been chartered by French oil giant Total, but its owner was unknown. French authorities immediately began an investigation to track him or her down. They first found a company named Tevere Shipping based in Malta. But Tevere Shipping outsourced *Erika*'s management to a company named Panship Management and Services, based in Ravenna, Italy. Panship chartered the ship to Selmont International, registered in the offshore haven of Nassau, which was represented by Amarship of Lugano, Switzerland. Thirty percent of Tevere Shipping's capital was owned by Agosta Investments Corporation of Monrovia, Liberia. It goes on and on, a dizzying Russian doll of ownership. By the end, French investigators found twelve shell companies standing between the ship and its "beneficial owner." Many of the companies were a brass plate in a Maltese or Monrovia street, but that brass plate can act as a mighty drawbridge, hauled up, when flag states provide such anonymity. All the power of the French judicial investigators could not go further. When *Erika*'s owner finally came forward weeks later—he claimed he had been skiing and had not realized he now owned an environmental catastrophe—he was revealed as a London-based Neapolitan, Giuseppe Savarese. The BBC reporter Tom Mangold asked Savarese why his ship's ownership structure was so complex. I only read the transcript of the interview, but I can hear the shrug in Savarese's voice: "That is normal in shipping."

Total, Savarese, and RINA, the Italian classification society that had certified the ship as seaworthy, were convicted of moral and environmental damage by a French court in 2008. An appeal two years later upheld the decision in a devastating 487-page ruling that is one of the best autopsies of not only a ship but also the shady practices of some shipowners including Savarese, who was found to have knowingly skimped on the quality of steel used to repair *Erika* (RINA classed it safe). The striking thing for investigators was not just the complexity of the ownership structure but how easy it was to put in place. A report by the Organization for Economic Cooperation and Development (OECD) found anonymity of ownership to be a feature in many flag states including Liberia, Hong Kong, Cyprus,

Marshall Islands, and twenty-eight others. Sometimes this was due to corporate rules in the nation rather than the registry, such as in Liberia. Usually it is sold as an attraction. All this amounts to what the report called "a multi-layered approach" and a "cloaking device." Total has already paid out nearly 200 million euros to injured parties, including the French state, environmental groups, Monsieur Cormier, a boat taxi operator who abandoned tourism after the spill, and Monsieur Lambion, who could not work as a fisherman for three months and was given 1,500 euros for "moral damage." The flag state of Malta, which had overall responsibility for *Erika*'s seaworthiness, pleaded diplomatic immunity.

Erika had passed all the required safety checks. And still she was corroded, poorly repaired, and her hull came apart at sea. I once wrote about *Erika* in a newspaper and was then invited to lunch at Lloyd's Register, the best-known classification society, in an elegant building in London that presents a Georgian facade to the street and hides behind it a modern construction of glass and steel. This is the headquarters of a business that began in 1688 in a coffeehouse in Lombard Street, when Edward Lloyd started providing the shipping news along with coffee. Now Lloyd's has a staff of 8,500, offices in 78 countries, and a turnover of $1 billion. It also has a fine boardroom and good food, over which important men attempted to politely educate me out of my mistaken views. *Erika* happened, but North Sea rigs make serious oil and gas spills about once a week and get away with little scrutiny. *Erika* happened, but much has changed since: the EU has tightened all sorts of safety requirements and regulations. Checks and balances have been strengthened and improved. *Erika* will not happen again, and anyway *Erika* was only one ship among the hundred thousand or so at sea on any given day, going about their business safely, securely, and vitally. My hosts were courteous. They offered to help my research in any way possible and kept their promise. They were persuasive.

Yet there are numbers to puncture that persuasion. In 2001, 63 percent of all ship losses at sea were registered to only thirteen flags of convenience. The five worst performers were Panama,

Cyprus, Saint Vincent, Cambodia, and Malta. Matters had slightly improved in 2009: only 58 percent of ships lost at sea belonged to thirteen flags of convenience. But there are suspect registries that are not classed as flags of convenience by ITF, such as Sierra Leone. Add those, and 70 percent of ships lost are flagged out. The top four registries according to tonnage lost are Panama, Liberia, Sierra Leone, and Mongolia.

For months, Martin Atkinson didn't know where his brother was. There was no body for his family to mourn. Frustrated, Martin found the website uglyships.com. This had become, strangely, the place where relatives and survivors left messages of support for each other. This was where someone unknown left several messages saying that he knew for sure that eleven missing Pakistani crew members were being detained by the Israel Defense Forces. And he was believed: for months, I received e-mails from a man named Ali, whose father worked on *Danny F II* and had not come home. Ali's English was not fluent, and his e-mails sometimes read like hallucinations, but they were haunting. He wrote that "accident is old for world." He was convinced his father was being held by Israelis. There was room for him to believe that when there was no official report to tell him otherwise. His father was old, which is a handicap on a sinking ship where strength is as useful as luck. He almost certainly went down with the ship along with Captain Milloy and Gary Beckett. Ali wrote that the Pakistani government had offered no support, nor had the shipping company. He wrote, "This world are door close for the missing crew and families."

Martin learned that bodies were still being washed ashore. He kept phoning the UK Foreign Office: Are the bodies from *Danny F II*? From flight 409? He researched survival rates: the water temperature was 18 degrees Celsius, which is half body temperature, which means Alan would have lost his body heat quickly. He thought there was a chance his brother had survived, but it was small. In fact, Alan's body had been found on the same day that the airliner crashed, January 25, in Samandag, Turkey. It had been classed as unidentified and was buried in March. By the time Strathclyde Police eventually enabled Martin to give a DNA sample in an acceptable format, it was May. The DNA was matched, the body was exhumed then flown home, and it arrived in a sealed lead coffin. "There was no way we could have had an open coffin," said Martin. "So that's what we got back." His twin brother, who had been in the sea for a month and six days, through Christmas, through New Year's, through all his family's waiting and hoping for a mythical life raft, for a miraculous open boat. Then his parents died, one after the other, within two weeks of Alan's funeral. Their death certificates list a physiological cause, but Martin is sure it was grief. He had no one left and still no clarity into this massive tragedy that had descended on the family. He didn't know whether his twin had died of hypothermia, drowning, or trauma. How had his brother died thirteen miles from shore, on a ship loaded with safety equipment, when there were rescue vessels and helicopters and the might of several states searching and rescuing? He wanted answers, but who should he ask?

He began to research. He learned, slowly, about flag states and how shipping works, and understood that his brother had been a Panamanian subject, really, while he was at work, however inconceivable a notion that was to a firefighter with his feet on the ground and never at sea. He wrote to his member of parliament and to the prime minister. He kept contacting the Foreign Office. He wrote to the Panama Maritime Authority via its website. He had no reason to doubt that Panama would immediately and comprehensively investigate his brother's death and explain why a ship classed as safe had sunk. He looked on the website and saw the headquarters of the authority, an imposing office building in Panama City. He followed the links—with difficulty, as most of the English-language site of the world's largest shipping fleet is filled with dummy text—to a list of casualty reports. There was nothing on *Danny F II*, all the way through 2010, then all the next year, then the next. For three years, his inquiries went nowhere. Other interested parties were also trying to get answers, from the Foreign Office to Nautilus International, the UK seafarers' union of which Captain Milloy was a member. Still no information appeared, because there was nothing to oblige Panama to do anything.

The procedure that should follow a marine casualty is clearly laid out in UNCLOS, the International Convention for the Safety of Life at Sea (SOLAS), and the International Convention for the Prevention of Pollution from Ships (MARPOL) all the major instruments of international maritime law: flag states are required to carry out prompt investigations into any casualty involving loss of life. MARPOL is the most insistent, requiring a report of an incident involving harmful substances to be "made without delay to the fullest extent possible." The European Union has more stringent legislation governing casualties within EU waters, but *Danny F II* was not European. Martin had appealed to the Foreign Office, but *Danny F II* was not British. There is no higher authority that Martin Atkinson can call on to force Panama to release a report.

Knowledge would be a comfort, but he has only competing stories and theories. Were there animals in the water? Nicolás Achard and Ahmad Harb say there were; the Foreign Office says there were not. Was there a washdown? Nicolás says there was; Kathleen Baker, daughter of Gary Beckett and a former employee on *Danny F II*, told Martin there was no way the captain would have authorized a washdown in storm conditions. Martin reads what he can, even in Spanish, in Uruguayan newspapers, which report crew members jumping into the sea holding on to a table. "Modern safety!" says Martin. "Okay, they lost a ship, but they should have been better prepared. They had nothing going for them." He is a calm-spoken man, but his anger is effective when quiet. "Everyone I talk to says, Oh, what do you expect with Panama? They say it's a get-out for lower standards. It seems to me it's such a casual thing that they expect so many people to die on ships. If it had been airplane safety, something would have been done about it."

Behind the scenes, there has been no lack of pressure on Panama. Diplomatic approaches, union entreaties. I spent a year writing and phoning the flag state, its ambassador, and had no answer. I tried back doors: industry associations that Panama belonged to, more reputable flag registries that might find Panama's behavior embarrassing. The director of one registry responded with frustration. "Many of us have struggled unsuccessfully to put some teeth into the international regulatory process that supposedly mandates prompt publication of flag state casualty investigations." He said Panama was one of the worst offenders at lax publication and investigation (the *Economist* calls Panama "delinquent"). Publicity, the director continued, was the only disinfectant until something stronger was in place. "Naming and shaming is the best tool we have."

Nicolás Achard now works ashore and plans on staying there. He has just married and wants to be at home, although he took another trip on a livestock carrier to blow away the ghosts and the fear. "I was scared and freaking out, but I had to do it." He and other Uruguayans are suing the agency that employed them, the Uruguayan Agencia Schandy, for the loss of their personal possessions. They are doing that because Schandy never bothered to contact them after they got home. "We would never have gone into litigation. But they never showed their faces and they behaved badly. All the companies claim they have no responsibility."

Martin has concluded that life must be cheaper at sea. "There's something like two thousand people a year getting killed at sea, but it's not grabbing anyone's attention. Once you're outside the twelve-mile limit, you do your own thing." He knows this now but still he checks his computer daily for a sign that Panama will finally tell him if his brother's death was due to accident, chance, or neglect that the flag state should have noticed. Ali still e-mails me regularly for news of his father, as if I can help as no one else will. They are two men adrift.

Kendal, *squeezing through sand*
(ROSE GEORGE)

5

SEA AND SUEZ

A Ditch in a Desert

WE HAVE TURNED THE BOTTOM CORNER OF EUROPE, PASSING through the narrow passage in front of Gibraltar that was a favorite hunting spot for U-boat packs in World War II, who waited there to pick off merchant convoys. In the twelve miles of territorial waters wrecks are marked; in international seas they are not. UNESCO estimates—because it can't do otherwise—that throughout the oceans there are three million ships or bits of ships on the seabed, beached or abandoned. They are common obstacles but also common treasure: diving companies can easily buy access to sunken merchant ships, even ones containing wartime dead. The ships are not automatically protected by war graves legislation although navy vessels are. In 2006, two daughters of a British man who died on SS *Storaa*, sunk in 1943 with a cargo of pig iron, steel slabs, and tank tracks, fought up to the High Court to have their father's wreck declared a military war grave and to keep it safe from recreational divers, treasure hunters, underwater desecrators, and busybodies.

Its salvage rights had been sold to one John Short for £150 in 1985, despite it sinking with twenty-two men.

These are sad seas in other ways, too. South of Sicily the captain tells me to look out for dolphins and flying fish, but I am also watching for small boats filled with desperate African migrants, because this is where you find them, if they are found. It is not in the captain's interest for me to spot any, because he would feel honor-bound to attend to them. This is not always the case: when a boat filled with seventy-two people escaping the war in Libya and problems elsewhere ran out of fuel, a NATO ship failed to rescue it. A helicopter dropped water then flew away, although women were holding up their babies in offering. "The helicopter did not save us," said a survivor. "Are we not human beings?" In 2009, a boat attempting the same passage from Africa to Europe was not picked up by Maltese authorities who spotted it, although passengers were clearly emaciated after twenty days adrift. Only five out of dozens survived. UN commissioner for human rights Navi Pillay, in language as angry as a diplomat is allowed, said afterward that "human beings adrift at sea are not toxic cargo." As usual, when I read a story about something that happens at sea, I wonder how many multiplications of the incident you would need to get the true figure of what happens in this wild place out of sight.

Even for me, delighting in landlessness, seven days without ports is a stretch. There is television, suddenly, as we near Sicily, but it is Italian and dreadful. I have been ignoring the invitations of engineers for days but it is time to go below. Mike, the second engineer, is becoming insulted. For days now our dining conversations have spanned the tasteless sadness of modern vegetables (and the beauty of his garden tomatoes in Romania, so large, so fresh), and the daily offer of a tour of his engine room. I can't postpone any longer and, besides, I want to see the sewage system. Down to upper deck, then, and through the door marked BEWARE: WHEN ENGINE FANS ARE RUNNING, THIS DOOR BITES. Mike seems delighted to have a guest to break up the noise, yellow light, and constant beeping, pinging alarms that fill the world of his engine room. They have been filling mine, too: the last supernumerary was a visiting engineer, so for weeks the alarm panel in my room has been beeping about a disturbed oily waste separator or a bilge pump in distress.

Mike offers tea and earplugs: he has a drawer full. Most engineers double-plug their ears with foam inserts, then ear defenders because the engines are three decks high and produce more noise than I have ever heard. They also make appalling heat. Sometimes the engine room temperature reaches 120 degrees, yet the men still work in boiler suits. The maximum temperature in which engineers are allowed to work, according to Mike, is "until they keel over."

He is proud of his machines. "Think how much cargo they have to push through water. This ship is a small island. There is enough power here to power a small town." He does some calculations and watches approvingly as I take notes. The engine produces 51,480 kilowatts, which is 80,000 horsepower. This is equivalent to one thousand family saloons or eighty Formula One cars. Maximum engine power can create a speed of 25 knots, which on land would be approximately 28 mph. At that speed, it would take us about two miles to come to a halt. All this power requires 260 tons of heavy fuel oil a day, which at current prices cost $30,000–$52,000 depending on market shifts. For this reason, we are doing only 14 knots, slower than an 1850s tea clipper, which could make 17 knots without all this fury and all this fuel. There is a phrase for this, and it is not "backward." "Slow steaming" is now common practice. Traveling more slowly through water reduces drag and friction and cuts down on fuel. So it saves money. It could also help to heal the planet.

Compared with planes and trucks, ships are the greenest of mass transport. Shipping produces 11 grams of CO_2 per ton per mile, a tenth of what trucks contribute. Air freight produces a great deal more, emitting 1,193 grams per ton per mile. Sending a container from Shanghai to Le Havre emits fewer greenhouse gases than the truck that takes the container on to Lyon. The Natural Resources Defense Council calculated the emissions involved in the journey of a typical T-shirt from a Chinese factory to an American back. An imaginary container was packed with sixteen tons of cotton in Urumqi, Xinjiang, and sent to Denver, Colorado. If it went by truck to Shanghai, by ship to Los Angeles, and then truck again to Denver, its emissions would be thirty-five times more than the same journey using only rail and sea. On the overseas leg only, a retailer would save ninety-nine tons of emissions sending the cotton by ship, not plane.

The International Maritime Organization calls maritime transport a "relatively small contributor to atmospheric emissions." It would be, if the industry weren't so enormous. Shipping is not benign because there is so much of it. It emits a billion tons of carbon a year and nearly 4 percent of greenhouse gases (although rival sides have different figures). That is more than all aviation and road transport. A giant ship can emit as much pollution into the atmosphere as a coal-fired power station. In 2009, it was calculated that the largest fifteen ships could be emitting as much as 760 million cars. Add shipping to the list of polluting countries and it comes in sixth. Ships create more pollution than Germany. And yet for decades nobody noticed.

In Joseph Conrad's *Narcissus*, the *Narcissus* has to be hauled out of Bombay harbor by a steam tug, which "resembled an enormous and aquatic black beetle." The tug leaves on the surface of the sea "a round black patch of soot . . . an unclean mark of the creature's rest." The coal is gone, along with the black gangs who worked in the engine rooms in their underwear, shoveling the black stuff, wearing the same minimal clothing as the men who had dug it out of the earth. Ships burn bunker fuel now, which takes its name from the coal bunkers it used to be stored in. Hence, "We will be bunkering in Rotterdam" or "Bunkers were completed at 3 a.m."

Residual Fuel Oil, to give bunker its real name, is dirty but cheap. Even now that fuel is ruinously costly—$600 a ton—bunker is still the cheapest. But it is horrible stuff. It is so unrefined that you could walk on it at room temperature. Even the spokesperson for Intertanko, an association of independent tanker owners, calls it "crud," and "one step up from asphalt." Burning bunker fuel releases into the atmosphere gases and soot including carbon dioxide, nitrogen oxides, carbon monoxide, volatile organic compounds, sulfur dioxide, black carbon, and particulate organic matter. On the high seas, *Kendal*'s smoke is disturbingly black.

Mike has endless environmental rules to follow. SOLAS requires shipping to "prevent, reduce and control pollution of the marine environment from any source." MARPOL, which entered into force in 1983 and has been ratified by 136 countries, has rules that govern the discharge of oil, garbage, and sewage. *Kendal* has rules that govern the discharge of paper (permitted twelve miles out) and plastic (never permitted). Sewage sludge can also be discharged twelve miles out, which is fine for a crew of twenty-one, but this rule also applies to cruise ships, which can carry six thousand people, the population of a small town. Sewage can add to ocean nitrification and the vastly increasing number of dead zones where excessive nutrients—present in sewage and agricultural runoff—have sucked oxygen from the sea, creating anoxic zones where fish and other life can no longer live. In 2003, there were 146 dead zones in the oceans; by 2008, there were more than 400.

Seafarers have cause to pay attention to their admonishing binders of eco rules. When shipowners can slip away behind flags and anonymity, the captain and crew are often the most visible people to blame for a disaster. In 2007, the *Hebei Spirit*, carrying a cargo of 250,000 tons of crude oil, was anchored off the port of Daesan, South Korea. Its captain was Jasprit Chawla, who I met on the tall ship in Glasgow's docks. He was a wiry man fizzing with the anger he still feels at having been imprisoned for something that wasn't his fault. *Hebei Spirit* was doing nothing untoward while at anchor, just waiting for the weather and its pilot. Chawla watched as a Samsung Heavy Industries barge approached on a collision course and kept coming. He sounded the whistle five times. He got on the radio to the Daesan authorities. He tried to call the barge and got no response, then watched in disbelief as the barge hit his ship, fracturing all three cargo tanks. Suddenly there he was in the middle of an environmental disaster "with hydrocarbons all around us." Imagine that the ship was an airplane. Imagine, for example, that it was US Airways Airbus A320, landed in New York's Hudson River by Captain Chelsey Sullenberger in 2009. Captain Sullenberger was an immediate hero, although fuel oil was discharged into the river, because all the lives were saved.

No one died either in the collision between the barge and *Hebei Spirit*. Yet Jasprit Chawla and his first officer were immediately thrown in jail. Chawla had been at sea for sixteen years without incident. But he was kept in isolation for a month, denied access to a lawyer, and held in prison for eighteen months. He became half of the Hebei Two and the cause of an unusually coherent and powerful lobbying campaign by shipping industry associations on their behalf. It worked, eventually, despite the fact that the barge was owned by someone with intimate connections to the South Korean government. A court found that Samsung was responsible for 10 percent of the pollution. Chawla said, addressing a seminar, "I salute the entire shipping community who came to support me when I thought I would never see my family or children again. Your letters were a great help in keeping my chin high."

Concern at the increasing and immediate criminalization of seafarers in environmental cases is growing. When the oil tanker *Prestige* broke up off Spain in 2003, twenty thousand tons of fuel oil spilled into Spanish waters. When it was finally towed to shore, its captain, a sixty-seven-year-old Greek named Apostolos Mangouras, was arrested and jailed for eighty-three days, despite having begged Spanish authorities for a port of refuge (disgracefully, they chose to send the tanker farther out to sea in gale force winds). The case finally came to court nine years later. "The ship was cracked and they sent it out to the ocean," Mangouras told the prosecutor, who sought to send the man to jail for twelve years. "It was the worst alternative. They sent us in a floating coffin . . . to drown."

No one has yet been imprisoned for the environmental damage caused by ships, because the International Maritime Organization has only just released regulations to increase energy efficiency and reduce emissions. That release took years of negotiation. The IMO is a member organization that rules by consensus, and with 170 members its pace can be slow. The new regulations require new ships to have 10 percent increased efficiency by 2015. Developing countries (including Liberia and Panama, the two largest ship registries) can apply for a waiver until 2019. By then, shipping will have grown still more, along with its emissions. Already the warming Arctic is freer of ice and freer for shipping. Russians have been sailing through the Northeast Passage for centuries. The *Oxford Companion to Ships and the Sea* refers with no irony to the "northward-thrusting men of Novgorod," who pushed their boats through seasonal thaws in the twelfth century. Now the ice retreats even more in summer so all comers who can pay Russia's fees and hire their icebreakers will come.

In 2006, Daniel Lack, a researcher at the United States National Oceanic and Atmospheric Administration, was aboard the NOAA research vessel *Ronald H. Brown* in the Gulf of Mexico, testing an instrument he had built that could measure black carbon in the atmosphere. It was frustrating because he kept running into ship's plumes. Lack was getting annoyed, but then realized that he had acquired some unique data. Before his accidental plume gathering, only six or seven ships had ever been measured for the particle contents of their smoke. Modeling studies led by James Corbett, a marine policy professor at the University of Delaware's College of Earth, Ocean, and Environment, produced startling data in 2007: that shipping emissions of particulate matter (what lay people call

"soot") are responsible for approximately sixty thousand cardiopul-
monary and lung cancer deaths annually. Seventy percent of the
pollution occurs within 250 miles of land, near coastlines linked to
busy shipping lanes in Europe, East Asia, and South Asia. In Los
Angeles, half of all smog from sulfur dioxide comes in from ships.
Corbett's predictions were dismal: annual mortalities would
increase by 40 percent by 2012.

When he looked into empirical research, Lack found that only
ten engines or so had been taken from manufacturers and assessed.
Despite the hundreds of thousands of ship movements in coastal
areas into ports barely a mile, sometimes, from human settlements
and the air they breathed, that was it. Lack didn't realize the importance of his data. He had never really paid much attention to ships,
being more concerned in his position at NOAA with the air. He
learned about bunker fuel and that it burns inefficiently. He knew
already that the more inefficiently a fuel burns, the more black carbon particles are emitted. Only forest fires produce more black
carbon than bunker fuel. Bunker fuel can have a sulfur content of
up to 45,000 parts per million (ppm). Low-sulfur diesel for cars is
supposed to contain 10 ppm.

The sulfur is converted into acid rain. "To combat the acidity,"
Lack says, "vessels have to burn lubricating oils, and not all the oils
get burned." He sums up, scientifically: "There is such a large
amount of particle emissions." The timing of his research was good.
The IMO was just beginning to notice emissions, as was the European Union and many ports. Nobody had had enough data, and
now they did. Lack was deluged with calls. People from local air
resource boards. Nonprofits that had been trying for years without
success to put pressure on the shipping industry. People working
on scrubbing technology that reduces emissions at the source.
Coastal peoples worried about their lungs. There was a hunger.
"The industry realized it had gotten away with a lot for a long time,"
says Lack. "They grabbed on to my study as a new start."

For a long time, protesting the environmental impact of maritime transport was a lonely job. The 1997 Kyoto Protocol didn't even consider ships. The big environmental groups had no marine teams, as they focused on aviation and cars. With those more visible forms of transport, they had had time to become inventive, strategic. They matched people who cared about emissions with people who cared about noise. They launched initiatives for people to "adopt a resident" who lived near an airport. But shipping presented a unique difficulty: it kept moving. When a ship leaves one port, calls at a dozen more, and ends up on the other side of the world, which country is responsible for its emissions? Who should be lobbied?

As with other regulatory challenges in this slippery mobile industry, this one fell to the owners of the coastline, which doesn't move. Emission Control Areas (ECAs) that limit the sulfur content of fuel now stretch two hundred miles from the entire U.S. coastline. They were already in place in the Baltic Sea and North Sea. This doubtless pleased the authors of a 2010 UK Parliament committee report, who were shocked at the "lack of urgency" shown about reducing shipping emissions by industrialized countries, and by the "blocking actions of developing economies." The IMO, they noted, did not announce a timetable of meetings to deal with greenhouse gases in shipping until 2006, and the first meeting took place only in 2008.

All shipping conferences now have some sustainability-themed components. There are clean ships, green ships. People are excited about wind power again, with either sails or kites. Why not? Even during the Second World War, windjammers such as the *Joseph Conrad* crossed the Atlantic carrying supplies, its sails tracked by submarines. But sailing ships need the right winds. They would be useful only to a modern supply chain with old-fashioned patience. Perhaps the answer is different fuels: *Maersk Kalmar* set sail in 2010 powered by two containers full of Soladiesel made from microscopic algae. Or cold ironing, meaning that ships don't keep their engines running while they are in port, as they do now, but are powered by shoreside electricity. There is some interesting thinking around the peculiar systems in shipping. Richard Branson's

Carbon War Room initiative now enables charterers to choose ships based on their efficiency rating, like a fridge or a house. It makes sense: charterers pay for the fuel but before now they were ill-equipped to choose the most efficient ship to burn it. On the Carbon War Room's predictably groovy video, a comfortably northern English voice explains that fuel-efficient ships can save the industry $70 billion a year and cut emissions by 30 percent. Every ton of fuel can cut CO_2 emissions by three tons. Going at 15 knots instead of 20 can save millions.

Slow boats to China, back to the future.

Until we reach the high-risk piracy area on the far side of Suez, watch officers have relatively little to watch out for. This is how Marius describes his watch keeping: "You look at the radar, nothing. The sea, nothing. The sky, nothing." Sometimes there is more excitement when cadets come up to the bridge with their mobiles, ready to grab a signal, because they see so many lights they think they are near a city. Instead they find masses of fishing boats with their candles or torches. You can't see them until you're almost upon them; they light a candle or flash a torch at you; and you must get out of their way, with your ship that needs at least a mile to stop. Also, fishing crews believe that passing in front of the bow of a big ship brings good luck. The closer they get, the better the fishing. "So you see them," says Marius, "and you alter course to avoid them and suddenly they alter course and you think 'Shit!' and they pass in front of your bow." How many collisions are there? "Who knows? You'd only know if you found the boat." In a forensic investigation into the loss of a scallop trawler, the *Lady Mary*, off New Jersey, journalist Amy Ellis Nutt asked a mariner the same question. He replied, "There are no skid marks on the ocean."

Otherwise, amid all that nothing, bored watch officers like to cause mischief with the radio handset. These are the seas of name-calling.

Marius tells me a merchant marine joke. A U.S. submarine captain sees a signal on his radar, so he gets on the VHF. "Signal on my radar, you must change course." No, says his interlocutor, I'm not moving. The submarine captain insists; so does the other man. The captain's threats escalate, but the other side still refuses to move, until the captain threatens extreme measures of the firepower kind if the other vessel won't change course. Here, a comedic pause. Then the response: "I'm a lighthouse, Captain, it's your call." (The joke was borrowed by the Swedish navigational equipment firm Silva for a 2004 ad.) The joke is not really anti-American, but anti-supremacy. No one is supreme on the ocean but the ocean. Marius tells another story about how dumb warship comms (communications) people are, so that you have difficulty believing that they are comms officers and not the junior baker taking over during a toilet break. Marius was asked to identify his ship. Okay, that's normal. Then they ask for the ship's port of registry, and he says, "London."

"Can you spell that?"

These days, ships are equipped with an Automatic Identification System (AIS) signal, and they are supposed to broadcast it, unless doing so would put the ship in danger. Navy ships are allowed to stay electronically unidentified. In principle, technology has removed much of the uncertainty relating to the movements of what Captain Glenn generally calls "other silly buggers." He is constantly alert for stupidities, for navigation officers who don't know the rules of the road or, if they do, will not follow them. The VHF is to be used for navigational purposes as a last resort. VHF-assisted collisions are common when officers waste valuable time on their radios trying to figure out whether they are talking to the right ship rather than looking at the radar or using collision regulations and common sense. Consequently, radio procedure is set out in rules and regulations. VHF must always be left on standby: Channel 16 is a hailing channel and for emergencies. You make contact on Channel 16, then agree to switch to another channel. In practice, that doesn't always work, particularly in calm waters and deep seas. Marius likes to listen to Channel 16 because all sorts of things happen on it. It's the closest a seafarer gets to TV. Sometimes you hear Chinese being sung. Often you hear Indian voices yelling, "Filipino monkey!" The captain finds this unpleasantly racist, but Filipino voices often retaliate. "Indian, I can't see you but I can smell you," or, "Does anyone know what IMO stands for? Indian Monkey Organization."

Any merchant seafarer is used to such radio-wave abuse. The U.S. Navy apparently is not. In 2008 a U.S. warship almost fired at Iranian ships in the Strait of Hormuz when it heard someone broadcast, "I am coming to you. You will explode in a few minutes." This, the *Navy Times* concluded, was the work of "a locally famous heckler known among ship drivers as the 'Filipino Monkey.'" A retired navy commander was invited to speculate on the heckler's identity. "Who knows? He could be tied up pier side or on a merchant ship somewhere." Or he could be any watch officer bored enough to make crank calls by the only means available.

Usually the VHF mutterings are beyond my understanding. Once I hear someone say, "Meow, meow." I look at Marius. "Did someone just say, 'Meow, meow'?"

"Yes."

"Why?"

"I don't know."

For a while, after piracy started up again in 2004 on routes to and from the Gulf, pirates played music over Channel 16 just before they attacked, both to unsettle seafarers and to block the channel so ships could not seek help. Marius has spent many a night listening to weirdness, including ghostly voices shouting, "Mario! Mario! Mario!" Friends of his on other ships have heard the Mario shouter, too, but no one knows who it is or the meaning of Mario. I don't think they want to know. Strange things happen at sea, and so they should.

* * *

I spend hours reading the charts. I note the names I find there: Terrible Bank, Herodotus Rise, Hecate Patch, a scrap of sea named for the goddess of dark places. Investigator Bank, Wadge Bank, Kurchatov seamount, named I suppose for the Soviet Union's atomic bomb creator. Wadge is a mystery. Igor finds my interest in the charts unfathomable. It is because of their words, I tell him, because I am romantic about the sea, and I like to think of the men who sailed through emptiness and tried to anchor it with names. Fairy Bank, King Arthur Canyon, Shamrock Knoll. Aren't they beautiful? "Words!" he says with scorn. "For us, it is just work."

Marius's job is to update the charts with the three hundred changes that have arrived by e-mail, so I usually find him bent over a chart, intent with a pencil. What changes? It depends. Sometimes the depth reading, sometimes there's no traffic separation scheme anymore. For example, he says, on the Cap Bon chart, a depth has been crossed out. Some measurements date from the 1940s. Neither the sea nor the earth stays the same. Today's chart travels from Ra's at Tin to Iskenderun. Those names excite me—I think medinas, Turkish delight, spices—but I am most excited about Suez.

A channel dug through a country by a Frenchman, where forty thousand ships pass every year (although it costs nearly $300,000 per transit for a ship the size of *Kendal*), Suez removed the terror and weather of the Cape of Good Hope, as long as the ship could pay for this new, shorter passage. A magnificent effort of engineering that shortened by ten days the usual twenty-four-day journey that ships had to make around Africa and up again to Europe. The canal takes fourteen hours to transit and has existed in some form since Pharaoh Senusret III, ruler in 1874 BC, chopped through the landmass to make a passage through open seas. The latest canal was built by Egyptian workers to the design of the French engineer Ferdinand de Lesseps; twenty thousand new workers had to be drafted every ten months, according to the official Suez Canal website, "from the ranks of peasantry." Alongside its banks run a railway and a "sweet water canal." I write in my notebook that somewhere nearby there is a vegetable oil pipeline marked on a chart, but I cannot find it again. The canal took ten years to build, is a hundred miles long, and earns the Egyptian government $5 billion a year.

Right, say the crew. But it's still just a ditch in a desert. Even laconic First Mate Vinton finds something to say about it, although the something is not much: "Sand, sand, sand." They go through Suez once a month, and it's a pain. Suez doesn't have locks like Panama, which at least are interesting, and the scenery is worse.

First, we park. Ships go through Suez in convoy. The channel is only two hundred meters wide and so can hold only one-way traffic. Our entry will be timed and staggered: first we have to wait thirteen miles out because we have a deep draught. Another Maersk ship approaches as we are heading to our anchorage. He is doing 11 knots and tries to overtake, then messes up and has to go behind us. The captain shakes his head wearily. He says, "It's 'mine is bigger than yours,' isn't it?" The other ship wanted to steal our anchorage space. It was the maritime equivalent of nipping into a supermarket parking space, and as pathetic.

There are more ships waiting. CMA-CGM, MSC (Mediterranean Shipping Company, though people using its nickname replace Mediterranean with Mafia), Evergreen, China Shipping. French, Italian, Taiwanese, Chinese. The cogs, wheels, and motors of the world and all its stuff. All these ships are Suezmax and above, according to the vital statistics of shipping, in which ships are sized by places they can fit through or around. Panamax is smaller than Suezmax, although Panama is now widening its canal in an expensive but surprisingly on-time development program known as the Big Ditch. *Kendal* can't yet fit through Panama, nor can an E class like *Emma*.

We stay in green waters until the order comes to move south, to the canal bypass of Great Bitter Lake. By now the convoy numbers thirty. They sit here, fishing boats or leisure boats dotting and darting between them. An Egyptian warship moves past lazily, maybe back from the dangerous Gulf at the canal's exit. When I walk the deck, I avoid the starboard side now because we have taken on Suez

crew, a requirement for any passage. They have their own cabin—
the Suez Crew Room—that is used for only eighteen hours a month,
but well used, because the crew hardly leaves it, doing nothing but
eating, drinking, listening to tinny pop music, and trying to sell
souvenirs. When they depart at the other end of the canal, they
lower their boat into the water, but stay attached to *Kendal* for a mile
or two, as if they don't even have the energy to let go.

The Suez crew is something of a scam: they are supposed to
board every ship in case the vessel has to tie up. Apparently they
have particular rope skills. There is also a special Suez electrician
whose job is to tend to the searchlight that is also obligatory and
placed on my fo'c'sle perch. The captain has never had to use either
the electrician or the rope-skilled crew in forty-two years of coming through and views them as an income-generating scheme to
add to the already significant fees. *Kendal* must also take a Suez
pilot. This one is fat and sleepy. At lunchtime, he asks what is for
lunch, so the captain rings down to the galley and conveys the menu:
split pea soup (without pork, after a previous cook caused chaos with
Muslims), spaghetti bolognese, fish cakes, french fries.

"Yes," replies the pilot.

The captain is nonplussed. "Everything?"

"Yes, everything."

A folding table is set up next to the pilot's chair and he eats.
Apart from that, he sleeps: on the sofa, on the captain's chair, on
the watch officer's chair. He is like a uniformed bridge cat, moving
around in search of sun. Marius has to keep waking him up for
instructions. Still, he is cheap, because he asks for food but not
much else. Suez is known as the Marlboro Canal because for smooth
passage, every ship's captain has to have a ready stock of Marlboros
to dispense. Immigration, port health, police, security guards. The
port captain takes four packs, to share. The shipping agent takes a
few. The electrician gets four; the boat crew get six. Sometimes
they want more than Marlboros, and the captain must go to the
bond locker when an agent or port official asks for "chocolate for

my babies." Not the Cadbury's Fruit & Nut? "No, I give them the plain crap." The captain dispenses £400 worth of cigarettes each voyage. The cigarettes are listed on the ship's budget as entertainment, port authorities, or gratuities, and accepted by company accountants as a needed expense.

I point out that they have chocolate in Egypt, and coffee and cigarettes. "Yes. They want it for free." In West Africa, officials come on board with empty shopping bags and empty the bond locker. The toll varies. The captain pays only seven cartons in Port Klang, for example, and none in Singapore. You don't dare give entertainment expenses in Singapore. The captain calls it the "fine city" because it fines you for everything. The crew like the Suez crew as much as they like the canal. They say, "The Egyptians can't have built the Pyramids; there were no Marlboros then." But the tobacco is worth it, because any penalties could be immense: an annoyed official could easily delay the ship for some pettiness. When *Kendal* costs $30,000 a day to run, Marlboro is cheap.

I wake from a nap to find we are in the ditch. The water is green; the banks are sand. From D deck I gaze at the desert, at an irrigated patch of green trees and plants that form a streak of freshness and life in the middle of the beige, at the homesick cadet on B deck below me, leaning on the rail to get some signal bars on his mobile phone, photographing and phoning. There are great ships in front of us, stretching along the channel, and more behind. We are a slow sandwiched procession, squeezing through sand.

No one else is out here photographing. They have all seen it before, and they need to save energy. Going through Suez means staying awake for pilots and port controls, judging when to get into the convoy. Suez is exhausting. The captain stays particularly alert. He would anyway, but once, a pilot ran the ship aground in the canal, and he has never forgotten it. By the time the captain realized they were going to run aground, they were beached on sand. He got the ship out "with skill and ingenuity" and went to the toilet with relief. "When I came back, I said, Where's the bloody pilot?

Then I saw his head popping up. He was on the deck, praying."
The captain felt sorry for him then. Losing a pilot's job is a big
thing. So is grounding a ship.

Our passage feels so stately and secure through the canal. It
seems that mishap is impossible. Wrong, says the captain. Even the
best captain can lose all his deck cargo. Boxes go overboard all the
time. The usual figure is that ten thousand are lost at sea, although
I find this figure hard to reconcile with an industry that would lose
commercial advantage by publicizing any losses. The European
Union calculates that two thousand containers are lost every year,
that 15 percent of those come ashore and 15 percent remain floating
at sea, causing a serious hazard to small boats. Some boxes become
notorious, such as those containing bath toys that were discharged
from the Greek-owned, Evergreen-operated *Ever Laurel* in the
Pacific Ocean between Hong Kong and Tacoma, which are now
remembered as yellow rubber ducks although they were plastic and
although there were also red beavers, green frogs, and blue turtles.
There were the 78,932 Nike shoes that were set adrift from the
Hansa Carrier between Korea and Los Angeles, then subsequently
tracked by the American oceanographer Curtis Ebbesmeyer, assisted
by a worldwide subculture of people who collect flotsam.

By tracking the movement of shoes through oceans, Ebbesmeyer established the route of two ocean gyres. From his work, I
learned that athletic shoes generally float with the tongues facing
upward (unless they contain feet, which is not unheard of); that
containers filled with computer and television monitors can discharge lead, mercury, cadmium, and other heavy metals into the
water. Eight pounds of lead for each monitor.

Some lost boxes are painfully expensive, such as the fifteen
forty-foot boxes that in 2004 fell from the *Med Taipei* off California
in bad weather, with their contents of wheelchairs, hospital beds,
ribbons, and cardboard. The owners of *Med Taipei* didn't report the
loss, a common practice—who would trust a company that can't keep
its cargo?—but the accident happened in the Monterey Bay National

Marine Sanctuary, and a box was found by a remote-controlled submersible belonging to the Monterey Bay Aquarium Research Institute (MBARI). Boxes have traceable numbers, and the owners were found and fined. The settlement was $3.25 million.

The money helped fund more research by MBARI: seven years later, the sub returned to the container. It was in good condition and presented a remarkable opportunity. No one knew how lost steel boxes and sea life interact. That is not surprising: there are species this far down in the ocean that have no names yet. Using a robot with long arms, tethered on four thousand feet of cable, the researchers, led by Dr. Andrew DeVogelaere, shot eight thousand hours of video and saw scallops they had rarely seen, all over the container, and snails that lay six-inch egg stacks. "It's interesting," DeVogelaere told a reporter, "in that when this container fell into the sanctuary there were negotiations with the shipping company about mitigating damage. They were arguing there was no impact because there was nothing living down there." They were wrong. The Aquarium team doesn't know yet if the container's presence on the seabed is positive or damaging. Other artificial reefs, such as two million tires scattered across the ocean floor off Florida, have been disastrous. The tires attracted hardly any sea life and drifted off to cause pollution in gyres, on beaches, wherever they ended up.

I hear about missing containers in passing comments. The Atlantic was bad five years ago, says the captain. Lots of damaged goods. But then they put stabilizers on ships and it got better. I see the disasters on YouTube videos, crazy stacks of containers, leaning and squashed and wrong. I find missing boxes in the pages of lawsuits. In 2003, *Canmar Pride* was sued by a division of the Ford Motor Company, which claimed that the *Pride* had lost containers filled with its automotive parts that were worth $6 million after rough seas in the mid-Atlantic. More precisely, the *Pride* lost containers that were "stuffed" with automotive parts. I like this word, sneaked in among the dry legal language like a pomegranate seed in dust. (It is actually a common freight term.) Reading the "precedents" section of the case, I dream up stories of what has disappeared, looking at the names of the companies suing shipping lines. Magic Sportswear Corp. v. OT Africa Line and *Mathilde Maersk* (athletic shoes?). Incremona-Salerno Marmi Affini Siciliani v. *Castor* (bathroom tiles?). Antares Shipping Corporation v. The Ship "*Capricorn,*" et al. (Greek marbles!).

Arranging six thousand or so heavy steel boxes into a logistic balance according to their weight, stability, and contents requires enormous skill. It is always the job of the chief officer. Vinton is remarkably relaxed in manner, and it is a surprise, when I ask him how many boxes are on board, that he can always answer sharply and precisely, though every port changes the number. Stowage is no easier now, just less manual. The rampant mechanization of shipping has not sanitized it. Everyone has a story about stowaways. Vinton found a man hidden inside a bunk. The man had drilled holes in the wood for air and hidden beneath the slats. Vinton says that you hear stories all the time. "There are so many. Particularly to transport, how do you call it, flesh."

On *Maersk Maryland* there were five stowaways who hid in the rudder tank. This is a tank around the rudder that doesn't necessarily fill up with water as long as the ship isn't too low in the sea. The five men knew to go there; the crew think they were organized. When their food and water ran out, they started banging, and when some Thai crew found them, the crew were taken hostage by the stowaways.

No, that's not right. It was the steward who was taken hostage, because he was bringing them their food.

Right. And at Algeciras the Spanish authorities wouldn't let them set foot on Spanish soil. It was a literal ordinance: they could go to the bottom of the gangway but no farther. The gangway was British territory protected by the Red Ensign. The company offered to pay for the stowaways' flights back to Dakar and for security guards but the Spanish still refused. No foot on Spanish soil. So they were taken back to Dakar by ship, "and they went mental. They fashioned knives and took the steward hostage and at one point were doing tribal dances around him."

I listen greedily to these stories and I don't mind if they have gaps. How many times can a steward be taken hostage? There are stowaway stories crazier and sadder than knives and tribal dances. In 2010, Ghana's authorities arrested three Chinese crew for throwing overboard three Ivorians who had hidden on their freighter. When two young Romanian stowaways were found aboard *Maersk Dubai*, in 1996, the Taiwanese officers put the young men off in an improvised raft. They were never found. The killing of eight African stowaways on MV *Ruby* by her Ukrainian crew became *Deadly Voyage*, an HBO/BBC film starring Danny Glover.

Read the IMO's stowaway database and you start to calculate the probabilities: If these are the numbers of stowaways caught, how many are not? In the more porous ports of Europe, where migrants think they will find a ship sailing to America, the dry database reads like an onslaught. One port: Igoumenitsa, Greece. One ship: the Ro-Ro cargo vessel *Ikarus Palace*. February 3, one Somali. Three days later, one Afghan. A Palestinian a week later. On the tenth of March, one Albanian. And then:

13.03.2010, 1 Palestinian
20.02.2010, 1 Albanian
10.03.2010, 2 Eritreans, 1 Palestinian
27.03.2010 1 Afghan
31.03.2010, 1 Afghan
07.04.2010, 1 Albanian
17.04.2010, 2 Albanian
24.02.2010 1 Afghan
28.04.2010, 2 Tunisians

I wonder, what is going on in Igoumenitsa? But I know what is going on in Igoumenitsa: ships call and ships leave and people see their movement as escape, as they always have done and always will.

Kendal's crew doesn't seem to mind stowaways. They are a headache, and the crew would rather not be taken hostage. But they are a part of life at sea. They are what happens. In Africa, you get worried if you don't find them.

Vinton must always keep an eye out for strangers on board and now he must watch for strangers overboard, too. We are not yet in the danger zone, but pirates are already affecting our passage. Stowage has to be calculated to accommodate the risk, so some boxes shouldn't be stored aft where pirates can fire at them. Imagine an RPG meeting that metal, those self-heating chemicals: what a prospect.

The time and place for such considerations is approaching even while we steam through this quiet green water, a majestic daisy chain of sedate ships. I don't know if "steaming" is the right way to describe our movement. Steaming is inaccurate, unless the black bunker smoke counts as steam. Driving sounds wrong, despite the engines. Sailing is daft. It is a small point of vocabulary, but I have time to make it into a big one in these listless days and thousands of nautical miles, so that it ends up as a grand theory about how we haven't bothered to update our language for these modern ships; the bigger they have become, the farther they have traveled from our vocabulary. Clearly there is an empty space in my brain that needs filling. It is too hot to be on deck; it is too dull on the bridge now that I've seen twelve hours of desert and canal and the rest of the miles look the same. There is nothing to do but wait. Steaming on, heading for danger, going south.

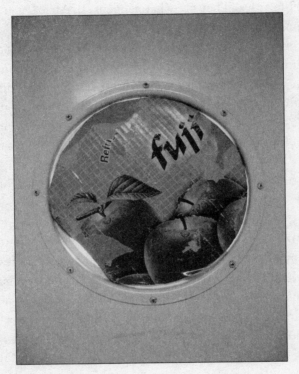

Pirate watch
(ROSE GEORGE)

6

HIGH-RISK AREA

Which Way Is It to Somalia?

The high seas shall be reserved for peaceful purposes—United Nations Convention on the Law of the Sea

THIS KIND OF HEAT SUCKS BREATH FROM BODIES. WE ARE IN THE Bab el Mandeb Strait, a narrow opening that marks the beginning of the Gulf of Aden. It is July now, and almost monsoon season. Monsoon weather is bad for nausea, but good for anyone scared of pirates, like me, because they travel in small boats that are upset by the force 6 waves that *Kendal* dismisses with ease. We are taking precautions, but much of our protection is weather.

On the internal e-mail system, the captain transmits two daily news digests—Tagalog for the Filipinos, English for everyone else—and a security alert from an agency named *Securewest*. By now, all the news is pirate news. The Yemeni Coast Guard has seen pirates move out of the Gulf of Aden and northward into the Bab el Mandeb Strait and lower Red Sea. In three weeks, pirates have attacked ten Yemeni ships and one oil tanker. All the assaults were repelled by armed protection teams traveling on the ships. But we don't have armed guards. Maersk doesn't allow it.

Instead, we have pirate watch. The ship has changed: the deck door portholes on every floor of the accommodation house have been blocked with circular pieces of cardboard cut from cartons from the bond store and Pinky's supplies. One porthole is now blocked by a Benson and Hedges carton, another by an image of rosy red apples. By sundown, all cabin windows must be covered with blackout blinds that are fastened into place with snaps, and a junior officer is assigned to patrol every evening at dusk, to monitor compliance. He does a lot of snapping. Pirate watch will last until we reach our next port, Salalah, beyond the far end of the Internationally Recommended Transit Corridor (IRTC), a 492-mile dual-lane sea highway skirting Yemen's southern coast that ships are advised to take. The corridor begins south of Aden near the island of Elephant's Back and ends just before Oman. The IRTC is patrolled by military ships from three coalition counter-piracy forces: one from the EU, one run by NATO, and one from the Combined Task Force (CTF-151) led by the United States, with a membership of nations that is described as "fluid." Beside the task forces, there are other navies acting independently of coalitions, including those of Russia, Korea, India, Japan, and China. It is the first major deployment of the Chinese navy since 1433, when Admiral Zheng visited the Sultan of Malindi and took home a giraffe. The Chinese navy is on piracy patrol, but it is also well placed to support its growing economic presence in Africa. If you want a window into future geopolitics, the Indian Ocean has a good view.

Since some Somalis took to piracy in the mid-1990s, their range and nerve have grown. At first staying close to the coastline of Somalia, they now operate across the Indian Ocean over to India's southern tip and south of Tanzania. This High Risk Area is 2,200 by 1,800 nautical miles. It includes the IRTC and also the routes of 70 percent of global oil traffic and 50 percent of container ships. Of these, fewer than 2 percent are successfully hijacked. But that is no comfort when portholes are blocked by apples and my imagination is running as wild as the waves.

Until Oman, no one is allowed on deck without a radio. There are no radios to spare for the supernumerary, so this means no more ocean watching for me. For the cadets and crew, there is nothing but watching, because the risk means two men are needed to stand extra lookout duty on the bridge wings, day and night, and there aren't enough officers. It is a boring and overheated task, particularly for the ones who for some reason choose to stand in hundred-degree heat in heavy engine-room boiler suits. The captain allows the watchers to come at reasonable intervals into the cool of the bridge. "Within reason" is how he defines a reasonable interval, but he can hear from his cabin when the bridge-wing door is opened and closed, and he knows that they take advantage. I'm not sure how useful the lookouts are, given the ship-sized blind spot caused by the containers, but I don't mind, because I am nervous.

One of the first things the captain asked me was: "Why do you want to go through pirate zones when you don't have to? Are you mad?" It is only now that I think the answer to the second question is yes. During the first night of pirate watch, I stay up until two in the morning, as if that will help. If I am awake, they won't come. This makes sense to me in the way that if any of my clothes are inside out in my suitcase, my plane will crash. Pirates like to attack in light, anyway, either the first or last of the day. They understand how to play with light and sunshine: sometimes they approach in the shadow cast by the ship, sometimes they arrive in the glare. I sleep finally and wake hours later to the singsong bong-bong that is the ship's alarm call. The ludicrous cheeriness of it would better suit a holiday camp, but I still jump out of bed in a panic, expecting the sunny bongs to be followed by an "Abandon Ship" or a call to the safe room where we have agreed to muster in an attack. Nothing happens but crackle. It's someone phoning home again. Someone always presses the wrong buttons on the satellite phone and makes an inadvertent public address.

Later, I tell Marius about my uneasy night. He laughs. He is convinced that we are protected by the size and speed of the ship. Even so, there were two alerts during his night watch. First, two fast craft, one ahead and one astern, doing about 20 knots at 2:00 a.m. That could be either pirates or smugglers. Drugs, diesel, weapons, alcohol, and humans flow illicitly across the Indian Ocean. *Kendal* shone searchlights on them, a passing U.S. helicopter did a flyby, and the suspect craft flashed lights back. Marius thinks they were friendly; the captain is more skeptical. Sometimes they pretend to be friendly. They lure you in. The captain's daily orders, written instructions that are kept on the bridge, instruct his officers to stay four miles away from small craft if possible. He has written, "Trust no one." Once, the captain was having dinner when the first officer made an announcement over the PA: Captain to the bridge. This is not an announcement a captain ever likes to hear. He thought, "Oh, shit," displayed no outward alarm, and took the lift up to the wheelhouse. Two fast skiffs, coming alongside. Finally they veered off. "I'm sure they did it to wind us up. They don't do it now; there are too many navy warships around." When the second incident happened during the night, Marius didn't alert the captain and now regrets it. It occurred to him later, he said, "if we're hijacked, I don't want to spend three months in Somalia with twenty-two crew saying 'It's your fault, you didn't call him.'" There were two fast boats again, doing 18 knots, coming too close. He shone the lights on them, and again the boats turned tail.

There is a U.S. warship off our port beam. I look at it through binoculars and Marius says, "You may as well wave. They have stronger binoculars than us. They can see you." He says that when the Americans first arrived in the Gulf of Aden, they wanted to get involved in everything. Anything that looked worrying, off they would go to check it out. Once an American voice came over Channel 16, trying to hail someone. "Merchant vessel, this is the coalition warship, what is your position?" Marius could see who they were trying to reach: a boat going about 4 knots, which means it was hardly going at all. It was obviously some little fishing craft puttering along. Anyone would know that. But the warship was new and kept calling to the merchant vessel, until someone took pity, got on Channel 16, and said, "It's a dhow. It won't have VHF or GPS. They navigate by the stars." The story still makes Marius laugh. "I pictured it like this giant, huge guy leaning over and shouting at a tiny mouse."

Still, I'm glad to have the warship nearby, especially when Marius pencils in the information from *Securewest* on the chart and writes that MV *Golden Blessing*, carrying a cargo of glycol ethelene and thirteen Chinese, was hijacked the day before. It is now on its way to Somalia. *Golden Blessing* was typical pirate prey: a low and slow tanker with no armed guards. Pirates have never captured a ship our size because our ten-meter freeboard (the height of the ship between waterline and deck) is daunting. It is difficult to climb onto an unwilling ship from a small boat, even if you have done it before, even with good grappling hooks and ladders. But there are still weak spots. Some points along the poop deck are more accessible, so those are barred with heavy nets. Astern, there are hoses port and starboard, jetting water to repel boarders. From the wheelhouse the hoses look like a pathetic deterrent, and I assume that a damp pirate can still perform piracy, but the jets are more powerful than they appear. Even so, says Marius, "I'm not going out there when they've got AK-47s, whether there are hoses or not."

The tension of pirate watch is hard on the crew. Some are genuinely unnerved, and being unnerved for a week out of every month is not nothing. The captain received an e-mail from the company inviting its fleet to order barbed wire for protection. He duly did so and was told that his ship was so big that it didn't need barbed wire, and his order was canceled. This infuriates him. There is always a first time. Most of *Kendal*'s officers favor armed guards as the best deterrent. At dinner one evening, I remark that the ITF has organized a petition against piracy. Igor nearly snorts into his soup. "So what do we do with a petition?" he says with scorn. "Send it to Somalia? 'Please stop attacking us!' The only thing to do is to send a petition with an A-bomb in the envelope."

Marius keeps quiet. Before he transferred to *Kendal*, he was on a smaller ship doing the run from Salalah down to Mombasa, Kenya. It was a sister ship to *Maersk Alabama*, which was captured by pirates in 2009 and whose captain was taken hostage and dramatically rescued by U.S. Navy SEAL snipers who killed three pirates in darkness through the doorway of a closed lifeboat.

Murderous, but impressive. The sister ship did the same route and was the same size and flag, but its captain was different and so were its tactics. Marius's ship stayed six hundred miles offshore for as much of its journey as possible, as company guidelines dictated. *Alabama* didn't and was known for sailing only three hundred miles off Somalia's shoreline. When Marius left the ship, he was sure he would see *Alabama* in the news. He was right. *Alabama* is still in the news: its crew is suing Captain Richard Phillips, although he became a national hero, for ignoring company policy.

Marius is not worried by pirates. But even he does not have the profound calm of Able Seaman Archimedes, to whom I talk one afternoon while he is on pirate watch duty on the bridge wing. It is the day after the near-attack, and he is dismissive of anyone who expressed concern about it. Scared of fishing vessels! So nervous! He would not have been scared because, he says, even three years earlier, when piracy was already a concern, they would stop for a few days in the Gulf of Aden to do some fishing, with no trouble (ships have been known to develop convenient engine trouble in good fishing zones). So Archie doesn't believe in pirates.

"What do you mean, you don't believe in pirates? Like fairies?"

"I don't believe. Suspicious craft, yes. But I won't believe until I see them."

I am not sure how to respond to this. It is such an outlandish thing to say. I tell him the latest figures of piracy: 544 seafarers taken hostage in the first six months of 2010, with 360 still being held. Thirteen ships hijacked. "Yes," Archimedes says. "I know all that. A friend was held hostage for three months. But it was good. Double pay! Overtime!" The Greek owners paid for three months' vacation afterward. The captivity was fine; the pirates were harmless. Harmless with guns? He grins again. Guns just for protection. They don't want to shoot you. Julius, a fellow AB, is also tranquil. "These pirates are not like Rambo or the Taliban. Then I would be afraid. But they are just normal people with guns." They only want the ransom. It is only business.

I had forgotten this when I asked the captain how pirates would reach the top stacks of containers. He was quiet for a second while adding the question to his mental list of daft supernumerary questions. "They won't. They're not interested in the cargo. They only have beaches in Somalia; they can't even unload it." All they want is the ship and the crew. Even so, expensive cargoes mean higher ransoms, so they would never turn down a tanker.

Forty-two thousand merchant vessels come through the High Risk Area every year, and the distances to patrol are dizzying. An EU-NAVFOR commander compared his force's task to patrolling western Europe with a couple of police cars whose top speed is 15 miles an hour. In testimony to a British parliament committee, Major General Buster Howes said, "Are we able to police the entire area effectively? No, we are not. What a [modern warship] can actively survey and influence in an hour is about a pinprick. If it has a helicopter, it is about three times the size of a full stop." A "suspicious approach" can become a successful hijack in only fifteen minutes. If a ship has a sensible reaction plan, if someone can cut the engines and someone radio for help, if the crew can stay out of danger so that a rescue is not risky, then drifting might give the navy time to arrive if it is in the same pinprick. But if pirates manage to take hostages, most navies will not attempt a rescue. When the British yachting couple Paul and Rachel Chandler were taken hostage in 2009, they watched as the British military supply vessel *Wave Knight* stood off, uselessly, from *Kota Wajar*, the pirated merchant ship where they were briefly held before being transferred to Somalia. The pirates "did not think they were going to be attacked," said Paul Chandler. "You can read something into the fact that they were standing on the deck of *Kota Wajar* firing AK-47s at a warship."

On day three of pirate watch, I rush up to the bridge when the ship starts rolling, in case it means something. It means only that we have left the sheltered waters of the Gulf of Aden and are in open sea, where the monsoon swells are stronger. Swells are good. The captain is on the bridge, as he is most of the time in pirate waters. At midnight, he is concerned about a tanker that has left the IRTC. But he consoles himself. "He's heading for Singapore so he's probably just set off that way." He worries in case the tanker knows something he doesn't.

I don't know what is going to change things, says the captain wearily at dinner. Not some bloody petition. He and his crew will continue sailing through this danger, month in, month out, and that's that. "I told you. Merchant navy. Scum of the earth."

Vasco da Gama, a Meko class frigate in the Portuguese navy, is on pirate duty. It is carrying 217 people, some marines, a helicopter, and much weaponry. It is also about to carry me for a week from Mombasa to Mogadishu and back, no port calls and hopefully no pirates.

Vasco da Gama is the current flagship of EU-NAVFOR, so it also carries an international staff of thirteen who run operations and who live on the flagship, whichever it is. When I asked EU-NAVFOR if I could watch them hunt pirates, *Vasco da Gama* was the option offered. The usual practice would have been to put me on a British ship, but there were none in any fleet. The flagship was already carrying internationals and could handle one more. The embed was strategic. EU-NAVFOR feels underappreciated and publicity could help make the case that it is doing good and being useful while costing 8 million or so euros a year. To get on an EU warship, I had to head for the unlikely setting of Northwood, a north London suburb usually described as "leafy." It is not the kind of place—quiet and bucolic—I expected to find the enormous Northwood Headquarters, base of the British army—all of it—as well as NATO's Commander Naval Forces North, the Commander in Chief Fleet, and EU-NAVFOR, the newest tenant. The base is huge, but not large enough to house some of EU-NAVFOR's staff, who have been living for months in a Ramada hotel in Watford. If you know Watford, you know that this counts as proper service to your country.

Wing Commander Paddy O'Kennedy was EU-NAVFOR's spokesman when I visited. He didn't stay long in the job: spokespeople do six-month rotations, as do the ships. A fluent speaker of Arabic, Hebrew, and sound bites, his next post would be as the British embassy's defense attaché in Tel Aviv. He was working for EU-NAVFOR despite belonging to the Royal Air Force, and his job was to talk piracy and counterpiracy. He had a talent for it. Even before we reached his office, he told me that once he was in the shower when his wife shouted up, "Paddy, there's someone on the phone; he says he's a pirate?" They phoned him all the time, because the spokesperson's number is on the EU-NAVFOR website, and although Somali pirates come from a failed state, they still have smartphones and Internet cafés. Pirates can Google. They are known to read up on their crews and hostages, so it is dangerous to make any information—a family photo of a captain standing in front of a decent house, for example—accessible online. A decent house could mean pirates push for a high ransom. Any excuse for a higher ransom.

The wing commander's desk was in a large open-plan office, but he spent much of his time in the operations room, where Finnish, Italian, German, and other European military personnel spent hours in front of a giant screen that displays Mercury, an information-sharing program between EU-NAVFOR and other coalitions and interested parties. Another screen showed a map of the High Risk Area. It was a real-time map, and as we entered, the screen showed that a ship had just been attacked. The crew, it was hoped, had taken refuge in a citadel, a panic room that ships are now encouraged to set up. There are good and bad panic rooms. Decent citadels are supplied with food and water to last for days, allow the ship to be steered from within, and cannot be penetrated by oxycetylene torches, dynamite, or other violence. If the crew are secured inside a citadel, a ship can be safely boarded by a naval patrol even when pirates are aboard. A poorly designed one can become a tomb. On MV *Arillah*, seafarers endured thirty hours inside their citadel while pirates burned ropes and wood near the ventilation grills of the citadel, trying to choke them out, or to death.

At his desk, which held a copy of *Pirate Latitudes* by Michael Crichton—a Christmas present from his wife, still unread in March—Paddy said, Okay, everyone knows the general situation in Somalia. Or they have watched *Black Hawk Down*, which they think amounts to the same thing. War, chaos, failed state. No meaningful government since 1991. By 2011, the Transitional Federal Government was nominally governing the country, but only in the sense that President Hamid Karzai—nicknamed the mayor of Kabul—was ruling Afghanistan: partly, and with backup. On the TFG's side was AMISOM, an African Union peacekeeping force that also wages war; and on the other side was Al-Shabaab, Somalia's native terrorists, affiliated with Al-Qaeda though without its global ambition. Al-Shabaab beheads, bombs, and terrorizes, it steals humanitarian aid, but it does all this at home. Between those two forces there are Somalis, including two million who require humanitarian aid because they are either underfed or starving. Consequently, EU-NAVFOR was formed in 2008 after UN Resolutions 1814, 1816, 1838, 1846, 1918, and 1950, to serve a dual purpose: to escort humanitarian supplies into Somalia and counter Somali piracy. Stopping illegal fishing came later.

Paddy didn't call them "Somali pirates." He was careful not to do so. Most are Somali, and they mostly operate out of and in Somalia, but some are Yemeni. A few may be Kenyan. Perhaps there is a Tanzanian or two. That is not the only question about their identity. When the Canadian journalist Jay Bahadur interviewed pirates in Somalia, they called themselves *badaadinta badah*, or "saviors of the sea," rather than *burcad badeed* ("ocean robbers"). Somali pirates understand PR, and this is their myth: that they are the descendants of the pirates of piracy's golden age in the early eighteenth century, when men like Edward Teach—better known as Blackbeard—and Henry Avery governed the waters of the Caribbean with considerable violence, but also by operating ships that ran democratically. Captains were elected and kept in check by quartermasters and a council of crew. Piracy was violent and awful, but it was also the best escape route from the more terrible life of a merchant seafarer, where there could be no respite from tyrannical, brutal captains.

The U.S. Congress has called piracy "violence against maritime navigation." As long as there has been maritime navigation, there has been violence against it. Augustine wrote of an encounter between Alexander the Great and a pirate. The emperor challenged the robber: What did he mean by keeping hostile possession of the sea? The pirate responded: "What you mean by seizing the whole earth; but because I do it with a petty ship, I am called a robber, while you who do it with a great fleet are styled emperor." I find this smug, but Augustine thought it "just and apt." The Romans saw piracy as a threat to trade and therefore to empire, but there were enough practicing pirates for Plutarch to write that they "already at that time controled the sea with large armaments and countless small vessels." When Julius Caesar was traveling to Rome from Bithynia, pirates captured him for thirty-eight days, and Caesar, "as if the men were not his watchers but his royal bodyguard . . . shared in their sports and exercises with great unconcern." Once his ransom of fifty talents was paid (equivalent to a modern $1.5 million), his equanimity became revenge: he equipped a fleet, hunted down his captors, and crucified them. Carthaginians preferred to dispatch pirates by flaying them to death.

Piracy may seem straightforward. Surely it is nothing more than the ugly business of taking the possessions of others through violence? But it can escape easy categories. What were privateers but pirates with permission? They traveled to rob foreign ships, just with authority from the nation-states that had commissioned them. The early American colonies, forbidden to compete with English ships for trade to and from Europe, found pirates brought useful income, as long as the violence was done against faraway maritime navigation. Colonel Frederick Philipse, who founded one of New York's great fortunes and families, funded a pirate base in Madagascar and sent privateers on revenue-generating voyages. Sometimes, piracy is a matter of opinion. In a café in Mombasa, a local man says to me with genuine contempt: "You have been on a warship called *Vasco da Gama* hunting pirates? But Vasco da Gama was a pirate."

This slipperiness, this shifting of shapes, has made room for myth and theater. Blackbeard knew that drama was an effective way to spread terror. His flag featured a skeleton stabbing a heart while toasting the devil. He wore his black beard in pigtails and somehow managed to set off sparklers around his face when he boarded ships. Pirates knew the importance of spreading stories of their brutality, but also of their bravado and rage against authority. Just before one was hanged in 1718, he was asked to repent. Yes, he said, "I do heartily repent; I repent that I had not done more Mischief, and that we did not cut the Throats of them that took us."

I haven't read of any humor coming from Somali pirates, although they did hijack a ship named *Buccaneer*. The way they treat hostages is not funny. But they also understand the power of telling stories. They have their own origin myth. After law and order fell apart in Somalia in 1991, chaos broke loose on and offshore. There was no police or functioning army on land and there was no coast guard at sea. Somalis prefer to eat camel meat if given a choice, but fishing is a common coastal occupation. Into the vacuum sailed foreign fishing vessels, come for booty. The pickings were good: lobster, tuna, shrimp. Local fishers, lobster divers, and other coastal professions found their living stolen by Taiwanese, Spanish, Russian, or Thai trawlers that scraped the bottom of their seas with shameless abandon and took all they could without license or payment.

Then, in the words of Abdirahman Mohamed Mohamud (Farole), president of Somalia's semiautonomous northern region of Puntland, this is what happened next: "The violation of Somali waters by foreign trawlers expectedly triggered a reaction of armed resistance by Somali fishermen [who] linked themselves with local warlords for protection, placing armed militiamen onboard the trawlers."

He calls this new breed of fishers "fishermen turned pirates." They then targeted unarmed commercial vessels, "inhumanly taking hostages for ransom and disrupting international maritime trade routes."

There are other versions of their origins. For Robert Young Pelton, who ran the *Somalia Report* news agency, pirates emerged originally from the Puntland coast guard. When the national government fell, the coast guard turned pirate "in about a day." A London-based Somalia expert told me that the modern pirates had never been fishermen or coast guards. He thought they came from inland criminal gangs and were operating a protection racket. Mombasa-based Somalis were already in the habit of selling illegal fishing licenses to foreign operators. You can do that in a failed state; foreigners used to the rule of law know no different. The foreigners would come and start fishing "and the [Somalis] would make their presence known." He meant that they demanded money. "Then they realized they could make more by pinching the ship." Thus the template was formed. "We would get a report of a vessel seized, journalists would ring up fishermen and get quotes about foreigners raping the seas and that Somali fishermen were furious. That becomes: Somali fishermen are doing the piracy." In fact, the UN Monitoring Group on Somalia estimates that only 6.5 percent of pirate attacks have been against fishing vessels.

What is certain is that in the first few years of the twenty-first century, pirates began to set out in fast, small boats called skiffs. They had powerful outboard motors, but could carry only the fuel that fit in their boat. They were hampered by distance, fuel, and weather: the rougher waves of monsoon meant even launching from a beach was difficult, never mind approaching a large ship at speed and throwing a grappling ladder at it. They had no GPS or charts. In the words of Major General Howes, a man with a silky turn of phrase, "they navigated by guess and by God." In this genesis story of piracy, these were "subsistence pirates." And then something changed. Either inland Somalis got involved, or those inland Somalis organized criminals, or it was a natural escalation, a progression of the blindingly obvious. Pirates began to hijack dhows, larger fishing vessels that could serve as mother ships, that can carry dozens of passengers or hostages, travel farther, and hold more fuel barrels. Now the pirates could hunt for weeks, not days, towing a couple of skiffs with them, so that they stopped being pirates and became a PAG (Pirate Action Group). They could travel as far as India and down to Mozambique. They could travel a thousand miles. They could be anywhere.

The truth about much of Somali piracy, though it involves solid weapons and solid violence, is as shimmering as Blackbeard's beard. Tales are told; myths shift. Facts change as fast as tactics. What is clear is that 2005–10 was another golden age of piracy, just as 1716–22 was the golden age for Blackbeard, Bartholomew Roberts, and colleagues. The *Oxford English Corpus* noted a fourfold use of the word *pirate* since 2007, with *Somali* the most common modifier. Behind the shimmer are some plain facts. Men, as a job, take other men hostage while they are doing their job, for doing their job. Other men and women try to stop them.

You will like *Vasco da Gama*, a colleague of Paddy's had told me. There is no sauna, as on the Swedish flagship *CarlsKrona*, but the Portuguese have long lunches and wine. As I see when I approach the gate at Mombasa's port, where a sleek pale green warship is waiting, there are also officers who wear Ray-Bans and look like models. Lieutenant Commander Pedro Silva Barata is in charge of communications for the international staff. He wears his name on a Velcro name badge, along with his blood group. I understand the military practicality of wearing this on your chest, but it never stops seeming oddly intimate, like seeing someone's underwear.

Three crew members salute as we board. Pedro salutes back while I shuffle. This is my first formal encounter with military life, and only the first episode of awkwardness. The last time I felt this socially inept was in front of the Crown Prince of Bhutan, when I hid a water bottle behind me as if it would dirty his royalty. I would have no idea what was expected even if I weren't arriving sleepless from London, sick to my stomach on malaria pills, still trying to absorb the fact that Mombasa's airport road is now called Barack Avenue. Next to the warship hundreds of people are emerging from the Linkoni ferry, their noise like a storm of oversized insects. The ferries still do good business, because part of Mombasa is an island, but the port has suffered otherwise. Since piracy began to grow in earnest in the early 2000s, cargo ships have stopped coming, even though Mombasa, Kenya's only seaport, serves five landlocked East African countries. Cruise ships also stay away, particularly after the *Seaborne Spirit* was attacked in 2005 and pirates were only repelled with high-pressure hoses and a sonic weapon. Four years later, when pirates attacked *MSC Melody*, another cruise ship, they were assaulted by deck chairs thrown by furious passengers. In 2010, a local shipping reporter tells me, there were forty-three cruise ship calls into Mombasa. By summer 2011, there had been only five. Still, the coalition navies are some compensation. They bring money and they spend it. When the U.S. ships come, girls arrive from all over Kenya, and Mombasa clubs fill with ship's officers and crew. R&R on a military ship consists of more than a disconsolate trip to a local overpriced shop or a lonely seafarers' mission. Hence the Ray-Bans.

Vasco da Gama has come to Mombasa from the Seychelles, where the crew had beach parties and got suntans. Before that it was patrolling the IRTC, the path for prudent merchant ships. Prudent merchant ships are advised to do a lot, these days, for better protection. They should report to the Maritime Security Centre for the Horn of Africa (MSCHOA). They should travel at maximum possible speed. They should employ "hardening" methods such as high-pressure hoses to repel boarding, barbed wire, or dummies placed in strategic positions to bulk up small crew numbers. They should be prepared to answer any suspicious approach by clever navigation: zigzagging is best. All these things come under the label of Best Management Practices, empty-sounding jargon for what is a set of good advice. Some of the techniques advised are tried and tested, such as using speed: ships avoiding U-boats in the Second World War were safe enough to travel independently of convoys if they could do 15 knots. Maneuvering: every wartime captain knew that zigzagging a ship made it harder to target. But despite these efforts ships have been brazenly hijacked in and near the IRTC, three miles outside Salalah's docks, and off the coast of India. Like all asymmetric forces, pirates can change quicker than complicated coalition naval forces governed by regulations, rules, and law. They can respond and dictate. They learn.

Vasco da Gama is crowded. There are 214 people on board on a ship half the length of *Kendal*. With more people and less space, I learn to walk differently. First, I brace my knees to counter the greater motion of a smaller ship. (Warships are no place for knee problems because you are constantly exerting your joints.) Then, I learn how to lean into the bulkhead to pass people in crowded passageways. *Vasco da Gama*'s crew do this sinuously and with skill because the passages are usually crowded on a twenty-four-hour ship. At all hours I encounter people on the narrow, steep iron gangways; on the black-as-night weather deck; at the sharp corners; in the hydraulically sealed deck exits that can take your arm off if you don't withdraw it quick enough and that keep out nuclear, biological, and chemical contamination and flies.

Supplies also take up room because the ship is refueling with all sorts of necessities in Mombasa. This is downtime after the tension of the IRTC, of the proper piracy work. Not that this week's job is not being taken seriously, as it consists of providing a military escort to *Petra 1*, a bulk cargo vessel carrying humanitarian supplies into Mogadishu. *Petra*'s top speed is 12 knots (nearly 14 miles an hour on land) but her usual pace is 4. She may as well have a target painted on her side, particularly as the supplies are for AMISOM, the UN's military presence in Somalia and Al-Shabaab's enemy. It was because *Petra* was fired on doing this supply run that the French military began providing informal escorts, and from that came EU-NAVFOR. Trouble isn't really expected, although the Spanish frigate SPS *Infanta Cristina* was attacked while on escort duty in 2010 by MV *Izumi*, the first merchant vessel to be used as a mothership—a floating headquarters—by pirates.

My accommodation is in the sick bay. It's the only free space on board. Only senior officers have cabins to themselves, and other cabins are so small only one person can change clothes at a time. Privacy here is prized because there isn't any. The sick bay is impressive, with comforting clinical steel, six bunks, and the only bath on the ship, useful in case of burn victims. Unlike *Kendal*, *Vasco da Gama* has a doctor and nurse, as well as six cooks and levels of staffing that would make merchant seafarers envious.

My visit has been carefully planned because it can be useful. "The navy has to get better at publicity," says Pedro. He tells me that the Portuguese air force is always in the news back home, because it does something derring-do and then sends press releases. In Portugal as elsewhere, the navy remains the silent service. (Not the most silent: in Tony Parker's book about lighthouse keeper life, one wife says that compared with the lighthouse service, "the Navy's a bunch of chattering monkeys in a monkey house.") The schedule involves a daily "walkaround" of a different department. There will be interviews with the flag commander, the captain, all department heads, and anyone else I choose. Four departments are run by lieutenants—logistics, weapons, mechanics, and operations—and the fifth is run by the XO, the navy name for the chief officer. The fifth department is the entire ship, so the XO is in charge of the crew's welfare and of mine. He is a shaven-headed man with a sunny temper but also a gravity that emerges in his delight in conveying things accurately; he will return hours after a conversation with a fact about Catherine of Braganza, or the proper definition of Portugal's Exclusive Economic Zone. I tell him my needs, which are vegetarian food and some pirate action. The ship is already catering to two Muslims on board—the bridge happily tells the Djiboutian translator which way Mecca is, when he asks five times a day—so a vegetarian is manageable. The pirates: who knows?

From the safety walkaround I remember little except the amount of Velcro sticking everything to every wall everywhere. "If we throw the ship against a wall," my escort tells me, "it will stick." The logistics walkaround is a shock after merchant shipping parsimony. It would make Pinky weep. The logistics chief, a harried lieutenant commander named Semide, won't tell me how much the budget per head is, only that it is more than seven dollars. From his expression, it is much more than seven dollars. The ship is crammed. We walk over boxes of orange juice. A carton of vin de pays has spilled and smells. Semide kicks it with disgust. "What a mess. It doesn't normally look like this, but we have no space." He has to store food supplies with spare parts. Tomato juice with wing nuts. As for the plenty, "Marines can eat twelve bread rolls for breakfast. Some guys eat five times day. You have to calculate for who you have on board."

The logistics department is also responsible for feeding and clothing any detained pirates. A small group of detainees would be kept in the nuclear, biological, and chemical decontamination compartment next to the hangar. More than a dozen would have to live out on deck in a space beneath the hangar, hemmed in by nets. They would be given clothes if necessary, though not the crew's fireproof overalls: they cost too much. Semide talks about pirates in the future tense, as *Vasco da Gama* has never yet detained any. There have been encounters. The closest was with a suspicious dhow departing a known pirate beach in Somalia. The XO describes the incident as part of a mission that "contained many heartbreaks." The ship fired its main gun. Boom! It landed in front of the dhow's bow. "For half an hour we fired. They didn't stop. They got on the radio and said, 'We are in national waters. You can't stop us. If you want to stop us, come and get us.'" This powerful warship was handicapped: it couldn't send its Rigid Inflatable Boat, a fast, zooming dinghy, because the distance was too great and the RIB could not be protected. They couldn't use the helicopter because a rotor was damaged. For snipers they have to be within 300 meters.

When they can get close enough, their choices are to detain, destroy, or disrupt. There is a notorious video showing how the

Russians, one of the independent naval forces, destroy and disrupt by putting pirates back in their dhow and then apparently blowing it up. (In reality, the pirates were removed before detonation.) Other independent naval vessels have been less scrupulous. *Vasco da Gama* can't do that, being bound by law and convention. Even if it did detain pirates, meeting the burden of proof required to prosecute them is hard. There are known signs of pirate activity: grappling hooks, ladders, too much fuel. All these things are now called "tripwires," signs of pirate behavior or intent. But it is not a crime to travel the Indian Ocean carrying ladders. Most fishermen in these parts carry weapons, and the ones with weapons who are not fishermen can easily throw their arms overboard.

Even if there are enough tripwires and *Vasco da Gama* ends up with a clutch of pirate prisoners netted on its deck, the chances of finding a nation-state to prosecute them are low. EU-NAVFOR releases 80 percent of detained pirates because it can't find willing courts. For now, the Portuguese can only fire at fast outboard motors or destroy pirate equipment, both imperfect solutions. The XO keeps a slow Honda outboard motor on deck that he would swap for the pirates' faster one if given the chance. He knows though that pirates who are neutralized simply go home and fetch more weapons, however slow their boat. After too many outboard motors had been destroyed, pirates began stationing men next to the motors as protection. When the navies started firing at the skiffs towed by the Pirate Action Groups, the pirates stationed men in the skiffs.

They are not dumb, or not always. A U.S. embassy cable reported that Seychelles officials had detained eleven Somali men in three skiffs near Marianne Island. "Someone must have briefed them on what to do when intercepted," a coast guard officer said, "because they dumped their guns and surrendered once we approached." The men were malnourished. From that, and from the supplies in the skiffs, the coast guard determined that the motherboat must have supplied the pirates with all the equipment and told them not to return without capturing a vessel. The same group, the cable

continued, had approached locals taking day-trippers to Marianne
Island and asked, "Which way is it to Somalia?"

The only likely action this week will come from drills and exercises
designed to keep the crew alert. Marines get easily dulled and the
warship's specialized diver has been relegated to his other job doing
the laundry. I see him laden with T-shirts near the laundry room
sometimes, and he never looks pleased. Also, there are many skills
to be kept fresh, if the list of the elements of a U.S. marine's antipiracy training is accurate: surgical shooting, combat conditioning,
diving, high-altitude low-opening (HALO) and high-altitude high-
opening (HAHO) parachute operations, rappelling, fast roping,
climbing, hand-to-hand combat, communications, knife fighting,
combat trauma, explosives, and intelligence gathering. Some drills
are more interesting than others: a ship fire is achieved with dramatic smoke. "It's water vapor. They use it in nightclubs." The XO
is keen to keep his passenger alert, so he will let me have a trip in a
RIB, a quick joy ride on the most dangerous waters in the world,
and a flight in *Bacardi*, the Lynx helicopter. I come to think of
Bacardi as the ship's pet, though one with nifty flexible rotor blades
so that it can fold in on itself to fit in the hangar.

I go out on the RIB and come back with exhilaration and a
bruised forehead from the steel safety bars combined with a choppy
sea state 6. *Bacardi* is more fun and less painful. First, because the
flight crew like to keep their morale up by playing 1980s pop, the
serious safety messages—if we ditch, jump into the sea on the right-
hand side because the pilots can see you better—are delivered to a
soundtrack of "Karma Chameleon." The flight detachment has the
best deal in this *Petra*-escorting downtime, as they do almost daily
reconnaissance missions over Somalia and out to sea. Loudspeaker
messages—known in navy language as "pipes"—begin at 5:00 a.m.
most days, announcing that the flight hangar is in use and that
smoking is therefore banned on deck. I guess at most of them, as

they are always in Portuguese, which sounds like Italian and Russian that have been put into a blender. Hardly any of the international staff speak Portuguese but there is rarely any translation provided. "I hear something," says a French member of the international staff. "But I have no idea what it means, so I look at someone Portuguese. I think, He's not looking worried, the ship isn't sinking, it's just that I'm allowed to smoke outside again."

Up in the helicopter, we fly over *Petra*. A crew member comes out on deck and waves. "That's how we know it's not a pirate," says the copilot over the headphones. "Pirates don't wave. They're always in a bad mood." He is joking, but knowing the difference is vital for the helicopter crew. It determines how close and low they can go. An RPG has a range of 500 yards. So they must get close enough to get good intelligence, but not so close that they regret it.

The flight crew do regular reconnaissance over pirate camps ashore, usually easily identifiable: huts on a beach, skiffs beached nearby, SUVs coming and going. Sometimes *Bacardi* gets close enough to see faces. There is no shortage of intelligence in counterpiracy. All the coalition task forces know where the hostaged ships are anchored, off Eyl or Harardheere or Garacad, pirate hot spots along the coastline. Pirates don't need to hide when they have human shields. The camps have been given code names. Great Pumpkin. Van Pelt. Spike. I see these names on maps in the operations room, a place of darkness and screens where I am asked not to look too closely. Next door in the comms room there are dozens of tape cassettes decorated with skulls and crossbones and labeled *piratas*. They hold recordings of boardings of suspicious craft and "other counterpiracy stuff, mostly flight operations," says my escort. "Quite boring." The skulls and crossbones are for fun. What is the point of all this information if you can't do anything to the pirates? The communications officers shrug. "We share information. That's all."

* * *

In the quarters that he has taken from the captain, the flag commodore—the chief of the EU-NAVFOR fleet—is everything I expect a flag commodore to be: talkative, weary, and sophisticated. Alberto Manuel Silvestre Correia knows what I will ask. Yes, counterpiracy work is frustrating. Yes, of an assumed pirate workforce of about four thousand, at least fifteen hundred have been held in navy warships and released. Some have been captured two or three times. If they were prosecuted, it would make a difference. If those fifteen hundred Somali men disappeared from coastal society, it would make a difference.

These are shameful statistics, and bewildering: if piracy holds no risk and capture promises nothing more daunting than three meals a day and a ride home, then it will continue. Correia knows this. He says, as everyone says, that the solution is onshore. There are no Kenyan, Tanzanian, Mozambican pirates because those countries have coast guards and law. Somalia must be rebuilt. Somalia must be saved. The commodore says that pirate attacks have diminished, which is true. Successful attacks are also down: at the time of our meeting, no ship has been hijacked for three months. In the Indian Ocean, by the summer of 2011, this is considered a great achievement. But the warships are handicapped by state cowardice as well as law. The UK has never prosecuted a pirate nor has Portugal. The United States has: in 2010 five Somali men became the first pirates since 1820 to be convicted under U.S. piracy law for an ill-advised attack on U.S. frigate USS *Nicholas*. The following year, Abduwali Abdiqadir Muse was sentenced to thirty-four years' imprisonment for his role in the taking of *Maersk Alabama*. His crimes were hijacking, kidnapping, and hostage taking, not piracy.

Mostly the job of prosecuting falls to locals: Kenya and the Seychelles have both been persuaded to prosecute pirates, with aid given and new prisons built. The Seychelles' prison is run by a former governor of HM Parkhurst prison on the Isle of Wight. Its staff include two former Parkhurst officers who, one tabloid delightedly wrote, usually guarded sex offenders. "There was a stampede when this job was advertised." Pirates must be better than pedophiles. When Seychelles inmates rioted in 2010, the eleven detained pirates were careful not to join in, locking themselves in their cells and refusing to cooperate. They were described as model prisoners.

Correia does not talk of eradicating piracy. He is realistic. "We have to contain it to a tolerable level of piracy. It is difficult to define what is tolerable." It is not difficult to define what could change things. "We have to provoke any effect that discourages them to fight. We have to produce an effect on their center of gravity." He thinks this is difficult for a civilian to understand, but I understand it fine. Everyone has a weak point on their poop deck. He read that the average lifetime earnings of a Somali is $14,500. "With one piracy action he can get double that. So why not take the risk?"

The media often speak of a "war against pirates." But although most ships are insured against piracy by war risks insurance, for the frigate's crew this is no war. They bristle at the word. "*War* is a very strong word for the military," says the XO. "We are acting as policemen." In official language, the counterpiracy coalition is a constabulary operation, and the frustration is familiar to any police force attempting to police an inner-city area, where you stamp out trouble, and it moves elsewhere like a bubble in an air mattress. It is like any asymmetric encounter, where guerrillas win through flexibility.

"We are being useful," says the XO. "We destroy their equipment. The frustration comes when I have seventeen pirates for twelve days and no one wants to take them. I have to leave them on a beach to be pirates again, two weeks later." When the Danish warship *Absalon* kept thirteen pirates on board for thirty-eight days they put on five pounds each: weeks in a skiff can easily become a starvation diet. I see an arrested pirate on TV whose legs are sticks. It is not an easy life, to spend weeks stalking ships, to run out of food. Perhaps this is why the XO has a strange sympathy for his quarry. "You have to understand," he says. "They are not just pirates. They are human beings. By the Geneva Convention we have to take care of them."

We are due to reach Mogadishu by 5:00 a.m. The ship is in alert stage 2. Not quite battle stations (alert stage 1), but prepared for trouble. I get up easily, thanks to the pipes, and go to the bridge, but there is only darkness to be seen. *Petra* is due to be escorted into Mogadishu's port—which has only two berths, though I am surprised it has any—by two AMISOM armed teams in fast boats, but they are late. Three hours later in the ops room there is an air of alertness. This is more action than the crew has had all week: in the time since I got up and then went back to bed, shots have been fired from the shore. No one is unusually worried: shots are always being fired from Mogadishu. At whom? "Who knows?" says a lieutenant. "Just because they want to, probably." Suddenly two fast boats emerge from the harbor and now there is concern. For some reason, the boats don't identify themselves. I ask why not and get a shrug. We listen to the crew of *Petra* calling the boats on the radio, using agreed code names. *Vasco da Gama* is Fox; *Petra* is Hound. Eventually the fast craft identify themselves as *Guardian 1* and *Guardian 2*. They are armed boats, but our armed boats. The comms officers managed to sound professional rather than frustrated. "Message to Hound: you can proceed to port over." Hound comes back: "Thank you for your very kind cooperation. We are happy with you."

Petra delivers its supplies safely. A few more boring days trundling back to Mombasa, and *Vasco da Gama*'s escort job will be over. Whether the supplies ever reach the people they are supposed to reach is not the escort's concern. Al-Shabaab has controlled the port before and may do so again. *Vasco da Gama*'s boarding parties have seen humanitarian supplies in pirate skiffs. "There is no one here who is not crooked," a shipping person tells me in Mombasa, and he means in East Africa.

* * *

In Mombasa, I see the crew around town now and then, on their generous R&R time. (A box outside the sick bay held antinausea pills at sea, free for the taking. When the ship is alongside, the pills are replaced by free condoms.) Some have gone on a two-day safari north; some wander in the old town, or have un-ship food in sea-front restaurants, as I do. My goal is the heavily touristed Mombasa's old town, but not for the usual attractions. The courthouse is a few hundred yards from Mombasa's historic fort, and this is where pirates will be. I want to see what they look like, even though I can guess: thin, and Somali.

I have made no appointment, but a court official welcomes me into his office. You want pirates? We have several on trial. They have dozens awaiting judgment and others in Shimo Latewa prison, already convicted. Seven presumed pirates are being tried for an attack on MV *Polaris* in February 2009. The court official finds me a chair and lets me take notes from dossier Kenya Penal INSOC 69 (1), 13/07. As attacks go, the only unusual thing about *Polaris* was that there was enough evidence to detain the attackers. They are still suspects two years on because trials in Kenya are slow, and because midway through this one, Kenya's supreme court decided it didn't want to try the world's pirates after all, and that there was no domestic law to justify trying foreign pirates who attack foreign ships and are detained by foreign navies. This caused some international panic. If Kenya wouldn't try them, who would? After diplomatic bargaining, a Memorandum of Understanding with the EU was signed, and now Kenya will try pirates on a case-by-case basis.

Prosecuting a pirate is difficult. Naval forces must do the job of police but without being prepared for it. They have not usually been trained in evidence gathering (although this is changing). Everyone involved in a pirate trial except the detainees is frustratingly mobile: the crew have long since gone back to sea, along with the naval force. People must be recalled. Flights must be made. None of that is simple or cheap. In the *Polaris* case, witnesses did come back to Kenya to testify, including an NCIS agent from USS

Vella Gulf, the warship that detained the suspects. In his testimony, he listed the damning baggage he found upon boarding the skiff:

Seven bags of personal belongings
One handheld GPS model no. 13476207
Four 1,000-shilling notes (Somali shillings)
137 rounds of ammunition
Six magazines
Five AK-47 rifles, serial numbers weren't readable
One pistol with a magazine with 5 rounds of ammunition
One rocket propelled grenade launcher
Three Nokia cell phones
SIM card and phone charger
In a separate bag, 19 1,000-shilling notes
Family photo and address book
One hook [attached to] a rope
One revolver with three fired rounds. Rounds were unsafe and
   we discarded them.
Two rocket propelled grenades. We were unsure of them as they
   were damaged so we photographed them and discarded them.

The following day, the case has a "mention"—a brief summary that seems to serve no purpose—in the courthouse. The judge is a large man who rarely looks up. From the *Polaris* dossier, it's clear why: he is furiously writing, because the entire official record of the case is handwritten by the judge. Kenya's judicial system is founded on the rule of law, but it operates with the rule of ballpoint. The accused sit in the dock. They have an interpreter and a lawyer, although only just: the attorney, Francis Kadima, had abandoned his charges, complaining that they couldn't pay him. He was now back in court on their behalf because the EU was paying his fees. The suspects are skinny. They complain, through their interpreter, that the prison food is bad, that they have contracted tuberculosis. "I feel pain all over," I read in the dossier. "Especially the bones."

Kadima does not inspire confidence or liking but he has created a shrewd defense. They are Somali, they say. They attacked a ship from the Marshall Islands and were arrested by U.S. forces. "The government of Kenya did not arrest us. We were told that the UN will take care of us as we are poor fishermen with no money."

The mention is swiftly concluded and no one is any the wiser, except that the suspects intend to go on a hunger strike to protest their treatment and lack of human rights. The judge seems shocked by this. "We are not animals," he says in his summing up. "We have no interest in keeping anybody in custody." (The two years of detention say otherwise.) The alleged pirates file out and mill on the porch with their lawyer. A policeman already stopped me taking a photograph, so I daren't try again. Instead I sit on a chair and look at them.

On my final day on *Vasco da Gama*, I roamed the ship, asking the crew what they thought of pirates. Their answers were surprising. A cook: "Pirates are human beings with problems." A helicopter pilot: "When we've been flying, we see the poverty that rules in Somalia. I don't sympathize, but I can understand how things started." The scariest of the marines: "Pirates are doing this because they are poor and don't have money. It's a way to get power." I found this compassion astonishing. I look at these hungry, diseased men who probably pointed automatic weapons at the crew of *Polaris* and terrified them for financial gain, and I don't care about their poverty or causes or problems. I glare at them. And one notices me, stops talking to the lawyer for a moment, and glares back at the white woman who thinks he is a pirate, when he knows he is a poor fisherman.

MV Iceberg, *three years in captivity*
(NEIL BELL)

7

NO-MAN'S-LAND

Veiled Faces in the Water

PIRATE FISHING, PIRATE RADIO, TERRORISM, ENVIRONMENTAL activism, downloading songs from the Internet: none of these are piracy, according to ICOPAS, an International Conference on Piracy at Sea held in Malmö that should not be confused with ICOPA, the International Congress of Parasitology. Pirates are violent criminals. You wouldn't know that from their usual appearance in film, in newspapers, at school sports events, where they are lovable rogues, child-friendly buccaneers, swashbucklers. They provide jokes: the Somali team at the Olympics didn't realize shooting and sailing weren't the same thing. They are saleable: a Mombasa firm that offers armed escorts to merchant shipping has called its pirate-chasing craft *Jack Sparrow*. Even EU-NAVFOR's communications with ships are sent on letterhead featuring pirate skull and cross-bones, to stand out among all the tedious stuff that is constantly spat out in ships' offices.

People love pirates. They are cartoons and thought harmless. I wouldn't mind the comedy peg legs if the distortion didn't continue in more serious quarters. I lose count of the number of articles and documentaries that focus on the pirates, on their motivation, on a one-sided story. Tabloid newspapers delight in the arrest of a pirate who has six toes on each foot. With that information, the *Sun* of course produces the headline "Yo-Ho-Toe." Here is another thin Somali in a yellow jumpsuit, talking to a BBC documentary maker in Hargeisa prison, saying it's only business. "There is no problem taking a ship. It will only be taxed and released safely. There is no harm."

For most of the last decade, it has been accepted that modern piracy is the bloodless kind, that these pirates are rational economic actors who understand that every ship is insured and that insurers will pay. They will not harm the crew, because the crew is their leverage. They operate according to understandable business norms. I read studies that analyze piracy as a "market-dependent crime." They decide that it operates best in a stable environment, not anarchy, which is why many pirates come from the less chaotic areas of Somalia, such as Puntland. Stability is needed to get supplies. I read that the average profit margin for piracy in 2010 was 25–30 percent, that pirates are "the very essence of rational, profit-maximizing entrepreneurs described in classical economics." In 2010, Harvard Business School chose Somali piracy as the best business model of the year.

Breakdowns of the pirate economic model have been done. One suggests that it costs $300,000 to kit out a pirate attack, including $2,000 for weapons and ammunition; $14,000 for skiffs and outboards; $1,200 for curved ladders; $4,000 for GPS receivers and radios; $7,000 for food; $30,000 for miscellaneous equipment; $180,000 for bribes. Once hostages are taken, add $15,000 for guarding costs. That must be the luxury version: a pirate financier interviewed by the British documentary maker Neil Bell was cut rate by comparison: $30,000 to finance a Red Sea attack; up to $40,000 for the wider Indian Ocean. He could get an RPG for $800 and ammunition for $200. There is no shortage of weapons for sale in

Somalia's markets, along with infinite supplies of khat, leaves of a plant that is chewed by millions in Arab countries, and on Africa's eastern coast, because it contains cathinone, which produces effects similar to amphetamine. It is cheap, and it is an efficient lubricant for violence. Pirates, Paddy O'Kennedy of EU-NAVFOR told me, live on khat and milk. They are high when they attack ships, because that dulls the fear. Navies that apprehend pirate groups often find clutches of fifteen-year-old boys in their number, small boys protected by weapons that reach their thighs, and an armor of intoxication.

Who runs these boys? There is talk of behind-the-scenes control from Internet cafés in London; Dubai; anywhere that the huge Somali diaspora, spat out by chaos and sent running, has ended up. Each year, *Lloyd's List* catalogues the one hundred most important people in shipping. I thought the most illuminating feature of its 2010 list was that it included only one woman. But attention focused on the fourth place on the list, because that was given to Garaad, one of the three most notorious pirates.

Here is another number: sixty-seven, which is how many hostages died between 2007—when Somali piracy began to flourish—and 2010. Here are the hostages killed in 2011 by this harmless business activity: Marie Dedieu, Christian Colombo, Jean Adam, Scott Adam, Phyllis Mackay, Bob Riggle, David Tebbutt, Wu Lai Yu, Captain Akbarali Mamad Sanghar, Jakku Suleiman Sandi; one bo'sun; twelve unnamed sailors. Some were killed by pirates; some were shot by navy crossfire in lethal "rescues"; at least one jumped overboard. In this rational business activity, attack rates on seafarers exceed violent assaults in South Africa, the country with the highest level of crime in the world (697.5 per 100,000 for seafarers, 576 for South Africans). Pirates holding the Taiwanese trawler *Shiuh Fu* amputated the hand of its captain, Chao-I Wu, to force a ransom payment. On at least one occasion, a captive seafarer was keelhauled, a sweet name for a terrible thing. A sailor is tied to a rope and dragged under the ship, from one side to the other. It is an old practice but even modern keels have barnacles and things that rip and shred, particularly on ships that have been static for months. If the man is not flayed, he will probably drown. That is the dramatic abuse: malnutrition and extreme mental stress are routine. Between the contours of this rational business activity, there is too much blood.

Shipping likes conferences: you could easily attend one a week, on financing, chartering, sustainable shipping, hull design. Supplying the world with nearly everything is an enormous and complex job: there are things to discuss. Maritime security and piracy conferences are now the fashionable ones to attend. This one takes place at the Museum of London's Docklands branch. It is a handsome building of high ceilings and old bricks that sumptuously preserves an echo of the warehouse's role while sanitizing it—along with the rest of Docklands—into a public-friendly waterfront in which no docker need set foot because no ships come to call.

The museum is running an exhibit on Captain Kidd, a famous golden age pirate. The show features historical documents as well as swashbuckling, treasure, and violence. A laughably hokey trailer for the exhibit is narrated by a man whose voice is meant to have Hollywood-style gravity but doesn't. Kidd, it says, is the man who inspired the pirate movies. He is the truth at the heart of the pirate myth. In a press release, the show's curator continues this tourist-enticing theme: "The story of Captain Kidd helped create much of the pirate mythology we've known and loved since the Golden Age of Piracy." I don't love pirates. The House of Commons 2006 report into piracy was written by people who don't love them either: "We must be clear what piracy involves," its authors write with dry anger. "Kidnapping, theft, assault, rape, wounding, murder. There is nothing remotely 'romantic' about the perpetrators of these appalling crimes, or their detestable activity."

Today's seminar is about detestable activity. For once, people are gathered in a room to talk not about the men who fire guns but about the ones who face them. A Maritime Humanitarian Response Programme is being launched to improve assistance to the families of hostages while their relatives are held and to the hostages once released. The discussion panel, squeezed behind a long table and trying not to look uncomfortable, includes two Vatican priests, one representative from a seafarers' union, one psychologist, one NATO rear admiral, and one former pirate hostage, whose name is Chirag Bahri.

The rear admiral says what I expect him to say: that the solution to piracy is on land not at sea, but no, he doesn't know how to fix Somalia; that the military solution is no solution; that he is not convinced that pirates are deterred by prosecution because the benefits of the risk taking are so high and "because they have nothing to lose. Their motto is 'do or die.'" I doubt this. I don't think this is in the pirates' cost-benefit calculation: they hope, as anyone would hope, that they will do or they will fail, but that they won't die.

The unionist is Roy Paul of the ITF. He is a large, plain-speaking man with a fatigued frankness. He laments, as the panel laments, that hostages released from pirates are left adrift. When they do seek help, the help is inadequate. He describes a released hostage who sought counseling. "The first time he came, he explained to the doctor what a ship was, and he explained what had happened. The doctor had no concept of maritime life. The second time he came, he had to do the same thing. He didn't go back." When you work in an invisible industry, you get tired of the effort required to pull it into the light.

Roy shows pictures. They are different from the images that usually accompany piracy stories. There aren't many of those to begin with: Somalia is a difficult place to be a journalist. Local reporters are frequently assassinated; foreigners get kidnapped. Colin Freeman of the *Sunday Telegraph* was kidnapped on his way to the airport by his own protection team and lived for forty days in a cave.

The most popular piracy image was taken by Agence France Presse. It shows the back view of a man holding an AK-47, gazing at a picturesque blue sea, the silhouette of a hostage ship offshore. Everything about the picture is calm. Even the weapon is draped without menace on the man's shoulders. I have not seen the images that Roy is showing now, of what ships look like when pirates have finished with them: the wrecked cabins, the filth, the comprehensive and violent theft of everything worth thieving. One image shows pages from a notebook kept by a hostage on a captured Thai trawler. They express an anguish that is not usually heard.

> Dream to the day Release Us.
> I want to back home.
> Help me please!
> Thank you for Soy Sauce made us do not starve to death.

Soon it is Chirag's turn to speak. I have never encountered a former hostage until now. I look at him with fascination, at his smart suit and neat hair, as if he is a specimen. He is young—twenty-nine years old—and speaks a strongly Indian English. His emotion is making it more accented still. Anger is a rare thing to see, as a hostage is a rare thing to see. Some sign nondisclosure agreements with their employers. Some tire of telling their stories and never want to see a clipboard or tape recorder again. Many go straight back to sea because that is their life. What else can they do? Chirag tells his story briefly. He makes people laugh when he tells how the pirates wanted him to convert castor oil to motor oil. How stupid they were. "We are not supermen," he told them. "We are seamen. We are just doing a normal job. What have we done?" He is passionate; he is politely furious. "It's very, very awful. I would request from my heart that something should be done with immediate effect."

Chirag's anger has pushed him into becoming a public ex-hostage, a spokesperson for the four thousand men and women who have been captured by pirates to date. It is an important position to hold. Sometimes, for fun, I ask friends and acquaintances—educated, sophisticated ones—how many hostages they think are being held by pirates. Usually they suggest a dozen, when it is often forty times that.

I arrange to meet Chirag the next day at ITF headquarters in south London. We sit in a small room and I try not to think that what I am about to do is indefensible, because I want him to tell me in great detail what he lived through. You can stop talking when you want, I say. I don't want to ruin your day. He nods. The interviews the day before were difficult. "Everything came in front of my eyes again; I was tied up, I was crying for help. I got a little bit emotional." He is also nervous about his safety. This sounds far-fetched in a secure, comfortable room on a noisy London road, but he is serious. Pirates have contacts and connections in London. Someone in the shipping industry told him he could still be attacked. You never know. But he will talk anyway. His world is so ruined, it doesn't matter. The first thing he says, with flat bitterness, is that he is getting divorced "because of the great Somalia." Behind Chirag's smart suit and anger, his life has been unmoored.

Chirag is from Ghaziabad in Uttar Pradesh. This is as landlocked a town as you can find in India: it is more than six hundred miles to the nearest coast. But Indians have a strong maritime tradition, with good maritime schools and good English that makes them popular with manning agencies. Becoming a marine engineer seemed like a good career choice. So in 2003, Chirag went to sea, and by 2010, he was on his thirteenth ship, a tanker named MV *Marida Marguerite*. He was the second assistant engineer, about to be promoted to second engineer. "But then, piracy . . ." He is quiet a moment. "Unlucky fellow."

The tanker's owner was OCMI, a German company. It flew the flag of the Marshall Islands and carried a crew of nineteen Indians, two Bangladeshis, and one Ukrainian. On that run, they were taking benzene from Kandla Port in Gujarat to Belgium. They had called at Salalah and were 120 miles out, eight days into

May, at noon, when they saw what Chirag calls "veiled faces in the water." It is a common belief among seafarers that pirates don't like to attack in full sunlight, but pirates know better than conventional wisdom. The crew were not unprepared. They had razor wire to repel ladders and boarders. They knew about and followed the latest version of Best Management Practices. But still, they were mostly dependent on luck, like all ships that travel slowly and without private security or nearby warships. That day, luck was somewhere else. *Marida Marguerite* was doing 13 knots; the two skiffs were doing 25. The visibility was good enough to see for five nautical miles, but the pirates could neutralize that advantage. They knew that the funnel casts a shadow on the sea, that if they approached through that shadow the radar couldn't see them. Chirag was in his engine room when he was told that skiffs were approaching. It took only fifteen minutes for the approach to become an attack. So fast and terrifying. I watch a video of an attack on another ship: the speed and unrelenting nearing of the boat have a menace that penetrates my computer screen. This must be the fear felt by the hunted, the kind that reaches your throat first.

Marida Marguerite began to follow a prearranged plan. Evasive maneuvers and zigzagging first, so Chirag was on his toes in the engine room, running up and down to push his engines to maximum power. Outside, the attackers launched two RPGs at the ship and fired their AK-47s. Nonstop, clatter clatter.

I ask him where the RPGs hit. No, he says, you don't understand. They deliberately miss because they don't want to harm the ship. It is just for the scare. I remember the pirate financier in Puntland, and I calculate the scare at $1,000. The pirates put their ladder amidships and climbed up to the deck. Chirag doesn't know how they got through the razor wire, but it was either with agility or wire cutters. Then they headed for the wheelhouse. The crew had removed the outside ladders because they expected this, but the pirates climbed pipes. The captain watched them climb for the three minutes it took them to reach the bridge doors, which were locked. You will let us in, said the pirates, or we will heat you out of there. I don't know what Chirag means by this, but it doesn't matter, because the fear is the important thing to be conveyed, and he is doing that easily.

The doors were opened, and the crew was told to assemble in the wheelhouse. There they all are, then: twenty-two men who knew they were in a high-risk area, who sailed with nervousness but thought they might escape because of the balance of probabilities or the size of the sea. A Danish family sailing a yacht from the Maldives to Oman thought the same thing. They hoped to "sneak through," they said after they were released from six months of pirate captivity. (A tabloid newspaper ran a gleeful article about how one of the pirates wanted to marry the thirteen-year-old daughter, although rumors ran in military circles that she had been raped.) This Danish family seemed so stupid. Who sails a yacht here anymore? The hijacking of the U.S. yacht *Quest* a few weeks earlier, and the murder of its four crew, had been unmissable news. NATO now advises yachters to put their boats on a ship to travel through this ocean. The Danes thought they were protected by geography. So did Paul and Rachel Chandler, the most famous kidnapped yachters. "When you explain to people that it's like sailing out of Falmouth," said Paul Chandler after their release, "and the pirates are based in Lisbon, you can see their minds thinking, oh, well, that's quite a long way away." That is an empty sea, he said. Just not empty enough.

There is still debate about whether pirates counter the vastness of their hunting grounds with planning. Most piracy experts think they linger and hunt by chance, waiting for a ship. George Kiourktsoglu, a piracy researcher at the University of Greenwich, thinks that they target certain flags. Perhaps this is because he used to be a nuclear engineer and does not believe in randomness. To Kiourktsoglou, pirates prefer ships flagged to registries that have no naval presence in the Indian Ocean. So ships flagged to France, Turkey, UK, Malta, or Cyprus, for example, run only a 0.26 percent risk of being attacked; for flags from Singapore, Marshall Islands, Antigua, and Barbados, the risk runs twice as high. The starving pirates who are captured, their legs brittle as sticks, reveal another reality: that the hunters are sent out with supplies and they don't come back until they find a ship or run out, and sometimes the calculations let them down. There are no firm figures for how many pirates starve or drown while out at sea, but some of them do. Major General Howes of EU-NAVFOR has calculated that fifty die each month. It is not a bloodless business for them, either.

On the *Marida Marguerite*, the crew didn't have a citadel prepared. There was nowhere to safely hide, so the crew stayed on the bridge as they were told and watched six pirates, pissed off and hyped up, shout at their captain to sail toward Somalia, six hundred nautical miles away. What could the captain do? He had followed procedure: he had radioed a distress call on Channel 16. He had alerted the UK Maritime Trade Operations Center in Dubai. In the past, some ships failed to do this when attacked, so the UK Hydrographic Office now issues an Anti-Piracy Planning Chart, where all the procedures and necessary numbers are listed alongside a stern warning not to use the chart for navigation. But these pirates had been too quick, or the crew had been too slow. By the time a naval helicopter flew overhead, the pirates were secure enough to fire into the air. This is our ship now. The helicopter withdrew.

When Chirag arrived from the engine room at the bridge, the pirates shouted at him: Sit! Sit! "I was terrified. For me to see these six monkeys with AK-47s: I thought, my god, this is the end of the day." All the crew was now sitting on the bridge floor. Some were crying. Others were comforting their crewmates, saying, no, they won't kill us. This is business. Some started talking about fighting back. There were only a few pirates: it could be done, surely? But the senior officers disagreed. At least one crew member would be killed. They would have to capture AK-47s, then fire them at night. They were merchant seafarers, for god's sake, not soldiers. They were unused to weapons. The idea was quickly dismissed.

So the crew watched the pirates and the pirates watched the crew, while the ship steamed toward Garacad, a small harbor town in north-central Somalia, where it was anchored four miles offshore. Here, the guard changed. The boarding party left and were replaced by forty pirates, a mixed group of teenagers and young men. This division of labor is common in piracy: good ship boarders are prized and not wasted on months of guarding. Half of the *Marida Marguerite* boarding party were on their third hijack, and off they went to try for a fourth. The new crowd brought a negotiator, an older, bearded Somali who spoke English. At this point, Chirag began to feel hopeful. Negotiations would be held; ransom would be paid; they would not be kept for long. He was wrong. At that time, the average period of capture was 250 days. This had changed over time. In 2005, charter rates were higher and fuel costs lower. It cost $150,000 a day to charter a tanker, and charterers pay that whether the tanker is freely sailing or captive off Somalia. A month of captivity could cost a company more than $4 million, making it imperative to solve any hostage situation quickly; $1 million ransoms were freely paid and captivity times were in months, not years. Now charter rates have been decimated by the recession. When it's only $10,000 a day to charter a tanker, companies can afford to let negotiations drag on.

The modern history of negotiation has been associated with land-based kidnappers. Only recently have expert ransom negotiators like John Chase learned to talk to pirates. Chase is a "response consultant" for AKE, a company offering services in kidnap and ransom (K&R) situations. He is dressed casually when we meet in a London café; he looks young for his fifty years, and he speaks quietly, so that afterward the recording of our conversation has the sound of coffee cups clinking in the foreground and the intricacies of bargaining for human life behind that. Chase's workload is unpredictable—he could be called in once a year or once a month—and it is in the interests of the insurance company to which AKE is contracted for him not to work, ever. In practice, that means he gets a good salary to spend plenty of time with his children, then has to leave them suddenly, for weeks or months, as long as it takes. Chase has been working in K&R for thirty years, and he has gripping and gruesome tales, such as the one about the Mexican gang known as the Ear-Loppers, after their favorite bargaining technique. The Ear-Loppers took exception when a rival gang also started chopping off hostages' ears and annihilated the other gang for stealing their brand identity.

Chase is pragmatic. He expects hostages to lose body parts sometimes. "We always say to clients and families, people may lose an ear but they are alive, they can lead a normal life." He has had only two failures. One involved a hostage who tried to escape and was shot in the back. The other happened in Iraq, when forces loyal to Saddam Hussein executed sixty hostages, all at once, after Saddam was hanged. That was unusual, because once there is money on the table kidnappers negotiate, a truth that applies to Colombian jungle rebels, Mexican ear-loppers, and Somali pirates. Chase's first piracy case was in 2000. He soon learned that pirates are more like land kidnappers than like Blackbeard or the lovable Captain Kidd, who would kill crew when it suited, and easily. The prize for Indian Ocean pirates is the ship with the crew. Either on its own does not have the value of both.

This is the procedure, usually: A ship is taken. Chase, or someone like Chase, will fly with a team to the headquarters of the company that owns or has chartered the ship. A crisis management room is set up, and far too many interested parties want to be involved. At this point, culling is required. "The crisis management team has to be nimble enough to deal with a piracy case. Often, they're built for, for example, if a tanker hits a reef somewhere and there's a spill. We pare down the crisis team to three, four, or five people to make decisions." This can involve trickery. "You always get some senior director saying, I need to be a part of this. We say, that's great, but we are going to be in this room for the next thirty days, twenty-four seven. They usually say, oh, I was going to the cottage next weekend, and suddenly they're not there." He really does mean 24/7. Frequently the team members are sleeping under the boardroom table for a month. They are rotated out every thirty days: that is considered the maximum time before mental and physical exhaustion begins. I think of Chirag and his crewmates, confined in a small space, dependent on other men confined in a small space.

The opposing sides of these negotiations have much in common. Each puts forward a special employee to do the talking. On the response team side, actors are often used. They can read scripts well, and they are always reading from a script. There is no ad-libbing in ransom negotiations. On the pirate side, there are now sophisticated, erudite translators. It is a new career opportunity for Somalis who left their wrecked country for Europe or the Gulf, who have come back with their overseas educations and language skills. Chirag won't tell me the name of the translator on his ship, or of any pirate, although he knows them. It is not worth the risk. He says only that the translator was English-speaking, Somali, and that he had spent time in India and knew some Hindi. He had also been to the United States many times. Negotiations began, "but he didn't get any fruitful result."

Probably the expectations were too high. By 2010, the size of ransoms demanded was escalating. Pirates were asking "crazy sums," says Chase. It is his job to manage expectations. Each region has its own known going rate and expected negotiation time. In Afghanistan, for example, the ransom paid is usually half a million U.S. dollars, and negotiations will take one hundred days. It makes no sense to deviate from that, to offer a million, because then the kidnappers hold out for more. If a million is offered within two weeks, but the accepted length of negotiation is one hundred days, then the kidnappers will start wondering: Is my hostage wealthier than I thought? Does he have government ties? Chase calls this putting the "expectation comfort zone out of whack."

For the first few years, all the negotiators operated with similar understandings. Then some shipowners gave in too soon or gave

too high: there are no formal guidelines or rules, so different negotiators do their own thing. The maritime lawyer James Gosling,
who has been involved in plenty of negotiations for shipping clients, gave a talk at the Vatican in 2012 about the peculiar economics of bargaining. These are not, he said, "what you and I would
call normal commercial negotiations. You don't start with one figure, counter another, and then finish somewhere roughly halfway
in between." If an owner gives too high a figure, pirates will retract
on sums they have already decided on and demand a higher ransom. Gosling called this the "yo-yo effect." Pirates now expect to
get $10 million for a small ship owned by one family who simply
cannot pay that much. When many ships are heavily mortgaged,
and owners rely on daily charterer fees to keep going, a hijack is
disastrous: the charterer stops paying, but wages must still be paid,
along with the mortgage. Several owners, said Gosling, have had
mental breakdowns or heart attacks when their ships have been
taken. Some have gone out of business. For Chase, expectations
out of whack mean negotiations take longer, hostages are held longer, and more get hurt or killed.

Chirag didn't know that there were these expectations. All he
could see was the day ahead. It was good that he could still work. A
ship's engines always need maintenance, even a ship stalled by the
limbo of a kidnap. The sea is still sea and salt is still corrosive.
Some ships released from captivity have sunk. Some of the sinkings
no doubt suited shipowners who possessed adequate insurance and
were anxious about the cost of repairs to a ship damaged by months
of immobility. Other ships were genuinely corroded, wrecked and
diminished. Chirag began to stay in the engine room for twelve
hours a day, keeping things going. The pirates didn't follow him
down there. They didn't like the dark or the noise. Once the engineers understood this, they deliberately set off engine alarms any
time a pirate came near. Also, for the first weeks, they hid beer in
the dark spaces of the engine room. A small triumph.

After twelve hours, Chirag would return to the bridge and

chitchat if possible, "if the pirates were okay." He became an expert at pirate watching, at guessing their moods. He soon learned that they were predictably unpredictable. Supplies were brought aboard from the shore, and the supplies often included goats, which were slaughtered on the main deck, to Chirag's disgust. He thought his captors were filthy, that they had skin conditions and STDs. But he also complained that they used all the water by showering. He was wary of the khat they were constantly chewing, which he tried once and didn't like because it changed the taste of his mouth and his mood. On the ship, afternoon was doping time and by the evening they were high. Chirag learned to read them more carefully when their eyes turned red. They became paranoid that a naval vessel or a rival pirate gang would dare to attack them, that the crew might call the navy somehow.

After twenty days, the hostages were allowed to move into cabins. Time passed with difficulty but it passed. Chirag says things like "for the first six months," as if it were nothing. I suppose he wants to forget it, but this empty time interests me. What happens to a brain over months of fear? Colin Freeman, held hostage in a cave by his Somali armed guards: "You realize that your mind, already tired and stressed, is not the limitless sanctuary you might expect. Rather than passing the time with intellectual, life-affirming insights, I increasingly found I could only manage things like listing old pubs I'd visited in my youth, and ranking the girls I knew in order of attractiveness."

At least there was food. At least there was more than soy sauce. The pirates brought their own cook, who prepared goat and more goat. The captives' diet was potatoes and bad rice, containing stones that fractured teeth. If they were lucky, the pirate cook made them chapatis. Supplies were meager, although there were regular boat taxis bringing food and goods from the shore, indicating that Garacad tolerated the pirate activity off its beach. This is not always the case. The northern Somali town of Bargal posted STOP signs with messages that piracy is *haram*, or against Islam. The town council presented local pirates with a list of demands, then posted an eighty-strong police force on the beach. When pirates came shopping as usual for khat, they were turned away. Other villages and towns in Somalia have also banished pirates.

But still pirates have no difficulty finding refuge. Perhaps they are good for the economy. Dr. Anja Shortland of Brunel University wanted to answer this question by measuring normal economic indicators, but on-the-ground research in Somalia is difficult. Instead, she used Google Earth, studying satellite images of areas where pirates were known to operate. She was looking for evidence of construction and electricity as indicators of prosperity and progress. Shortland compared images from 2005 to those from 2009. None of the notorious pirate towns—Eyl, Hobyo—had enough light to show up, then or now. They had the darkness of unelectrified poor places. Then Shortland looked at walls. Somalis like to live in compounds. If they have money, they build walls. They do home improvements, like anyone else. By 2009, compounds in Eyl and Hobyo had grown in size, and more had cars parked outside, suggesting "a combination of a rising value of stored goods and increasing community tensions." The walls and snazzy compounds showed that pirates were prospering, but that common good—in the form of electricity—had not been shared among other residents. There were no other visible improvements to infrastructure. Being a pirate town did not pay.

There are plenty of tales of wild parties, prostitutes, drug taking, and more. But in Mombasa, a local shipping journalist thinks he knows where the money goes: into that new apartment building and that money changer's office; into that block of offices and that villa there. The journalist had bought a piece of land for 330,000 Kenyan shillings in 1993, and in 2010 a Somali offered him 1.5 million shillings for it, in cash (about $16,000). He didn't sell. He doesn't know that the buyer was a pirate, but the rumors are powerful around these men with such cash from such a poor country. "Some who have done piracy several times are here." He says the godfathers—the land-based pirate controllers—come here to spend their gains, that the money changers are mostly Somali-owned. "The government turns a blind eye, maybe because of corruption. They can make you not see them."

There is no need for secrecy in piracy. John Chase's negotiators often communicate by Skype. It's not like in Afghanistan or Iraq, where you are trying to negotiate out of sight of governments who want to rush in and rescue the hostages. Somalia is different. "The pirates will talk on the phones for hours at a time. Everyone knows where they are; it's not an issue of trying to locate them." Everyone knows where the hostages are, but no one is rushing to rescue them. Bryan Toki, a maritime security consultant, once rescued an Indian ship that had been held for 332 days. He was "haunted by the sight of Chinese sailors, rail-thin with beards down to their waists, waving for salvation on a nearby ship." He wanted to fire at them, "to open up on those bastards who were holding them and free those poor souls. But I had to remind myself, this is a business."

On *Marida Marguerite*, the beatings began at the end of August, three months after the ship's capture. This was when the negotiations began to go badly. The second officer had turned turncoat, whispering information to the pirates about the size of the company, the value of the ship and its cargo. The pirates seemed to believe him. In Chirag's description of his captors, they are part knowing and part gullible. They knew enough to research Chirag's name on the Internet, to bring him a printout of a letter his sister had written to the Indian government begging them to do something to release her brother. But the Indian government would do nothing when the ship flew the flag of the Marshall Islands. "They can only pressure the owners. German owners, Marshall Islands flag, crew members from all over, cargo from some other country going to some other country, vessel of some other make. The problems are bad because of that." When the pirates sequestered every cell phone on board, they knew enough to scorn some because they were old models. But they were dumb, too. They found a phone in a drawer that didn't have a SIM card, so the screen read Emergency SOS. "They saw that and said, you have called the navy. The captain and chief were beaten up day and night because of that."

There had been slaps before, if the pirates didn't like the crew talking. But at the end of August, they began the torture. The captain was first, then the chief engineer, then down through the ranks. On September 9, the pirates came to the engine room. They saw the intercom phones as if for the first time and said, those are satellite phones. (On another ship they thought a coffeemaker was a sat phone.) They said, you are calling the navy. You are calling the company and telling them not to negotiate. There was no protesting to be done. There was no point saying that of course he wasn't delaying negotiations, he couldn't give a damn how much the company paid, he just wanted to go home. At 6:00 a.m., he and a fellow engineer were taken to the bridge deck and told to lie belly down. Three pirates came and tied their ankles to their wrists in a classic stress position. The heat was one hundred–plus degrees by early morning. Then Chirag's genitals were bound tightly with plastic cable ties. "They were such torturous people. They used to have fun with that. Lots of crew had their genitals tied up." Cable-tied genitals and cooking on a hot deck: this continued for four hours.

Chirag's left hand was paralyzed for a month and his sperm count suffered. He knows who decided this new policy of violence. There was a young pirate, under thirty, but who looked fifteen. He was the most dangerous one. Chirag won't say his name, but I learn that it was Budiga. He was the devil. "Some older pirates had some heart in them. They used to tell the young chap, leave them alone. This is not humanity. The crew have not done anything." Harassing the crew, they said, would not move the company quicker.

But it might. So there was more slapping, kicking, "like you would kick a donkey." The senior officers had it worse in this "torturous period." They were taken to the meat freezer, ice was put in their undergarments, and they were left there for forty minutes, at below-zero temperatures. Another was hung by his wrists from a mast. This sounds so antiquated, both the hanging and the mast, as if it belongs in the romantic mythology for which we love Captain Kidd. The sailor passed out after two hours.

The longest-held ship so far is MV *Iceberg*, whose twenty-four crew were reduced to twenty-two over three years of captivity. Chirag knew about *Iceberg* because he could see it every day, anchored a mile or so away. I am drawn to *Iceberg*, to the absurdly long time it was held hostage and because it was abandoned by its owners, Azal Shipping of Dubai, and by its flag state, Panama. Throughout all its captivity, it was visible off the coast of Somalia. In 2010, documentary maker Neil Bell took a handheld camera on board *Iceberg*. In his film *The Pirates of Somalia*, we follow his camera into the ship and into the cabin where twenty-three men lie shoved together like sausages. Their faces are Yemeni, Indian, Ghanaian, Sudanese, Pakistani, and Filipino, and their expressions are dull with despair.

In London's Imperial War Museum, in the small Merchant Navy section, there is a logbook from a raft that fled SS *Culworth Hill*, a ship torpedoed in the Second World War. It is written on sailcloth. The words are plain and the wretchedness is clear.

King, 11pm, 11 April: Out of mind
2nd engr 5am 19 April GANGRENE
Leak, D.E.M.S., 6am Out of mind
Bolt Army Gunn 10am 19 April Out of mind.

What does an old logbook have to do with a Panama-flagged ship? *Iceberg*'s third officer, Wagdi Akram, went out of mind. He was Yemeni, a father of four, and a well-liked member of the crew. But then he deteriorated. First he disappeared, and his crewmates found him hiding in a ceiling. They chained him up because they saw that their friend had become "mentally incapacitated." For three days he was chained, but on the third day he seemed the old Wagdi, as gentle as he used to be. They released him. The next day he went to pray, but he didn't finish his prayers. The bo'sun found him in the sea near the anchor, dead.

The crew of *Iceberg* were not allowed to not forget Wagdi Akram, because they were still living with him. Bell's camera heads into a room that holds a freezer chest. "This freezer for fish," says the crew member who opens the lid. Not for fish anymore: he lifts up some packets and there is the calm, dead face, its skin brown and its mustache black, of Wagdi Akram, out of mind.

When *Iceberg* ran out of water (and also electricity, making that freezer of death more dreadful), Chirag was ordered to resupply it with water from *Marguerite*'s own stock. He also resupplied other hijacked vessels and "needy fishing trawlers." *Marguerite* was the pirate water fountain, supplying three hundred tons in all to other ships. Chirag describes a strange community of frozen ships and boats, anchored in limbo just off Somalia. *Asian Glory, Samho Dream, Al Nasir, Iceberg*, all captive, all nearby. The artist Allan Sekula, in his book *Fish Story*, writes about Michel Foucault's definition of a heterotopia, a displacement habitat, a place that exists between places. Cemeteries, fairgrounds, retirement homes, psychiatric hospitals. But the best heterotopia, he writes, is the ship, "a floating piece of space, a place without a place, that exists by itself, that is closed in on itself and at the same time is given over to the infinity of the sea." Foucault is wrong. There is a better heterotopia: a ship lying at anchor off Somalia, crippled and crewed by crippled people, visible but untouchable.

Marida Marguerite had exhausted its fuel supply after two months. This derailed the pirates' plans to turn it into a mobile mothership. This is when they demanded that the engineers turn castor oil into fuel, an impossible request against all laws of physics. Anyway, the ship was in no fit state to be sailed. Chirag smiles. The machinery was not fit because Chirag had temporarily sabotaged it. "I personally did some small thing. I opened some of the machinery parts and I did all I could to make them feel that the machinery is not in a working state. I don't want my vessel to become a mother vessel." He sounds very pleased. "I got some tortures for that but I'm okay with that."

Chirag elides the next few months. There was hope in October then more waiting. Somewhere in a conference room, where people were sleeping under the boardroom table, details were being worked out. Money was being arranged, as it usually is. John Chase is strict about when to pay out. "They'll demand several million and then say, just send two thousand, I can buy medicine and food. Of course your loved ones sound sick, you think you need to send this. But for $2,000 in Somalia you could feed a whole family for a long time. If you send a few thousand every few months, they will keep going forever. You have to resist temptation." Sometimes negotiators have sent food out on a boat when a captive ship has run short. This did not always go smoothly: if pirates ask for halal food, you have to send livestock. But how do you get a live goat up the sheer twenty-foot side of a ship? With difficulty and dexterity.

The ransom is sometimes not the biggest cost in freeing a ship. John Chase's team charges $3,000 a day for negotiation, a fee regulated by the insurance industry. But then there is the drop. Before, when the amounts were smaller, it could be sent out in tugs or boats, like the goats. A million dollars could fit into a rucksack. When the crude tanker *Irene* was released for $13 million, the cash weighed as much as a gorilla.

This is how the conclusion is supposed to happen. Money is arranged, usually from friendly banks in Dubai or in other offshore environments that permit the payment of ransoms to criminals. Both UK and U.S. governments publicly discourage the payment of ransoms, but their laws permit it, as long as the recipients are criminal gangs, not terrorists. This distinction would probably baffle Chirag, hog-tied on a scorching deck for hours, but fortunately for pirates no one yet has linked them convincingly to

Al-Shabaab. So men with small planes are hired, because the ship is too far offshore for a helicopter to be useful. A pod the size of a mini torpedo is attached to the underside of a Cessna or Otter. The ship is told to set sail, if it can, into the wind and code words are established so pirates don't mistake the money drop for a navy assault. The crew are made ready: for proof of life, they are lined up on the deck. They wave, sometimes, or stand impassively and hoping beyond human expectation. The pods are dropped into the sea. The pirates go out in skiffs to collect them, and all is usually well.

This procedure can go wrong. In 2010, rival pirate gangs fought over a $5 million ransom that had been dropped on the laden oil tanker *Maran Centaurus*. Only the arrival of navy helicopters broke it up. With *Marida Marguerite*, it went right. Chirag and his twenty-one crewmates were on deck, watching nervously. "It was a moment to cherish. A chartered plane counted us first." The right codes were transmitted by radio. "Hellfire calling, beta beta hare or something." The money was dropped a mile away into the sea and fetched by skiff. And Chirag, who knew his captors well by now, could see that this was a dangerous time, when the paranoia rose in the pirates. "You knew from their faces. The person who used to smile at us, you see his face and, oh my god, you had better stay away."

The counting of the money began. This is something that would probably interest Harvard Business School, because it is an organized and complicated business. Pirates use logbooks and accountants. The accountant on *Marida Marguerite* had been there all along, tallying how many goats had come on board, what the rice cost, making notes. Chirag reckons 150 to 200 people arrived during the next twenty-four hours to get their payment. A village of people come to be paid for services rendered.

Finally, the pirates ransacked the ship, taking whatever they could find, from cell phones to clothes—but not Chirag's new leather jacket, which he had hidden in the engine room—and left with money stuffed in their pockets, in their stolen clothes, in plastic bags, in the crew's suitcases that the crew no longer needed because they had nothing to put in them. By ten o'clock on the morning of December 28, all pirates had gone. Some had left earlier, saying they had a long way to travel. Then a U.S. naval vessel arrived and Navy SEALS came on board. You must have been pleased to see them, Chirag? But he is dismissive. He thinks they took pleasure in the condition of the ship. His pride was damaged.

This was still a dangerous time: there were a thousand miles to travel to safe anchorage, back to Salalah. Released ships have been attacked by rival pirate groups on their way home. I read about letters of safe passage given by pirates to released ships like old-fashioned passports. *Marida Marguerite*'s pirates left behind a phone number instead. Call if any other pirates attack, and they will leave you alone. Chirag doesn't know who the number belonged to, and he doesn't care. He says the captain threw the number away anyway. It mattered only that the ship was sailing away and under its own power. When the pirates finally left, laden with money and other people's possessions, the crew got back to work. No way were the engineers going to let their ship be dragged off by a tug. The shame of it. "Why should I lose money for the company by paying for tugs?"

This loyalty is a surprise. The German owners had behaved decently enough, continuing to pay the men's salaries and "extra basic" while the ship was captive. They sent a fuel barge to replenish its oil and a fresh set of clothes for every man. Later, the crew were paid $1,000–$2,000 in compensation, depending on seniority. I work this out to be about $8 for every day of abuse, fear, and loathing. This is not a calculation I have seen done by Harvard economists.

Chirag does not want to go back to sea. Other released hostages have gone back to ships. At least one crew member of *Maersk Alabama* went back to the same ship on the same route, though never again without armed guards. By now, two-thirds of ships carry armed private security guards, even while the status in law of these rent-a-marines is still fluid, even while you hear stories still of them dropping weapons in the ocean rather than paying expensive export licenses, or worse. They are permitted by several flag states, the IMO, ITF, and the UK government. The business is popular, attracting former marines and Special Boat Service men leaving service or their postmilitary mercenary jobs in Iraq and Afghanistan, rushing to this new money zone where they will earn better money than a government salary and not get blown up. There are now thought to be fifteen hundred armed guards working, and a couple of dozen floating armories where weapons are stored. Now, ships advertise their armed guests in their AIS, so that where the display reads "destination," there is "full armed guards" or "3 armed guards O/B (on-board)." Armed security costs around $50,000 per transit—though security companies are coy about figures—through the High Risk Area, but it is an economical expense: some insurers now reduce premiums if armed guards are on board by up to 75 percent. No ship carrying armed guards has yet been hijacked.

Ashore, proper investigation is finally being done by the UN Offices on Drugs and Crime into the financial flows of piracy, with a view to blocking them. Somalia has a new government stable enough for prisons to be built, and for pirates to be tried, as the MV *Polaris* attackers wanted, in their own country. Other countries have taken on the pirate task. Yemen, the United States, Germany, and Italy have prosecuted pirates. India, meanwhile, wants to prosecute Italian marines who shot two Indian fishermen off Kerala, mistaking them for pirates. As for other shootings of innocent, AK-47-carrying fishermen at sea by marines or ex-marines, certainly they happen, and certainly we never know about them.

All these efforts have dulled the second golden age of piracy: attacks are down. Perhaps the ex–military men whose messages I read on close protection forums, exchanging information about weaponry and sun protection and how many DVDs to take on ship (a lot; it can get boring), will do what the commander of the EU-NAVFOR fleet wanted and keep piracy to a "tolerable" level. Or they will move their services to West Africa, where piracy is growing while East Africa's is dimming. And then, cynics say, the young men of Somalia will get back in their boats and set off again, hopeful and hunting.

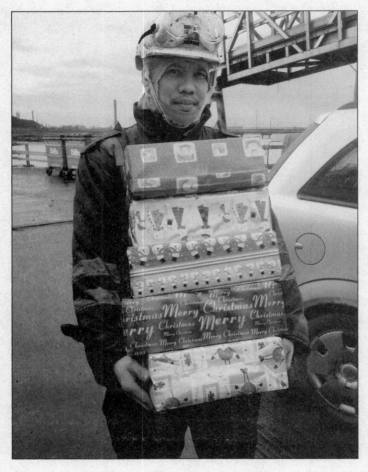

A ministry of small gestures
(ROSE GEORGE)

8

SANCTUARY

The Merchant Navy Comforts Service

THE VIEW—CRASHING WAVES, A SANDY BEACH—IS SPECTACULAR. It is unexpected, because all I knew of the Port of Salalah, in the Gulf state of Oman, was its status as *Kendal*'s sanctuary after pirate waters, as the relief at the end of the Internationally Recommended Transit Corridor. I wasn't even sure how to pronounce its name until Captain Glenn told of a girl in the office who pronounces Salalah like "Ooh-la-la!" The spectacular view is from the terrace of the Oasis Club, a bar restaurant on the cliffs above the port. I go there twice in twenty-four hours, with whoever can grab a few hours' leave to come with me, enough for a quick Skype home; perhaps a drink—nonalcoholic of course—a meal that hasn't been cooked by Pinky, and some fruit that doesn't look as sad as ours.

In the better ports around the world, sailors always head for a mission to use those precious hours. Run by church organizations—the Norwegian Church, the Seamen's Church Institute of New York, and the UK's Mission to Seafarers are the best known—these missions, or seafarers' centers, offer Internet, food, drink, and a small period of solace and different company to that on your ship. The Mission to Seafarers alone runs 230 centers worldwide, and it is a godsend, because most are in or near ports, and seafarers lack either the time, money, or visa to go farther.

The Oasis Club is not godly; it is a private establishment that has become a de facto mission because of its location near the port, its free transport, and its chefs who produce steaks the size of plates. Also, in this dry state, it serves alcohol to those seafarers allowed to drink it, which includes the entire U.S. Navy. I travel in with Francis and a bunch of the Filipino crew. At passport control, Francis begins to speak Arabic to the staff while we look at him in shock. I suppose it shouldn't be a surprise: really he is speaking globalization, because he used to work in Jeddah, one of the satellite destinations of Filipinos' enormous reach. This is the first time Francis has seen uncovered Arab women. The bus driver wants to sell him a sword, and Francis fingers the metal and says, "Wow," politely, but doesn't buy it. Overseas Filipinos often take home a box of gifts, known as *balikbayan*, a word meaning "one that is returning home to the country." A sword wouldn't fit.

The club is packed because a U.S. warship is in port and its crew is making full use of their R&R. There is no table without chasers on it. One sailor swats a fly and says, "Yeah, baby." In this atmosphere, you would pronounce Salalah as the girl in the office does, and it would fit. The Filipinos gather around a table to Skype home and to talk; I check e-mails and wish I hadn't. They are an intrusion into my ship brain, which has become different. It must have, because it regularly and routinely spits out dreams of such violence and vividness that I wake in my cabin in a daze, shaking the dreams off like sand. It is rare that I wake up without having dreamed a murder. The crew nod with recognition when I tell them this. They think it is the vibrations, that the noise gets into your head and shakes your thoughts.

I take refuge on the club's terrace, for some air and some view. There is a drunken sailor already there who is sober enough not to reveal what the warship has been doing, but I presume it has been on antipiracy duty and thank him with some force, as the keen comfort of seeing a sleek gray ship in Gulf waters—Chinese, Dutch, American, who cares—is still fresh. The sailor seems to be drinking off months of stress, and so would my crew if they could. Maersk seafarers aren't even supposed to drink in airports when transiting to a ship.

Despite the Oasis Club and the plate-wide steaks, despite the tax-free income and the duty-free goods, despite the view of a glorious ocean that the crew can't wait to be rid of, the life of the seafarer is one of isolation. *Kendal*'s welfare standards are higher than many ships, but providing socializing or solace is difficult, even for Maersk. "Ships' crews today are subject to constant change," write the authors of a report into transnational seafarer communities. "As a result, crews tend to consist of strangers-become-shipmates and consequently the social relations of seafarers' employment are experienced as a series of discontinuous encounters."

One day, Julius and Pedro want to know my purpose in asking them so many questions, and I say it is to write about seafarers' lives. Pedro nods. "The toughest job and the loneliest." Yes, echoes Julius. "Definitely the loneliest."

For most of history, the seaman's life has been one of adventure, perhaps, but also of weevils, awful food, terrible weather, press gangs, pirates, constantly possible drowning or injury. Sea life was underpaid, underfed, and so often lethal that Marco Polo thought a man who went to sea must be a man in despair. There has always been concern for the souls of seamen, who were thought to belong to a heathen parish. When the English king Stephen sent a fleet to Spain in 1147, the articles of agreement included a priest for every ship "and the same observances as in parishes on shore."

In the high times of evangelism, seafarers became a noble cause. Victorian missionaries, who could travel through the British Empire to save souls, instead wandered to the local docks. Mariners' churches, missions, centers, and accommodation houses abounded in the nineteenth century. Naval officers, impressed by missionary efforts in the South Pacific, had begun work among the destitute seamen of East London docks in 1827 and opened a sailors' home. The Seamen's Church Institute in New York opened in 1835, the same year that an Anglican reverend, John Ashley, fitted out a cutter named *Eirene* to become the first floating chapel of the Mission to Seafarers.

This was not an easy parish to minister to. In his history of the Mission to Seafarers, L. A. G. Strong writes that "the visitor who was unwise enough to interrupt a card game could expect anything, from the ship's dog at his trousers to a howl of derision and the routine inquiry, 'Does your mother know you're out?'" But the rowdiness was misleading. "Behind their grim exterior, their beards, their tobacco chewing, and the menacing knife at their belts, these Victorian seamen were lonely." They were also sometimes emerging from months or years at sea in slave conditions. Flogging was banned on American ships only in 1850 (although when the secretary of the navy asked senior naval officers their opinion, only 7 out of 241 replies wanted it discontinued). It took another sixty-five years for seafarers to be protected from other forms of corporal punishment, with the 1915 Seamen's Act, legislation nicknamed the Magna Carta of the sea, that aimed to improve the welfare of the U.S. merchant marine. Until then, captains could and did chastise their crews with "fists, boots, pieces of rope, brass knuckles, pistols and ship-board items such as belaying pins, marlin spikes, hand spikes and other tools."

Nor was there peace and harmony ashore. Sailors in a strange port were easy marks for exploitation. Dockland touts known as crimps or landsharks abounded. These were colorful names for unscrupulous people. They were expert at their work: they waited for sailors dockside or boarded their just-berthed ships to trap them on board. Most sailors wouldn't get their wages for a few days, leaving them with nothing to live on ashore. You haven't been paid yet? Then have this gin, this woman, this boardinghouse bed on credit. It's no trouble. After three days of such underhanded openheartedness, the sailor usually had a bill long enough to push him straight back onto a ship and out of the way of home.

The crimps—they had names such as Timmy, Dutch Charley, or Flash Tom—were making the godless world of seafaring worse than it need be, so the Reverend Robert Buckley Burton, a seafarers' chaplain in Bristol, took action. In a scene more *Mission Impossible* than Mission to Seafarers, he bundled sailors into a line of waiting cabs and took them to the station and to trains home. Police at the station helped the good reverend oversee the purchasing of tickets and the delivery of seamen onto the trains. "Victory was complete," wrote Strong, "when the trains pulled out of the station, and the crimps stood behind the railings, shaking their fists."

Chaplains were installed in overseas ports of empire and trade: Madras, Singapore, Vancouver. In San Francisco, the chaplains were considered so trustworthy that seamen would leave gold coins with them for safekeeping. This was a broad church. The Strangers' Rest Mission in London's Spitalfields catered to West Africans, Caribbeans, and Chinese, although the Chinese were given their own dedicated shelter in the 1900s. There were homes for Destitute Sailors, Coloured Sailors, an Asiatic hostel for Indians, which showed Hindustani films and provided "native washing facilities." There were floating boats of worship: the first three churches of the Seamen's Church Institute of New York (SCI) were full-sized chapels attached to a barge that floated up and down New York's waters as required. The Floating Church of Our Savior for Seamen was, wrote Leah Robinson Rousmaniere in SCI's official biography, a "pinnacle, Gothic-style church with a seventy-foot steeple." It was a stunning example of "ecclesiastical maritime architecture," possibly not an overcrowded branch of architecture studies these days.

Accounts of the early missions abound with not obviously religious endeavors, such as chaplains sourcing a piano for a musical captain at short notice, or recruiting compliant young ladies—but not too compliant—for seamen's dances. Some chaplains visited ships carrying lists of Old Testament names for crossword enthusiasts. The third and last floating chapel came ashore in 1910—tethered to the ground of Staten Island and becoming All Saints Episcopal Church—and by 1913 a magnificent new sanctuary for sailors had been constructed at 25 South Street, flying flags on its roof that in code spelled "welcome." By the early twentieth century, it had accommodation for 714 seamen, over 200 employees, and an excellent reputation amongst seafarers for all sorts of services, expected and less so.

The SCI's most famous employee was Mrs. Janet Roper, known to all as Mother Roper, famous for her efforts to match families with their lost seafarer relatives. Seamen often went missing, but Mother Roper located two hundred a year on average. In 1934, she gave a radio interview to Captain Phillips Lord and ended like this:

> Boys who are sailing out on the sea and listening in tonight: find for me—Smoky Joe—his mother is dying. Tell Harry Kelly— Punch Kelly—his father has died and his Mother has got to go to the Poor House. I want to hear from Frank Pazana, Mike Murphy or sometimes called Lemon George—tell Blinky— that's one-eyed Blink Ross, his little girl is sick and needs him. Pass the news to Punch Smith his wife is seriously sick. Shorty McGuire has been looking for his wife and little boy for ten years. Tell him I've finally located his wife and little boy—and they want him back. Goodnight boys—and see that you write your Mother and your sweetheart once every month and let them know where you are. That's only fair play. Goodnight, boys.

What resonates most from Mother Roper, from the archives of all the seafaring parishes, is a constant and unwavering kindness, offered in all weathers and all ports, and for no obvious gain. Polish sailor Józef Korzeniowski, Joseph Conrad, well knew the Sailors

Home on London's Well Street, with its tiers of small rooms offering shelter. It was, he wrote, a "friendly place . . . Quietly, unobtrusively, with a regard for the independence of the men who sought its shelter ashore, and with no other aims besides that effective friendliness." In the Port of London, a chaplain reported taking visiting Chinamen sightseeing, before feeding them supper at his home. This, wrote the authors of the Port's 1966 report, was "men who are strangers [being] taken into a world of friendship." Two years later, a Chinese-language padre, Peter Kao, reported taking Ng Sing, a chief steward on the *Benvrackie*, on a similar tour. This was a big event: Ng had been with his company for more than twenty years, and this was his first ever time ashore.

There is much that Ng or Mother Roper would not recognize about today's shipping world, but some things are unchanged. In 2007, a seafarer working on an LNG tanker reported that his regular route—between Qatar and Japan—left him only eighteen hours in port at either end. He hadn't had shore leave for fifty months. When Erol Kahveci of Cardiff University asked seafarers how long their average shore leave was, 36 percent said two hours. Nearly two-thirds spent all that time in the port area. Now that 4,000 to 6,000 foreign seafarers arrive in British ports every day, the missions have changed their mission. From looking after Britons abroad in a strange land, as they used to do, they now care for the world coming the other way.

Immingham, a port on the northeastern coast of England, doesn't look much like a sanctuary. It is not stunning like the terminals of Singapore or Shanghai. Nor does it have the waves or views of Salalah, because it is perched near the mouth of the flat, dull Humber Estuary. I had never heard of Immingham, though I grew up only fifty miles away. When I researched it, the first story was not about its impressive annual tonnage—it is the largest port in the UK by volume shifted—but about Graham Cardwell, an assistant dockmaster who faked his own death in 1998 by leaving a life jacket and hard hat on the docks' mudflats. He was assumed to have been carried out to sea while carrying out routine inspections, but had carried himself instead to the East Midlands, where he lived under an assumed name and worked in a pub, before a passing tugboat captain recognized his voice, having heard it so often in the docks over the VHF radio. Cardwell told police he believed he had cancer and didn't want his wife and children to know. "A family reunion," said a police spokesperson, "is not expected for the foreseeable future."

Perhaps this is a place that drives you mad. You would think as much if you drove in through its gates and saw the huge refineries and the vast dumps of coal and iron ore, if you wiped from your car dashboard the layer of coal dust that soon settles with a window open, or saw nothing but the flat warehouses, no greenery, nothing but toil and production.

You would think so, but then in the middle of the mucky docks you would reach a modest building and a modest Irish priest who would change your mind. Father Colum Kelly arrived at Immingham as a temporary chaplain for the Seafarers' Centre, on loan from his inner-city Catholic parish in Leeds. It was meant to be a six-month loan, eight years ago. The parish is too broad and the needs are too great, and he is still here. The view from the center is nothing much, unless the *Ernest Shackleton* research vessel is visiting, sheltering at bargain prices in these temperate waters from her Antarctic survey work. Yet Colum waves his arm to the view, to the industry and muck. It was a shock when he arrived, but now, isn't it beautiful?

Inside, the building is warm and spacious and has been equipped with consideration for men who spend their lives among metal. There is a trickling fountain surrounded by plants, pool tables, a large bar, and a shop that carries freshly made sandwiches, hair dye, and Fisherman's Cough Linctus, a local remedy. That fishermen require particular cold remedies is not a new notion: Fishermen's Friends lozenges sell billions every year, and were invented by a

Lancashire pharmacist to resolve the bronchial problems of local fishermen working in the freezing Atlantic. Now they are bought by local dockworkers who come for their lunchtime sandwiches—there is no other shop on the docks—but also by the citizens of the Philippines, Cape Verde, Russia, Ukraine, Bangladesh, China, and India, who regularly arrive in Immingham and head to the nearest source of supplies.

When missions are the only touch of land that seafarers get, they get reputations. Felixstowe is well attended but the beer is considered overpriced. Also it is less jolly now: children racing through it were a common sight when seafarers could take their families to sea, before piracy. Felixstowe's shop is more popular than its bar prices. It sells London souvenirs to seafarers who will get no closer to the capital than one hundred miles away, but their families don't know that. The shop manager in Felixstowe had learned her clientele well: Taiwanese drink Guinness in the morning with a bar of chocolate; the Italians love Cadbury; Indians prefer Quality Street. Everyone likes souvenirs that are lightweight and easily packed. Seafarers travel home by airplane with the same luggage restrictions as anyone else. Felixstowe's manager sources her souvenirs from a nearby warehouse, so she often finds herself following a container out of the docks to the warehouse, buying its contents and selling them back to the men who have brought them. Bristol's mission is liked, according to a port welfare survey, "because it has many phone boxes." Chinese and African ports are hopeless and sometimes dangerous. Of course African ports don't have welfare facilities, wrote one seafarer, because "how could they provide it for visitors since they don't have it for themselves?"

Immingham is popular. Transport can be provided, but the docks are not so giant that visitors can't walk or cycle from their ship, if they have a bike on board. The building is spacious and its staff are kind. There are books in the library, and a mail-order catalogue, far cheaper than chandlers, that can supply the shopping needs of the hurried. There is a small chapel in the corner of the games room, but most seafarers prefer to have Mass on their ship, so it is rarely used. Colum usually has music playing there: Rachmaninoff's Vespers are popular, "and not just with Russians." Felixstowe's chapel when I visited had no music but a noticeboard filled with modern prayers, including one asking God to help "with the smooth processing of my son's dependent visa and also pray for my wife's blood transfusions that she will have a Christian blood donor." Another, from Anonymous: "What you are doing is so loud I can't hear what you are saying."

From the beginning, church welfare groups tried to cater to the needs of their seafaring parish. It was not necessarily going to be a happy meeting, given the Latin prayer *Qui nescit orare, discat navigare.* He who does not know how to pray, let him go to sea. In 1942, the Seamen's Church Institute statistics recorded 106,362 visits to its 138 entertainments, but only 14,021 attendances at church services. The Port of London Mission in 1965 fared even worse, evangelically: only 2101 seafarers attended services, but 18,475 used its entertainment facilities.

In her history of SCI, Rousmaniere quotes an old sailor introducing the institute to a young boy looking for a ship: "You can eat there; sleep there; they'll stow your gear. It's cheap and it's clean. They got a job board—tell you what ships are lookin' for a crew. They got it all; and they ain't *too* holy." The cultural and geographical shift of modern seafarers, though, makes for a more receptive audience for proselytizing: there are Filipino Catholics, Russian and Ukrainian Orthodox, Indian Hindus. Visitors to Immingham's center can choose from three kinds of spiritual comfort: Catholic from Father Colum, who works for the Apostleship of the Sea; Ecumenical from David, a lanky Methodist who represents the Sailors' Society; and Anglican from the Mission to Seafarers chaplain. He is replacing the previous incumbent, who was prosecuted for immigration offenses (he married his own wife twice). The Anglican for now is on vacation and probably deservedly, as his last posting was the Red Sea port of Aqaba, where he regularly attended to seafarers arriving on ships punctured with pirate bullet holes.

Colum lives above the shop. He is the only residential chaplain of the three and the only full-time priest working for the Apostleship of the Sea. There are a dozen rooms on his floor, but most are empty and forlorn: the center used to provide accommodation for seafarers, but there is no call for that now. Colum's small apartment features a decor that has placed function over beauty. There is a utilitarian mismatching of things, though no necessary thing is lacking. He has a single bed suitable for a child or a priest and one comfortable chair next to which there is usually a book of poetry. There is something of the ascetic about Colum: he never eats lunch, and he forgets that other people do. He is sustained by his own energy between breakfast and dinner. I don't mean that he is an impoverished personality, far from it. The energy he gives off would fuel his boiler, which remains broken despite attempts by a visiting ship's engineer to fix it. Colum says not to worry, he has adequate heating, and he indicates a tiny fan contraption that wouldn't warm a flea.

The rooms are dismal, but the view is not. Colum's office faces onto the lock that leads from the outer waters to the inner docks. He looks up sometimes from reading that poetry or working on his computer to see a window filled with a ship sliding by. Today, a wind turbine ship slowly passes, heading for the North Sea, where it will plant wind farms. It has four columns reaching one hundred feet up; these will drop beneath the ship when it begins its work, perching the ship above the water. "It's amazing," says Colum. And it is. He also likes the cable-laying ship that passes through sometimes. Its crew gave the center a varnished cross section of cable, which is kept behind the bar. It is about two feet tall, looks like the veins of a giant, and is worth $5,000. The ships keep him awake at night sometimes, but he loves this place. How could he not? Every day the view is different yet the same. The surroundings never depress him. "Never. The whole world comes here."

Colum had no seafaring links. His family in Ireland is not a maritime one. After thirty years in city parishes, though, the assignment sounded like a break. The first step was to go to sea. Apostleship of the Sea training consists of taking a passage on the *QE II*. Colum's voyage was no sinecure. It was right after the 2004 tsunami, and the Thai crew was distraught when they watched the TV news and saw "doors and bits of houses floating through their villages." It was his first exposure to the modern seafarer's predicament of quick information and eternal impotence. He understood then that even a seafarer on the most advanced, most expensive of ships may still need comfort. He still needs effective friendliness.

Colum's duties are various. A typical day contains nothing typical. He might be asked by seafarers to buy batteries, if they can't come ashore. He might give them a ride to the stores to buy decent coffee, noodles, or laptops, where they will encounter checkout staff who say, making conversation with foreigners, where are you going next? And when the seafarers say Panama or Brazil, she'll say, "Oh, how exciting" but she has no idea that their Brazil is different to hers, that hers is palm trees and beaches and theirs is a concrete dock. An Indian crew arrived at Immingham, and Colum went aboard their ship. He asked the captain his usual questions: "What can I do for you? Shall I take you shopping?" The captain said no, thank you, but he had another request. His crew would like to walk on grass. Green, green grass. "We have been ashore," said this captain, "but most of the time we walk on steel. It is unforgiving." The priest was not flummoxed. He put them in the center's van and drove them to a churchyard near Hull airport. "And they all took off their shoes and walked barefoot on the grass for an hour, then they went back to the ship."

Batteries are a common request. A battery can mean a lot when you have been for several weeks without one. "Never underestimate," Colum says, "the value of a small gesture." He often buys things for seafarers—electrical goods, children's toys—and delivers them to the ship the next day. Sometimes he pays for the goods himself and trusts he will be paid back. He looks bemused when I ask if that trust has ever been betrayed. No. Sometimes seafarers give him fistfuls of dollars and send him off to shop for them. The faith goes both ways.

His is a ministry of small gestures with great impact. A SIM card, a battery, a gift for a man who has spent yet another Christmas at sea. At Christmas, Immingham's center delivers thirteen hundred shoe boxes of donated gifts to seafarers. In mid-January there are boxes still left over from the Christmas deliveries, so Colum approaches a group of Filipino seafarers sitting near the fountain. The fountain has toy penguins perched on its edge. "They were part of the Christmas crib," says Colum, as if that is normal. He asks who was at sea for Christmas, then gives a box to a seafarer named Jude, who seems pleased. He has time to talk, and as usual with seafarers big things enter quickly into the conversation, so that he tells us he has yet to meet his youngest son, Elijah, born four months ago. Other than that, he says, life's okay. He works on a tanker and the food is fine. Everything is fine, and now he has a Christmas gift, too. The box holds toiletries (toothpaste, shower gel, a hairbrush) and woolen items: a sweater, socks, and a hat. All seafarers' charities provide woolly hats and other comforts. In the Second World War, the Merchant Navy Comforts Service, established in 1940, sent parcels containing a woolen helmet, two pairs of socks, a scarf, a sweater, and woolen gloves to men leaving for convoys and trouble.

The Sailors' Society runs a Woolly Hat Week every February, with the dubious aim of getting the general public to wear a woolly hat to appreciate seafarers. There are now 386 knitting groups listed on the Sailors' Society database, including Pam Richardson from Bedford, who was knitting when I phoned her one evening. A maroon bonnet, since I asked. She tried a balaclava but thought it was a bit too complicated. Pam had been knitting hats for sailors since 2008, although she has no maritime connections. She didn't even like ships: you'd get her on a plane first. She met a priest at a Sailors' Society once who asked her how she was involved. "I told him I just knit hats." He said, "Don't ever say 'just!' Wherever we go in the world, sailors always ask us if we have any bonnets." This is true: I watched one seafarer leap over the ship rail and sprint down the dock when he saw that the visiting chaplain had a car boot full of hats. He was headed for Norway and it was winter. Once, a seafarer approached the same chaplain and gestured to his head. He didn't speak much English, and the chaplain wasn't sure what he wanted. A scarf? A hat? A headache pill? "No!" said the seafarer. "Terrorist!" A balaclava.

Jude takes the hat. He appears grateful. But he earns $1,390 a month. He could have bought a hat and everything else from the shop fifty yards away, and probably has. That is not the point. "They can really help us," said one sailor to researcher Erol Kahveci. "They can share my emptiness."

The International Labor Organization (ILO) defines seafarers as a special category of worker. The seafarer's special identity does not change the fact that he spends most of his working life stuck on a confined metal box where intimidation is easier than in most work-places. A ship's call in port is then a precious chance for outsiders to inspect, to inquire, to minister. Colum does ship visiting daily. He is a man of God in high-viz and hard hat. He never calls ahead: ship visitors turn up and hope for a welcome, and it is invariably given. Any visitor is a fresh face. "The chaplain asked me how I slept here," a seafarer reported to a welfare survey. Such a simple inquiry, but "even that was very important for me. It is nice to hear another person talking to you."

The first ship is Norwegian. It has a good, sturdy gangway, good paint, no rust: all the signs of a decent ship. We are a priest and a woman: each bringing more bad luck than the other in seafarer superstition, but the AB on gangway watch doesn't flinch when he hands us ID badges. Colum makes conversation: Where have you come from? What are you carrying? How long have you been at sea? Murmansk. Coal. A long time. The watchman is Filipino, as are the three men we find in the lounge area, lounging. Colum's greeting consists of "What can I do for you?" before he reaches into his pocket for a cheap SIM card they can buy, or gives them a flyer about the center with useful phone numbers, or asks if they need him to buy anything. He can bring it to the ship tomorrow. It's no trouble. They ask if there is a charge for the mission bus, and he says no, it is provided freely, although the center is funded only on goodwill and donations, which means it is funded with great difficulty. "There is a voluntary port levy, about ten pounds," says Colum. "But you'd be astonished how many companies cross it out. The majority don't give it. Ten pounds on a bill of fifty thousand, and they cross it out. If every ship calling here gave us ten pounds, we would fly."

Last year, the center lost £4,000 when someone broke in and raided the safe. Colum knows who it was. Everyone knows who it was except Immingham's port security. It was a late Sunday night. "He drove here but not a single camera in the whole port picked up his car. We asked security about it. They said that their cameras can't read license plates at night." Colum and David, his Sailors' Society colleague, form a double act of disdain about the security. Immingham, like all major industrialized ports, must conform to standards set out in the International Ship and Port Facility Security code (ISPS), devised after September 2001 and enforced by 2004. This has various requirements such as keeping a gangway watch at all times on ships, so that seafarers must be guards as well as everything else, and more guarded gateposts ashore. It is probably most economically summed up by a student at a Swedish engineering college, who wrote in a paper that "The ISPS code forces the ports, ships and all organizations who work in the marine industry to keep their security gates more tightly."

Colum drives a gas-converted old Lexus, but he also likes to ride his motorbike in and out of his dock homeland. He wears different helmets, so the guards at the entrance gates can't see his face, but he has never been stopped. Lesley, who drives the seafarers' bus, one night saw two men loading a BMW onto a trailer from a yard full of new cars. Sometimes you see those new cars being driven from Immingham to somewhere else, by drivers wearing dark glasses even in the Lincolnshire gloom. The drivers are part time: they are called upon when needed. I like this idea, of a force of drivers in suspended animation, reactivated for a Nissan Micra arrived on a Ro-Ro from Zeebrugge.

Lesley thought, you don't usually see single trailers taking cars away. She phoned security. "Where? We can't see them." But Lesley could, and she followed them in her bus until help arrived. They were caught, but there must be hundreds who are not. For all the tightly closed gates, docks are porous places, though you hear about their holes only through anecdotes.

Colum's combination of dog collar and hard hat puts him in a unique and useful position. He can be a minister, but also a listener. Often, seafarers tell him things they would not dare tell people they consider to be more official. He is a safe pair of ears. Once, he visited a ship at Immingham where the crew were silent and wouldn't look at him. This was striking. It is rare that he is not made to feel welcome. He left knowing something was seriously wrong, and that evening saw some of the crew in the center, their day's work done. They saw him and began to cry. They told him they had just come through the Bay of Biscay in a force 10 and knew their ship would sink when they went back that way. We know we will die, they said. They begged him to help. They knew that he was in a special and delicate position. Mission chaplains must be careful about their role as human help line. They cannot be seen as snitches, or they might be refused access. But they have to be a comfort service that doesn't just provide woolens. Colum phoned someone he knew at the right authority and the ship was officially inspected. A bilge pump, supposed to pump water out, had been put on backward and was pumping water in. The ship would have sunk. "But the crew didn't dare say anything on the ship. The captain had called them to the bridge and made them sign forms saying they were happy with everything." He shakes his head. It's sad. Such exploitation.

Priests cannot be everywhere, though. The ITF runs a global network of inspectors from its affiliate union. Once, on the other side of the country, I visited the port of Birkenhead, near Liverpool, where Tommy Molloy was the ITF inspector. He works out of Mariners' Park, a retirement community for ex-seafarers that overlooks the Mersey, a wide and majestic river. The park has green lawns and pensioner-suitable speed limits. There are individual houses and a residential center, where rank is still respected and old mariners call each other chief and captain. Molloy's job is to inspect ships that come to call and to check on welfare.

Some ships have signed agreements with the ITF to pay decent wages and provide proper conditions. Plenty have not. Molloy knows his place: it is to work at the dirty end of shipping. He shows me images of moldy food, moldy upholstery, shocking sinks. At sea, Captain Glenn moans about chandlers who supply ships with green bananas that will never ripen, fruit that goes moldy obscenely fast, substandard meat. He swears that he used to see meat stamped with "For Merchant Navy only," and it was the rancid kind. Seafarers with constricted time, little local knowledge, and ready cash are easy marks for all sorts of profiteers. Molloy heard about a taxi driver taking Filipinos into the city center who swore that both tunnels under the River Mersey were closed (a legal impossibility) and charged them $200 for a fifty-mile detour on a four-mile trip. Don't get him started on what they were charged for Manchester United tickets.

There are more serious concerns than green bananas or soccer. Exploitation of seafarers is easy when an owner can slip away behind his flag and brass-plate company. The nonpayment of wages is common and blatantly done. When Molloy visited one Greek-owned ship, he found that the Filipino crew and officers hadn't been paid for months. "The captain got on the phone to the company and told me $48,000 was being wired immediately. I said, hang on, but I haven't calculated the total yet, then I did and it was $47,600. They knew exactly what they owed."

When MV *Most Sky* arrived in Liverpool in the winter of 2010, its crew had to pool their small change to buy a loaf of bread. They were warming themselves with a kebab grill. *Most Sky* was a scrappy-looking ship, but MV *Philipp*, which called the following year, was not. The ship was flagged to Gibraltar, part of the reputable Red Ensign group of registers, and owned by Vega Reederei, an established German shipping company. Its crew were employed by a Vega-owned staffing agency in Manila. Its books seemed to be in order, except that they were false books. Visit any Filipino seafarer's forum and you will find plenty of tales of double bookkeeping. One set of salary rates to please ITF, another set of figures that are the true wages paid. On MV *Philipp*, the crew was getting a third of the official figure in the books and was owed $230,000.

The German owners of MV *Philipp* promised to pay the money, then a staffing official flew over and persuaded the crew to return it. Molloy kept fighting, and the crew were paid again. Then, on arriving in Manila, according to the ITF inspector there, "they were bundled into two vans, taken to Vega Crewing's office, and the money taken from them under duress." Who could the crew complain to? Blacklisting by staffing agencies is a career-ending risk. About ten thousand Filipino seafarers are thought to be blacklisted. No one will admit to the practice but it is considered widely used among the staffing agencies in the Philippines. Someone easily gets work for four or five years, makes a complaint about a racist captain, for example, and suddenly there is no ship. There is nothing to be done.

Good port authorities have systems in place to detain ships.

In the worst cases, they can impound and sell them. The UK's Maritime and Coastguard Authority, regulators of all Red Ensign flags, can detain a ship if it is dangerous or if the owners have abandoned it, but not for unpaid wages. Abandoned ships can be impounded and sold by an Admiralty Court, but the process takes at least twelve weeks. Twelve weeks in winter with a kebab grill for heat is a long twelve weeks.

Abandoning a ship is defined in law rather lyrically as "the severance of ties between the shipowner and the seafarer." It is usually a calculated and cynical economic decision. If insurance premiums or port fees are too high, or the company goes bankrupt, the owner disappears, leaving unpaid wages and a stranded crew. Molloy has tales that might seem preposterous, such as seafarers selling blood to earn money—this happened in the United Arab Emirates in 1999—or worse. The worst he has yet heard was the case of *Ionian Sprinter*, a ship owned by Greek Adriatic Tankers until the company went bust and left its ship and crew in St. Petersburg with no money or food. They got so desperate, they caught and ate a stray dog. "Not because Vietnamese like eating dogs," said Trinh Vinh Thang, the Vietnamese radio officer. "We were just too hungry."

Abandonment peaks during deep recession and then subsides, but it never goes away. Seafarers often stick it out even when they are eating dog, in the hope of claiming wages they are owed. Often, they have taken out loans back home to cover the unpaid wages. Molloy remembers the case of *Kyoto One*, a ship owned by Panaygis Zissimatos, a Greek shipowner notorious for defaulting on debt and bank loans in the 1990s. The ITF got some of the back wages for *Kyoto One*'s crew and urged them to go home. They wouldn't, and the ship ended up in Durres, Albania. "The Russian chief phoned me and said the Sri Lankan bo'sun had lost his mind. I spoke to the bo'sun on the phone and he said, if you send me home, I will cut my throat." Like thousands of seafarers, he had coped with not being paid by taking loans from moneylenders. The wages did not cover his debts, and he had been assured the moneylenders would kill his family. Russians and Ukrainians are more likely to stand up for themselves, in Molloy's experience, but Filipinos will stick it out longer because of blacklisting.

There is no international instrument to stop shipowners doing the equivalent of a night flight, although there is hope of setting up a global fund to pay seafarers at least enough to get home. In 2009, the worst year of disappearing owners and stranded seafarers, the ILO's database recorded that fifty-seven ships and 647 seafarers were abandoned, including the *Tor Atlantic*, left in Argentina, the *Prince*, abandoned in Dubai, and the *Fiona*, left in Ancona, Italy. Hardly any cases were listed as "resolved."

As we descend the gangway to return to the docks of Immingham, the air filled with the faint dust of a nearby grain silo, Colum says, "People get outraged about sweatshops, but they don't realize that once the stuff is loaded on a ship, that can be another sweatshop." The position of the Fairtrade Foundation is one of defeat. The complexities and realities of shipping are too overwhelming. "We work with nearly nine hundred producer organizations in sixty countries across the developing world," a spokesperson said, "who ship to thousands of traders in over twenty different markets. Incorporating shipping requirements into our standards and certification processes would add to auditing costs." They would like to have ships that have signed agreements with unions to guarantee good conditions. They would like to avoid flags of convenience. But without any way of monitoring, "this would be merely an empty gesture."

In the face of the difficulties of seafarers' lives, is a bonnet an empty gesture? Shipping is an industry that thinks it is acceptable to use the phrase "the human element" to describe its workforce. It may seem frivolous to confront this hard, fast, pitiless world with woolen comforts or a battery. Colum disagrees. "Anything we can do to humanize this harsh industry, we should do." He visits churches and schools to give talks about the shipping world and hears people wonder that such a life exists "in this day and age." They say, I can't believe that people have their wages stolen, or must sail on unsafe ships, or that the crooks can get away with it. "But the people on ships are invisible. Ports are invisible. We have to make these people matter. They do matter." If the priests and the unionists didn't look out for seafarers, who would?

Colum dreads being moved back inland. He won't go. "I'll do this as long as my knees hold out." He stays for the times when he walks through what he thinks is an empty center and hears a strange noise. He finds a young Ukrainian seafarer at an Internet terminal singing to his baby for the first time. He stays because the one constant is that his parish will always be different from one day to the next. He stays because the newly ratified Maritime Labor Convention might fill the gaps between paper and practice and make decency required and indecency impossible. But if not, Colum will be there with his hard hat, comforting strangers who come to a strange land that they fed, clothe, and equip, with friendliness and a simple acknowledgment of their worth. On the wall of Felixstowe's Seafarer Centre library, a schoolchild had posted a prayer: "Make all the people on the ship safe, so we can have all the food from the ship that the seamen bring us. If other countries were not so nice, we wouldn't have so much food. Thank you. Amen."

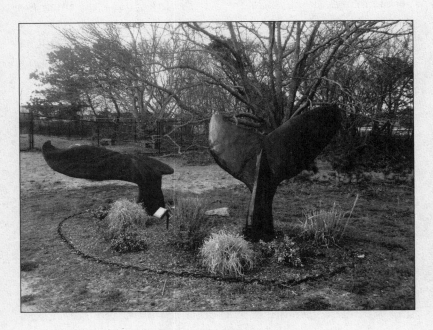

Whale flukes in Provincetown
(ROSE GEORGE)

9

ANIMALS BENEATH

So Remorseless a Havoc

On *Kendal*'s chart table, I leave a note for duty officers. It says, "Watch keepers, if you see whales or dolphins, please call me on 227." For days, southward slowly through the Indian Ocean, grazing India, heading for Sri Lanka, the note reaps nothing.

Off Colombo, we drift. Because *Kendal* zoomed through the pirate zones, the captain is left with a day of spare time. He can't arrive early in port because the berth is not arranged. The only option is to float back and forth across a square of water he has designated. We are like a strange sea video game: first we steam to one corner, then the engines are turned off so that we meander back, then steam again. Zigzag.

I go to the fo'c'sle and at first can't figure out what is so unsettling there. By now I am used to the powerful stink of the animal hides that we loaded at Salalah, which gets stronger and stronger as I walk forward, a pungent chorus. What unsettles is not the smell but the quiet. Even in port *Kendal* is noisy. This is the first quiet for four weeks and it is sweet, although sailors of old would dread such calm, creating a passive verb—to be becalmed—to express the malevolence they felt, as if they were assaulted by something beyond just weather and chance. In *The Mirror of the Sea*, Conrad encounters a fellow captain who has just emerged from a becalming and drifting.

> "We had three weeks of it," said my friend. "Just think of that!"
>
> "How did you feel about it?" I asked.
>
> He waved his hand as much to say: It's all in the day's work. But then, abruptly, as if making up his mind:
>
> "I'll tell you. Towards the last I used to shut myself in my berth and cry."
>
> "Cry?"
>
> "Shed tears," he explained briefly, and rolled up the chart.

I love the calm. The water is green, blue, and clear enough to display unmistakably a trail of trash coming out of Sri Lanka and heading into the ocean to add to the millions of bits of plastic that roam there already, unstoppable and tragic. I spot a brown splodge. A sponge, maybe, or a plastic bag. It is an endangered sea turtle. It swims merrily, or swims with no thought of my silly anthropomorphic adjectives. On the fo'c'sle now there is also a large dragonfly, golden and black and dead. Perhaps this will be my allotment of ocean wildlife. That accidental passenger pigeon, long disappeared into an Algerian saucepan, a turtle, and a dead insect.

The next day Marius says with careful innocence, "I saw whales the other day, and hundreds of dolphins." I ask him what kind of whales. He says, "The blowing-spout kind." He tells me that in the Strait of Gibraltar, ships are allowed to do only 14 knots so that they don't run over whales. That is considered the maximum speed that allows the animals time to get out of the way. (Actually, it's nearer 10 knots.) On one ship Marius worked on, the captain was doing 18 knots in the Strait and a cadet dared to speak up. "Captain, we are killing the whales!" There is the odd grumbling from grumpy columnists in *Lloyd's List* about slowing down for little purpose, but in general, seafarers like to see sea life. It makes a change. Some ships carry whale-spotting books. But the captain on that ship was different. He said he didn't care. His ETA was more important.

Did he kill any whales with his 18 knots? Who knows? The only evidence of ship strikes against whales is when injured animals are beached with gashes and horrible injuries, attracting huge crowds and headaches for authorities charged with disposing of the carcass. The most notorious whale disposal incident occurred in 1970, when the Oregon State Highway Division was tasked with destroying a forty-five-foot sperm whale that had arrived on the beach at Florence. Perhaps because of their experience with moving large boulders, the highway officials decided to use dynamite. A crowd gathered, the charges were blown, and then everyone ran as giant chunks of blubber rained from the sky and crushed the Oldsmobile 88 of Walter Umenhoefer, who became known as "the blubber victim" forevermore, to his annoyance. The tale of the exploding whale was singular enough to have been investigated and authenticated by the myth-puncturing website Snopes.com. It is more singular that the detonation of whales still occurs.

Off Western Australia, for example, in 2010, a whale was exploded. A courteous man named Douglas Coughran e-mailed me from the Senior Wildlife Office of the Nature Protection Branch of Western Australia to explain why. It was, he wrote, an example of the "very challenging issue of human/whale interaction." Whales that are beached on unpopulated shores are left to break down into the nitrogen cycle "as nature has done for millennia." A carcass on a more public beach is a health hazard: those animals are usually removed with ingenuity and earth-moving equipment and buried elsewhere. This particular dying humpback had beached on a sandbank and could not move or be moved. It was too big to shoot, so it was dynamited while not quite dead. The Department of Environment and Conservation tried to give reassurance: sandbags would be placed around the whale's head before it was exploded to death, and a helicopter would patrol afterward to prevent a shark feeding frenzy.

At sea, whales are bashed, battered, gashed, pinioned, and stuck. The true scale of trauma is unknown, like much else about whales. The size of big ships means they can hit giant sea animals, lost boxes, or yachts and not notice. A bump, maybe, a faint jolt among all the pitching and rolling and jolting already. Visual evidence of fatal encounters is rare enough to draw crowds. When a tanker brought a whale into Baltimore in 1940, newspapers reported that it attracted ten thousand spectators. In June 2012, *Maersk Norwich* arrived in Rotterdam with a whale, long dead, draped over its bow.

Off Sumatra, the animals come. I am watching and peering as usual, with little hope, and there is something off to the corner of my eye, and then there they are. A dolphin gang, zipping and zooming beside the bulbous bow right beneath my fo'c'sle perch. Perhaps it is because I have been at sea for a month, or perhaps I would do this anyway, but I talk to them. In fact, I shout. Get out of the way! You will be hit by the bow! I don't want any deathly draping on this ship to provide some preserved horror on YouTube. The dolphins laugh at me. They understand ships. They are fast enough to outpace us, even at 14 knots. So they come and go, racing against the red bow pushing through the underwater, taking turns, propelled by the bow wave. They can feel the action that the bulbous bow makes in the water, flattening it, creating speed and giving them some. Half a dozen gangs come and go, veering and carousing and bow surfing, using the ship to their advantage. It is fabulous, a treat, a beautiful harmony of animal and machine. This is not how the sea's animals and its machines often get along.

In a laboratory about eight thousand nautical miles from Sumatra, I am peering again, now at creatures in a plastic specimen container.

They are minute but not microscopic. My eyes can see them fine, and their little bodies and shrimpy legs that would be terrifying if magnified. They are such tiny things to be linked to such huge matters as devastation, pollution, and extinction, of man and beast.

The creatures are copepods. They look like nothing much. When I ask if they have brains, one of the laboratory researchers needs to look up the answer because she had never considered it before. (Yes, they do.) Another researcher says her friends call her the Bug Counter because they think she works with sea bugs and that's funny. The brains aren't of much interest because copepods are fascinating as food. Specifically, as the major food source for fifty-ton animals that for some reason have chosen to survive off minuscule, elusive bugs.

Copepods feed the North Atlantic right whale. The right whale's beautiful Latin name is *Eubalaena glacialis* (the true whale of ice), but whalers gave it a more prosaic one, because this, they concluded, was the right whale to hunt. It was plentiful, slow, and it floated when it died. Also, it contained satisfying amounts of whale oil and baleen, the keratin fringes and fronds that span its huge mouth and filter seawater, and that were, confusingly, sold as "whalebone," a substance so essential and ubiquitous it was the nineteenth-century plastic. A Mr. J. A. Sevey of Essex Street, Boston, sold fifty-three varieties of whalebone items, including divining rods, tongue scrapers, plait raisers, and policeman's clubs.

The Basques were the first to hunt the true whale of ice, a thousand years ago. Then came North Americans, Portuguese, British, French, Danish, and German. Everyone wanted this whale. For two hundred years, through the high times of whaling, mothers, fathers, and calves were harpooned and slaughtered. Whale researchers don't know how big the population was before that, but it was devastated enough for the right whale to be given protected status in 1935. Now there are about four hundred North Atlantic right whales left. This figure makes *Eubaleana glacialis* one of the most endangered large whales, and one of the most endangered species in the world, despite having no natural predators in the ocean. But it still has an unnatural one: the greatest threat to their survival is the ship itself. Because of its habit of feeding and breeding close to the eastern shores of the United States, the right whale now has a new name. It is the urban whale, because its habitat is usually within one hundred miles of the U.S. coastline and in busy shipping lanes.

The laboratory is in Provincetown, on Cape Cod. It is off-season now, and the town is quiet. It is so determined in its off-season quietness that its status as a famed hedonistic summer destination— popular with gay visitors because of its tolerance—is difficult to imagine. I like the stubborn seasonality of places like these, in the way that I miss the half-day closing of shops on Wednesdays. There is time to breathe.

Provincetown is mostly closed. Though it is early April, the weather is also off-season, with a biting wind on the pier where I wander, stretching car-crunched muscles and shaking off soda sugar, looking into the beach-hut kiosks that are quiet as sentinels. One belongs to the Provincetown Coastal Studies Institute. Its purpose is instructional as well as commercial. A display board educates about the particular, peculiar currents of Provincetown's bay, about the way that the movement of currents brings waves of copepods, which make whales come every year as punctual as the seasons to feed their fill. Opposite the booth is a large white boat named *Dolphin VI*, a whale watcher. Provincetown is one of the places where whale watching began. Dolphin aren't running now, but there are other ways to see whales even off-season.

My whale-watching facilitator is Stormy Mayo. His legal first name is Charles. I forget to ask him where "Stormy" came from, and then I think, it doesn't matter. People who are interested in whales learn to accept not knowing something because they soon learn that they will never know very much. The Mayo family is tenth generation in Provincetown, arriving sixteen years after the Pilgrims. Stormy has inherited land in the east end of town and a private beach. It was there, thirty years ago, that he set up a summer school with his wife. This led him to whales.

He knew of them before that. Anyone who grows up in Cape Cod knows that whales come there. Stormy used to go out with his father on boats and saw them. But whales were not his calling. He had a marine biology doctorate from the University of Miami in marine ichtheoplankton, "the planktonic state of big fish." That meant his interest dwelled in the midlayers of oceans. His wife, Barbara, worked on the flora and fauna of the *benthos*, the bottom layer, where clams live. After university in Miami, the Mayos returned to Provincetown so that Stormy could build a schooner, a wooden square-rigged sailing boat. He is still building it. But having a family beach, two PhDs, and a clientele of seasonal summer people, Stormy and his wife decided to give outdoor lectures. The title was Marine Ecology and Oceanography; the venue was the beach or sometimes a boat; the dress code was bathing suits. It was successful. Tourists who wanted more than the beautiful light that has attracted artists to Provincetown for one hundred years could sign up for a few weeks of instruction in wave action, moon action, and the day-to-day activities of clams.

The course did not cover whales. The Mayos didn't think of that. This was the 1970s. No one was yet saving the whales. Scientifically, says Stormy in his office next to the bug-counting lab, whales were "a blip on the radar. They were thought to be insignificant in the ecosystem." He has a spare and dry delivery. When I ask what is in a plastic specimen jar on his desk, he says, "Well, I'm prepared to call it a blob." Back in the 1950s and 1960s, he says, "Who gave a damn about whales? Just big blubbery cowlike things."

Then Albert Avellar, a Provincetown skipper, noticed that the tourists he was taking out fishing were more fascinated by the big blubbery cowlike things than by the fish. Stormy and the captain didn't get along, because Stormy was known to be an environmentalist, a protector of the ocean, while fishermen were the ones who consumed and plundered. They were supposed to be on different sides. But the captain thought a whale-watching cruise would be a good idea, and having a PhD on board talking about seabirds and whales was an even better idea. Stormy was dubious. How could they be sure to find whales? Avellar was certain. Right whales, he said, come to Race Point every April 15. And still Stormy doubted. "I didn't know much about them but one thing I know is, this is a rare animal. But we went out to Race Point on April 15 and there they were." Since then, the Avellar family has built one of the largest whale-watching operations in the country, and Stormy—his wife died in 1988—is now head of Right Whale Habitat Studies at the Provincetown Center for Coastal Studies, counting bugs and trying to save whales.

The Coastal Studies boat is RV *Shearwater*. RV stands for "research vessel." Often, research vessels are expensive and technologically advanced to be quieter, greener. *Shearwater* is more low-tech. The center is not richly funded and the boat was a donation from a wealthy inventor, so Stormy took what he was given, and it was a fishing trawler. Modifications were made for its changed purpose, such as plastic seats installed on the observation deck for marine-mammal watching, but the engine still belches diesel and smells of fumes. It is not quiet.

Today the research team is all women. The principal investigator, Christy, will decide where to go according to what sightings we get. We will follow the whales. Up top there is Beth, a former biology teacher, whose task is to help Christy gather water samples to count copepods, and Eliza, a Harvard student interning for her third summer and who is today's photographer. It is the task of everyone to watch for whales, constantly. The captain is Ted, standing in for the regular skipper. Normally he takes tourists out on dinner cruises from Chatham. He has a calm air that I associate with sea people, though that may be fanciful.

Stormy can't come along because there is a conference call to be made. He sits on many boards, task groups, and committees, including the Atlantic Large Whale Take Reduction Team. He used to be one of the few official whale disentanglers, which explains the two lacrosse helmets on a shelf in his office. Whales get entangled in fishing ropes and lines and gear with heartbreaking regularity—75 percent of right whales have been or are entangled—and humans try to disentangle them. It is extremely difficult to remove ropes and cords from a thrashing fifty-thousand-pound animal at sea from a small boat. Things fly at you. There are poles being thrust. The helmets aren't protection from the whale: one flick of a tail, says Stormy, "and my head and helmet are over here and my body is over there, so it really doesn't matter."

Today's mission is bug collecting. The day is fine, the sky is blue, the weather report is not alarming, and we set off, hoping for the right whales. They arrived in January this year, far earlier than their usual appearance in April. No one knows why their schedule changed, just as no one can explain why they are not calving as much as they should, after ten good years. The southern right whale population, which lives in the southern hemisphere, has been growing by 7–8 percent every year, but figures for North Atlantic right whales are gloomy. Researchers hoped to spot thirty to forty calves by the end of the calving season in March, but by February they had seen only five. Already, northern right whales have a Potential Biological Removal (PBR) of less than 1, the number that can safely be removed from their population each year by human causes. When their feeding grounds coincide with shipping lanes—traffic in and out of the Cape Canal toward Boston passes through here—a strike rate of one a year is hardly unlikely.

On *Shearwater*, instructions: if anyone up top sees whales, they should stomp on the roof. The instruction is definitely to "stomp." That is the quickest way of getting attention in the cabin and from Ted. The engines should then be immediately cut because propellers can be lethal, even if they belong to a well-intentioned boat. There is also an aerial team out today, who will help with spotting from a small aircraft. The whale aviators are seasonal, working only in feeding and breeding seasons. They are also women. A disproportionate number of right whale researchers are, says Beth. She thinks it's because women will work for no money. You don't go into right whale research for riches.

We head out of the harbor toward Race Point. The point got its name from two currents that meet here and seem to race each other. Copepods like the currents here and so do the whales. Their favorite food is a variety of copepod called *Calanus finmarchicus*, which whales follow to all their known feeding grounds: Cape Cod, lower Bay of Fundy, Great South Channel, and Jeffreys Ledge. A chapter in *The Urban Whale*, a compilation of right whale research that manages to have scientific rigor and to be gripping, is entitled "Enormous Carnivores, Microscopic Food, and a Restaurant That's Hard to Find." In it, Mark F. Baumgartner writes that right whales "are among the Earth's largest animals, but they feed on creatures that are the size of fleas." The ratio of a right whale to a copepod is 50 billion to one. It is like humans choosing to eat only bacteria. It makes little sense. Perhaps it's the taste? Beth can answer that. She has eaten copepods blended to a paste, with crackers. They taste like the sea. If they are eaten alive, they zip around the mouth like Pop Rocks candy.

Northern right whales have a whole ocean to live in, but they still stay close to humans, feeding in Cape Cod and the Bay of Fundy, migrating south to Georgia to give birth, then back up north to feed again. The aerial team reports in. A group of whales has been spotted "sagging." I hear Beth say this and think whale talk would sound rude to the hard of hearing. Whales can also take a "fluking dive," with their tails—flukes—last to disappear. *Sagging* derives from "Surface-Active Group," which sounds like a World War II battle formation but describes a group of right whales getting friendly or frisky. Right whales can dive below for twenty minutes at a time, but for friendly socializing or determined mating they stay in surface waters. Beth and Eliza point out the SAG in front of the boat. There: look. But there is only a mass of black shapes just under the green water, rolling, seething, and rolling. I can't distinguish a whale, and neither can Eliza. She exhorts them to be more identifiable. Come on, she says to the SAG, show me a ped scar. She means a scar—probably from a propeller or boat strike—somewhere along the peduncle, a part of whale anatomy reaching from the tail fluke to the midback. But scars mean nothing to me. Right whales have no dorsal fins, so they are just black slabs. Even if I could see them, they would not impress. These are not poster whales. Stormy Mayo calls them ugly as sin. He thinks our fascination with them is a size issue. "If the right whale were the size of a cockroach, a slimy thing, slippery, looking like that, crawling around behind your cupboards, you're going to tell me that you would take it out and cherish it? I'd say you'd step on it."

Other whales have more charm, however slippery and slimy. When a northern bottlenose whale swam up the Thames in London in 2006, it drew crowds of thousands. A rescue operation cost $150,000, although the whale died while being transported on a raft back to the river mouth where its doomed navigation had begun. An *Observer* journalist wrote that he would never forget "the day a whale sailed through the middle of London; and the people of the city, rather than trying to hack it to death, came in their thousands and lifted it and tried their hardest to sail it back."

The bottlenose was headline news, but in fact marine mammals strand with dismal regularity. Cetacean stranding databases list their causes of death and location. Most die of infections. But there is also starvation and physical trauma caused by propeller or a mass of ship. Between 1970 and 2007, sixty-seven right whale carcasses were reported. At least twenty-four had died from the consequences of being struck by a ship. No wonder the roof-stomping signal has been devised: our research vessel propeller could cut through whale skin like any other. We can approach up to five hundred yards away, a distance granted only with a federal permit and not permitted to commercial whale watchers. Researchers used to puncture right whales with identifying tags—Stormy calls this practice "sticking things into whales"—until they noticed that there were swellings around the tags, that the whale's body responded as if to a wound. Right whales had enough stresses to deal with and the tags were stopped.

Identification in the hands-off era comes down to photographs and pattern recognition. Both natural and unnatural markings are useful: propeller scars, but also callosities, patches of rough skin that are white because they are infested with cyamids, licelike parasites. Eliza thinks she has recognized one of the frolickers from a scar. It's Minus 1.

Pardon?

Minus 1. That's his name. She doesn't know how he got it. All right whales we know of are listed in a photo identification catalog, an effort that is comprehensive, exhaustive, and impressive in its scale and in the level of collaboration required to achieve it. Any glimpse of whale, in calving or feeding grounds or anywhere, is photographed and given a catalog number. As whales become known, they are given mnemonics, names to aid with identification. That sounds sober and rational, but the names can be enchantingly odd. There are the mother and calf, Kleenex and Snot. There is Van Halen, named after a callosity shaped like a guitar. There is Yawn and Etch-a-Sketch and Rat, named for a scar on her side that really does look like a rat chasing a ball. Some whales are named for their deeds, such as Shackleton, a young male who swam up the Delaware River into the port of Philadelphia in 1994. Like Ernest Shackleton, he got stuck, though in his case under a pier, and like his namesake he escaped and survived. Later, Shackleton was understood to be the calf of Eg #1140, also known as Wart. The names are a pleasing dash of color amid scientific rigor, somewhat like scientists who have wild tattoos of DNA chains and molecules under lab coats. But whales would be better off if there were too many for names.

Whale fieldwork is a slippery business. Researchers must understand their subjects only by glimpses, bodies on beaches, or by what RV *Shearwater* is doing today, which is taking samples of water, squirting them with formaldehyde, then analyzing how rich the water is in copepods and what that means for the reproduction, health, and survival of the right whale.

The SAG splits up. Who likes to be watched while they are mating? I assume that *Shearwater*'s presence is audible for miles ahead, with its relatively noisy engine, but then I see right whales feeding. Their activity is called skimming, because they feed just below the surface. A right whale eats like a bulldozer: opens that great mouth and takes in tons of water. The baleen fringes strain out the copepods from the water. We see two right whales skimming, but they do not see us. Or they don't care. I don't know how they give off an air of ferocious intent, but they do: it is something in the directness of their line, in the tenacity of their purpose. Head down, mouth open, go. One theory about why whales keep getting hit by ships—which they should hear coming, when the engines are the size of houses—is that they are too intent on eating, so nothing will disturb them. Stormy has another idea. He thinks they are tethered and handicapped by themselves. "They're feeding, they've allowed the boat to get close because they're oblivious, they're moving slowly, and then at the last moment when they could apply huge power to diving out, their mouths are full of tons of water and they're anchored just like a sea anchor on a ship." A sea anchor that reduces their speed to about 2 knots, too slow to escape a ship. He is not certain, though. This is not scientific fact. He calls his theories "all my imaginations."

Imagination is important in right whale research, because it fills in some of the unknowing. Some of the things that have yet to be conclusively proved include why right whales have periodically disastrous low reproductive rates but sometimes recover; or how whales arrive at feeding grounds that other whales have found. Chemicals? Calls? Smell? We don't know how whales know to go to places that their ancestors have gone to, like a young whale named Porter who was discovered far from the usual feeding grounds off North America, in a fjord in Norway. We don't know where they go in winter. We do know that right whales travel distances that make any human achievement on land seem laughable. When a young male named Churchill became entangled in fishing gear in 2001, a quarter of a million dollars' worth of attempts to disentangle him failed. He was tracked using a tag linked to satellite. He was called Churchill because he was an obstinate animal. He stubbornly survived, although the fishing gear had wrapped around his mouth and he couldn't feed. The scarcity of right whale food means they can fast for long periods, but not this long. Churchill swam for two months, and apparently unerringly, while starving to death, up to Georges Bank off Canada, into the Gulf Stream, and the Gulf of St. Lawrence. Then back, though not using the Gulf Stream because the current was against him. To Emerald Bank, southwest of Sable Island, 186 miles off Halifax, Nova Scotia, which is known for its wild horses and shipwrecks. Then down to the Roseway Basin, known for rich plankton, back to Georges Bank. There, the dying animal visited the heads of deep ocean canyons that are cut into the North American coastal platform before returning to Georges Bank and, in Stormy's words, "hanging out." In two months, this crippled, insulted whale had swum 5,000 miles on no food. Sightings showed that he was getting thinner and thinner. The roll of fat behind the blowhole that indicates a healthy whale was long gone. And then so was he, somewhere off New Jersey. There was no body: dying whales who don't strand sink and drown.

The *Shearwater* team think the whales we have sighted are skinny. Also, they are not as numerous as expected, despite Beth's superior ocean-gazing skills. She sees gray seals—Over there! A head like a dog!—porpoises and fin whales where I see only waves and water. You get used to it, she says. Your eyes get better. You learn to see what she calls "funny water," which might mean a whale is in it, and which she calls "a highly technical term." The copepods they gather are also meager, another worry. Maybe the whales aren't getting enough food. It is another stress on them. But one of the greatest pressures on them is not something Beth can spot even with her sea vision, because it is to do with waves, but not the kind you might expect.

Oceans are not quiet. Millions of cruise passengers go to sea for the peace, but underwater and in water there has always been noise. Waves, rain, disintegrating icebergs, other animals. The sea is a place of sound, because when light can penetrate only a hundred fathoms below the surface, sound is the best way to communicate. A great whale swimming in the deep can't see its own flukes, but it doesn't need to. Because water is denser than air, sound travels faster, farther, and more resonantly in it. Consequently, marine animals are vocal beings. They can transmit singing, clicking, calling. With sound, they can gossip, search for mates, avoid fishing gear, communicate. They send out clicks and understand from the echo what is around them and where they are going, just as bats do. The humpback sings in complicated sequences the length of a concerto; the blue whale makes great moans; the fin whale sends out pulses that divers used to think were the creaking of the ocean floor. Minus 1 and his companions in that SAG group were probably producing sounds that have been described as "scream calls, warbles, gunshots, noisy blows, and up-calls," and the watching humans in the air can hear none of them.

Sounds underwater can travel astonishing distances: a right whale can hear another from ten miles away. The ocean has natural sound channels, like noise byways: if a sound falls into a channel, it can travel hundreds of miles and perhaps thousands. It can travel an ocean. When a foghornlike signal was transmitted from Austra-lia in 1991, it was heard off Oregon three hours later. Sound is not the preserve of mammals. Dutch biologist Hans Slabbekoorn estimates that eight hundred species of fish use hearing. Every species of fish he has investigated has been able to interpret noise, either through an inner ear or by understanding vibrations on their body. I don't know what is more astonishing: that fish can hear or that I never considered such a possibility.

Sound means life for aquatic animals. And now, because of us, it can mean death. Humans are thoroughly embedded in din, from traffic, people, construction. It is known that excess or overloud noise can have physiological effects on humans, disrupting concentration, sleep, and reproductive patterns. It can bring insanity into a living room or prison cell. There is no reason why noise would not do the same for mammals who live in water where sound is more powerful still.

How do we pollute the ocean? With plastic and chemicals and sewage, but also with noise. We lay cables across its bed and drive piles into its floor. We fire air guns that have the force of dynamite to carry out seismic surveys. Our fishermen send out constant pings—echolocation—to find fish. Our militaries deploy sonar that induces the bends in dolphins, porpoises, and whales, so that they arrive in mass strandings on beaches with blood on their brains and coming from their ears; with air bubbles in their lungs; with all the signs that unfortunate divers display when they rise too soon through water. All this is acoustic smog. It is pernicious, widespread, damaging, and preventable.

Modern ships the size of *Kendal* run on machinery that produces noise and vibration above the water but also beneath it. The movement of propellers in water produces something known as cavitation: a constant creation of tiny bubbles that constantly pop. Aquatic bubble wrap. The cavitation of a freighter leaving Cape Cod Canal can be heard all over the bay. A supertanker can be heard in the sea a day before its arrival.

Noise research is a recent field for oceanographers. Until

recently, the tools required to study noise—underwater listening devices known as hydrophones—were too expensive to be widespread. Only classified military circles could afford them. The first significant civilian research was done in the 1950s, but the data were analyzed only forty years later. No one had thought to do a comparative study of long-term noise levels before. Researchers had been looking at daily, weekly, or monthly noise rates. When they compared levels over a longer timescale, the results were shocking. Ambient noise in the deep ocean was increasing by 3 decibels every decade. Every ten years, noise from commercial shipping had doubled.

The quality of the noise is a greater problem. A ship produces sounds that fall below 100 hz. This is the same frequency used by right whales and other ocean animals to communicate. I ask Russell Leaper, a researcher at the International Fund for Animal Welfare (IFAW) to translate what the noise of a shipping lane might sound like to a whale. He calls it broadband noise. I want more of a translation. He says, "white noise," background traffic, something like the constant noise of the freeway that I can hear from my office. It depends on the frequency and proximity of the shipping. Up close, the noise of a ship to a whale would be like standing next to a jet engine, or almost in it. In the vast spaces of deep sea, it will be quieter. But in the habitat of the urban whale, in the coastal areas of the Eastern Seaboard, there are many ships and less space.

There are other acoustic polluters. If the ocean floor is rocky, the loud pulses fired by seismic air guns—to generate waves that can be used to image the ocean floor—can travel immense distances. Researchers studying fin and blue whales in a 100,000-square-mile area of the Atlantic Ocean found that their entire research area was polluted by a single seismic survey. Sonar, pinging, and air guns are intense but discrete and short-lived. Shipping noise is always there. Christopher Clark, a Cornell University professor and acoustic specialist, calls commercial shipping "by far the most ubiquitous anthropogenic contributor to ocean noise."

Sometimes, whales can adapt to it, in the way we raise voices in a nightclub or beside a noisy road. Some whales have shifted into higher frequencies when disturbed by noise. Sometimes they find ways around it or away from it: plenty of animals and fish have exhibited avoidance behaviors, fleeing the sound by swimming or diving. Beluga whales have taken evasive action against icebreakers thirty miles away. Gray whales alter their migration routes by up to a mile.

None of this should surprise. Who wouldn't flee unwanted, terrific sound? But dramatic behavior change is only part of the damage. Of increasing interest and worry to scientists is what the cumulative impact of decades of constant low-level noise can do.

Roz Rolland is a right whale researcher at the New England Aquarium. A veterinarian by training, she arrived at whales twenty years ago and has not left. Like many right whale researchers, Rolland spends time every year out on boats, and she has been doing this for years. She coedited *The Urban Whale*, which is where I discovered her work with scat and dogs.

Rolland was looking at hormone levels in right whales and it was proving difficult. It is tricky enough to trap wild land-based mammals using helicopter chases, rocket netting, or aesthetic darts. Whales are even worse. Their blubber is too thick for blood samples to be taken easily. Helicopter chases are neutralized by a simple fluking dive. Also, Rolland writes, "There is no safe method for capturing a free-swimming large whale. For biologists accustomed to working on other animals, the sheer impossibility of capturing large whales, and the near-complete lack of information on their basic physiology, is astounding."

Creative thinking was required. Animals excrete whether on land or in water, and like the excreta of land mammals, whale poop, or scat, is filled with bacteria, hormones, and debris that can yield data about stress levels, food intake, and toxic burden. Even better, right whale scat is pungent enough to be detected by human olfactory systems. It also floats, but only briefly. Initially, scats were harvested opportunistically, if someone smelled one or if a whale defecated while being photographed. This made for a scanty research harvest, until Rolland thought of dogs.

Sniffer dogs sniff. If they can sniff on land, why not on water? She contacted Barbara Davenport in Washington State, who runs a sniffer dog training company. Davenport gets her dogs from city pounds or humane societies, because the worst pets often make the best sniffer dogs: they are rambunctious and lively and have a strong desire to play. These are good qualities for a reward-based training system. The first dog Davenport brought to meet Rolland was a three-year-old rottweiler named Fargo. He was trained, on land at first, to detect the scent of a right whale. Then they went to sea along with a small platform that became known as the fecal flotation device. It was a piece of wood with a hole cut in it: a plastic jar with whale poop was inserted into the hole; the platform, the dog, and the scientist went to sea; and the dog had to find the platform. Everybody was learning. The dog had to learn not to jump out of the boat when it tracked the scent. Rolland had to learn to read the dog's signals when it zeroed in on the scent: pricked ears, a moving tail, a different facial expression, quicker breathing.

Scat collection rates rose significantly, allowing Rolland to track stress hormones in the right whale population. They also enabled her to make one of the biggest breakthroughs in ocean noise research in decades. It was one of those delicious happenstance moments in science. An inadvertent illumination, a lucky fleeting thought. Rolland hadn't anticipated that whales might be damaged by noise, concentrating instead on causes of stress such as red tides, toxins, and disease. Then in 2009, she attended a workshop organized by the U.S. Office for Naval Research on the effect of underwater noise on ocean creatures. Rolland says that science is all about the question you are asking and she began to ask a new question. She had ten years of stress data and she started to look back through it. Susan Parkes, an acoustic data specialist, mentioned how much quieter the ocean had been after 9/11. And Rolland remembered that of all her boat trips over all those years, some had been special.

On September 11, 2001, she was about to set out on a boat into the Bay of Fundy, as she did most years. The weather in those parts is unpredictable, but that week it was good: high pressure, very low winds. She would be foolish not to go out. But still, in the morning, it was foggy, so the six o'clock departure time was postponed, and then some more, and then someone on the dock said a plane had hit the World Trade Center in New York City. They rushed back to watch television and cried as the second plane hit. "Then we sat around looking at each other and said, we can't just dissolve into a heap. We have to get on with our lives." So they got on their boats and went out to sea. It was weird. There were no whale-watching boats or fishing vessels. There were no planes flying overhead. There were no container ships passing to and from the Cape Cod Canal or in and out of Boston. There was just water and silence. "It was very much like we were the only ones out there with the whales. It was a remarkable experience."

For the whales, it was even more remarkable—they were swimming in a preindustrial ocean. Rolland was on an ocean quieter than it had been for over a century. It stayed that way for most of the week. After the noise workshop, when she checked data for the eleventh, twelfth, and thirteenth of September, she was shocked. Usually, researching what noise does to right whales is extremely difficult. "You're not able to take the noise away and then put it back and see if there is a response by the animal." Even if you analyze hormones, the results can be inconclusive: stress markers such as glucocorticoids could be produced for other reasons. But the message of the quiet ocean data was unmistakable. During the week that ships were stilled, underwater noise was lower by 6 decibels, and the levels of whales' glucocorticoids (stress-related fecal hormone metabolites) were lower, too.

This story is not what it seems. It is not a question of bad shipping and good environmentalists or innocent creatures and metal villains. Amy Knowlton, a colleague of Rolland at the New England Aquarium, has been studying the right whale since 1983. On her first day, she saw a young male with its tail fluke severed. She was mystified. If right whales can hear each other, why can't they hear massive ships coming? Why don't they get out of the way? In the 1990s, Knowlton read an article about how sailboats can get sucked into the wake of big ships. She wondered if that could also be happening underwater to whales, and she began looking into hydrodynamics with the ocean engineering team at MIT. The team discovered that a ship's speed could be a factor in a whale's survival, and that a whale emerging from depth could get sucked into the force around a propeller. Other theories were advanced elsewhere: that there is an area in front of a ship that is somehow soundless (it's called a "bow-null" effect). Remedies were considered. If whales don't get out of the way in time, then maybe more time can be given to them by slowing or moving ships? Knowlton began to study marine policy: how the shipping industry operates, how policies are enacted, and what policies might help right whales.

By the mid-1990s there was more urgency. Every carcass found seemed to be the result of a ship strike. A ship strike committee was formed. Port authorities, industry people, and whale people sat together. Ideas were put forward. Can ships be slowed? Can whales be satellite tagged and ships warned in time so they avoid them? Maybe acoustic buoys in shipping channels were the answer, although experiments in using signals to deter whales from shipping channels had not been successful, as the whales headed straight for the signals. The best options were rerouting, changing shipping lanes, and imposing speed restrictions. All these may sound simple, but they are not: they require the cooperation of a huge global industry of competing actors and changing international law. Even so, it was done. For a start, there was goodwill from the shipping industry. No one wants to accidentally kill a whale. Knowlton once met a seafarer who had been on his bridge while passing through the Indian Ocean, when he spotted a whale. "It was swimming along and coming toward the ship. He thought, I assume it will get out of my way. But it didn't, and he ran over it and killed it. This totally upset him." The seafarer said that he understood now to actively avoid whales, because they don't hear him coming. He hadn't realized there were actions he could take.

Proposals to govern the actions ships take in coastal waters were submitted to the Fisheries Service of NOAA, where a "tremendous advocate" named Lindy Johnson worked. Without Johnson, says Knowlton, it would have taken longer and probably never happened at all. But Johnson went to the IMO and somehow pushed the new rules through. Speed restrictions were put in place on a seasonal basis, once it was understood that a ship traveling at 17 knots would have a 90 percent chance of killing a whale, but 10 knots gave it a fifty-fifty survival rate. And, incredibly and impressively, shipping lanes in the Bay of Fundy were moved. It was a matter of only miles, but the implications were wider than that: the Canadian Hydrographic Service had to change seven nautical charts at the cost of $30,000 per chart. It is too early for any serious assessment of the results, but Knowlton is sure of the difference, at least anecdotally. "When we're out in the Bay of Fundy now, we see ships on the horizon. Before, we'd see them bearing down on us, where we were and where the whales were. The difference, to our minds, is dramatic." She doesn't think ship strikes can be eliminated, but she is sure they are being reduced.

As for the noise, pro-whale people have a strong argument: a noisy propeller is an inefficient propeller. Inefficient propellers waste fuel and now that fuel costs a fortune, increasing its efficiency has a receptive audience in shipping circles. But that is only for new ships. There is no chance of retrofitting the existing fleet of big, small, and medium-sized vessels that chug across oceans, trailing noise behind them. There is still no international regulation of noise in the ocean, and IMO talks only of installing voluntary guidelines. Anyone can sign a voluntary guideline and voluntarily not follow it.

Without global regulations, acoustic pollution will grow because shipping is growing (by 2 to 6 percent annually). Already, the acoustic habitat of the right whale—the range it needs to hear around—has been reduced by 90 percent. Humpback whales now have 10 percent of the acoustic range they used to have, so that their chances of finding a mate, food, and probably surviving have all been decimated.

Stormy Mayo is not particularly optimistic. He believes that the best thing for whales would be to leave them alone. He gave a talk once and remembers that he was "feeling poetic" and said this: "These creatures live in an ocean that once was theirs and now it's walled by nets and crossed by ships. They once lived in a silent ocean except for the sounds of animals. They now live in an ocean whose noise impairs their very livelihood, that is perilous. They live in an ocean that arguably is changing in such profound ways that thousands of generations of them have never seen anything like it." He thinks the future of ocean creatures and right whales is "pretty tenuous," as much as Herman Melville did when he wondered whether "Leviathan can endure so wide a chase and so remorseless a havoc." The chase now is inadvertent, but the remorselessness remains, of noise pollution and other kinds, of a sonified, plasticated, damaged ocean.

Torpedoed seamen, World War II

10

RESCUE

The Bride in the Boat

Going back to the sinking of the Britannia, *it must have been horrific when shells were hitting the ship?*

Yes, but somehow one seemed to be rather busy at the time.—Ian McIntosh

IT HAPPENED WHEN *KENDAL* WAS FIFTEEN DAYS OLD. AS THE SENIOR captain in Maersk's container fleet, Captain Glenn often took new ships out from the yard. This time he was sailing this new K class from the shipyard in South Korea to Tanjung Pelapas in Malaysia. The weather was poor, but as the captain wrote in the ship's log, the crew "felt safe, comfortable and proud on their new vessel, the weather having little effect on such a large ship." Cargo: containers. Wind southwest force 6, sea/swell height twelve feet, southwesterly direction.

On August 7, 2007, *Kendal*'s bridge team began to hear messages from Singapore Port Operations Control Center about MV *Pailin Maritime*, a Thai general cargo ship carrying twenty-four men and 4,700 logs, that was in trouble. The ship was thirty years old and ill-kept. Even as she set off from the Solomon Islands with her cargo, hoping to reach Ho Chi Minh City in Vietnam, her chief officer had worried about a frame in number two hold. It had recently been repaired and patched, so before departure the chief had had a diver inspect the hull. Everything fine, sir. But the weather was bad, and *Pailin* pitched heavily, and the hull cracked exactly at the frame that had given the chief such concern. Captain Glenn, telling the story of *Pailin*, calls the ship "this tired old girl."

The tired old girl was listing heavily. If she had been a motorbike, the rider's left knee would have been scraping the ground. That made it impossible to launch the port lifeboat, which was almost underwater. Then *Pailin* rolled violently so the starboard lifeboat was crushed and the crew could only jump into the water with life jackets and life raft pods. One crew member couldn't swim, wouldn't try, and went down with the ship. The rest "took their chances in the warm seas," where some waves were thirteen feet high. From the water they watched as the lights on *Pailin* flickered, then failed. Fifteen minutes later, the ship had disappeared beneath the surface. The crew were left in darkness in furious seas. Shark territory.

Kendal was 170 miles from the last known location of *Pailin* when the first distress message had come through at 3:45 a.m. By 8:25 she was only eighty-eight miles away and no other ship had responded. It is no small thing for a great modern vessel—huge and time-pressured—to change course, and yet they do so frequently to help other ships in trouble. I read often of freighters and container ships that divert to rescue small ships or boats, of costly rescue exercises and efforts that seem at odds with a just-in-time stressed industry. The old code of honorable conduct at sea is surprisingly intact, though not always. In December 2009 British crab boat *Étoile des Ondes* was run down by the bulk carrier *Alam Pintar*, which did not stop. Several merchant vessels did not respond to distress signals, flares, or messages from the French and British coast guards. It was, wrote Admiral Stephen Meyer, chief inspector of the UK's Marine Accident Investigation Branch, evidence of "a dereliction of one of the most fundamental duties of the mariner, the moral and legal obligation to go to the aid of those in peril on the sea." Even in wartime, "civilized combatants went to great lengths to save the lives of sailors from enemy vessels they had sunk. Yet here we are, in the twenty-first century, finding ships failing to respond to Mayday messages."

The International Convention for the Safety of Life at Sea (SOLAS) is plain, in its Regulation 33, Distress Situations: Obligations and Procedures. "The master of a ship at sea which is in a position to provide assistance, on receiving information from any source that persons are in distress at sea, is bound to proceed with all speed to their assistance. This obligation to provide assistance applies regardless of the nationality or status of such persons or the circumstances in which they are found." It is a comfort to find this old-fashioned notion of honor and duty in the middle of both dry legal documents and the wildness of the ocean. Of course the wildness is why the duty exists. All assistance is gratefully received, from whatever source. Sailors used to call their highest-placed sails Trust-to-Gods, because who else could you rely on when you had to climb to their heights? (They were also known as Hope-in-Heavens.)

Four ships agreed by radio to proceed to *Pailin*'s distressed crew. They were *Al Laila*, *Cap Colville*, *Rio Imperial*, and *Maersk Kendal*. By 11:30 a.m., *Kendal* was close enough to hail *Pailin*, but fruitlessly. At 12:08, she contacted *Kirmar*, a passing merchant ship. The language of the captain's log is spare, but telling: "*Kirmar* was on scene but maintaining her passage."

Kendal had already abandoned her passage, although there was a berth booked for her in port. Captain Glenn risked costing the company thousands of dollars by diverting and delaying. There was no question of doing otherwise. "I think I was put on this planet for that." What about the ships that did not respond, the ones whose passage was more important than anything else? Perhaps they didn't receive all the messages. Perhaps their VHF was turned down, which was one excuse used by some of the ships that failed to assist *Étoile des Ondes*. Others, wrote Admiral Meyer, said they didn't see the distress flares, or they hadn't received the coast guard's alerts. This is so improbable that the chief inspector, whose role is constrained by diplomacy, nonetheless adds an exclamation mark in brackets, the only indicator with which he is probably allowed to express his disbelief. Most alarmingly, "some masters claimed not to understand they have a legal (and moral) duty to react." Captain Glenn, in an account he later wrote of the *Pailin* incident, kept his dismay polite. "The number of ships in the area that did not respond . . . was disappointing. Time-honored traditions are slowly eroding."

Kendal was farther away than *Al Laila* or *Cap Colville*, but *Kendal* arrived and the other two did not. These were not seas empty of ships. MV *Liuhe* was six miles west of *Pailin*'s last reported position, but also continued on her passage. Singapore reported that a Vietnamese warship was in the vicinity and would arrive, along with a search and rescue craft. Instead, as Captain Glenn's log records, "Neither vessel sighted during search and rescue operation so will not be mentioned further in this report." *Rio Imperial*, a car carrier, was on its way, but two and a half hours away.

In the hours that it took for *Kendal* to reach the scene, the captain prepared his crew, who had hardly any search and rescue experience besides the practice kind. They were as inexperienced as the equipment on their brand-new ship. None had been used beyond testing, including the rescue boat, a fast open craft. Even so, when the captain asked for crew to take the rescue boat out into stormy seas, three volunteered. Everyone was nervous. Even the captain "was half-hoping we were not first to arrive, as then he may be responsible for the organization of Search and Rescue overall and thus success or failure."

Kendal arrived on scene at 12:30. Nineteen minutes later, an empty life jacket was seen in the water. This was enough for the captain to set in motion his search plan: he knew from the currents, the winds, and the drift rates that any survivors would probably have been carried northeast by now, but in case *Pailin*'s position had been wrongly reported, they also did a four-mile survey southwesterly. Nothing to see: they went north. By this time *Rio Imperial* had arrived and began to search north of *Kendal*'s search area, with the bridge officers communicating by radio.

What does the search part of search and rescue mean? It means looking, peering, staring at choppy seas, hoping to see something. It means tensing your eyes, screwing up skin, constantly straining. It means keeping the bridge windows wiped with the big wind-shield wipers, binoculars for all in all directions. It is extremely difficult. Human eyes work best with things they can differentiate—a branch, a bollard. They are not built to look at endless water. When the German sail training ship *Pamir* sank in 1957, five hundred miles from the Azores islands, its survivors in a life raft watched in amazement as a ship failed to see them, although it was only three hundred feet away.

There was other work to be done. The captain and his first officer needed to calculate where survivors might be, using charts, math, physics, and brains. This was what the captain was good at (Henry the Navigator). But it was the first mate who drew his attention to IAMSAR, the International Aeronautical and Maritime Search and Rescue manual, which contained a series of tables showing the drift rates for life rafts. "I'd forgotten about that. I knew what the wind had been doing and what the current was doing, but I didn't know how far a boat would drift." Now they did. They knew they were on the right path when wreckage floated past later in the day: bits of blue plastic, some ropes. The officers' calculations had predicted that survivors would be twenty-nine to thirty-six miles away. Then, the captain writes, "after hours of just staring out to sea, it all began."

At 17:20, many large logs were seen in the water. Five minutes later, a body went past, facedown, his naked back exposed, his shirt rucked up to his neck. The sight unsettled the crew, but the man was obviously dead, so the captain ordered the ship to carry on, in search of the living. One and a half miles and five minutes later, the crew saw orange smoke, then a small rocket, though it was more of a damp squib. Imagine the hope behind that damp squib, the fierce and desperate hope: the sight of a ship, a ship. Later, *Pailin*'s chief officer, one of the men in the water, told the captain that they had made out, only just, *Kendal*'s funnel. Perhaps they had seen the white star. They realized that they had been noticed only because of the smoke: the chief officer was a good enough seafarer to understand that it meant that *Kendal*'s engines were going astern. The ship was braking. They had been seen.

By now light was dimming, but the captain decided to launch the rescue boat anyway. He did not do it lightly, but he did it quickly. His crew were reluctant because they were scared. The captain had no room for fear alongside his adrenaline. The sight of the dead body had upset everyone, but he was not scared because he knew what his ship could do, and he had faith in his crew. He is careful not to sound emotional, but the setting off of the boat is where his emotions emerge, because it meant the crew trusted him. "You put them in harm's way and they trust you. They trusted me with their life, and I found that great."

Everybody was alert. The chief engineer, even in his windowless undersea engine room, understood that dusk was falling and sent up extra lights, although no one had asked him to. And the crew in the rescue boat headed toward the site of that orange smoke, careful to stay as long as possible in the lee of the ship, inside an area that the ship's mass turned into a shelter, because the captain was constantly positioning her to protect the rescue boat from wind. He doesn't say this, but that must have required great skill. He had promised the crew that he would always be between them and the sea. The conditions were dramatic. There were dark logs everywhere, the seas were blackening, and then suddenly there were two black heads among the logs. The captain says, "They looked like two black tires in the water, or two tennis balls." Two tiny tennis balls that were the heads of men grasping life jackets as floats. At 18:03, they were hauled into the rescue boat. The mood on the ship lifted. (In his log, the captain wrote, Bingo!) The nervous crew found the search and rescue exciting, almost fun, even though they had discovered that the all-in-one immersion suits they were wearing made moving their fingers almost impossible. Luckily you can haul a man, one of two black tennis balls in black waters, into a boat with mittens on.

The five men in the boat—three rescuers, two rescued—returned safely to *Kendal*. The Thai seafarers were "alright, but only just." One was Thanasan Kumsup, the forty-three-year-old chief officer of *Pailin*, which was a family concern: his brother was the captain, and another brother owned the one-boat shipping company in Thailand that operated the vessel. For all those hours in the water, he said, they had fended off furious logs. Their chests were deeply bruised by hours of blows and assaults. They had found themselves in the water with only the life jackets, but during the hours they were in open sea, one smoke float, one rocket, three life buoys, and three packets of survival food had floated past, near enough to reach. Without them, Captain Glenn is sure they would have died. Once the swell subsided, there would have been sharks. For anyone wrecked in this ocean, there are sharks. When USS *Indianapolis* was torpedoed by a Japanese submarine on a July night in 1945, 900 of its 1,126 crew members made it alive into the water. The shark attacks began at dawn. When rescue arrived four days later, only 316 men were alive. *Pailin*'s crew had been seventeen hours in the water and traveled thirty-five miles.

Rio Imperial reported in by radio. She had seen a life raft three miles northeast of *Kendal*, so Captain Glenn proceeded northeast again, as the survivors had told them that two life rafts had survived the sinking. *Rio Imperial* retrieved thirteen people from the life raft it had spotted. At 19:03, the lookouts on *Kendal*, still peering, still straining, saw something orange off their port bow one mile away. It was too dark to launch the rescue boat, so *Kendal* became a giant rescue ship instead, slowing by the raft and skillfully drifting to it. A squall began to blow, but the pilot ladder was lowered, four survivors climbed up it, and the raft was then cut loose and allowed to drift away. The survivors were traumatized. They didn't speak much. *Kendal*'s crew figured out from communicating with *Rio Imperial* that the captain and four others were dead. The survivors' moods, wrote the captain, ranged from "visual depression, fear, relief, at the same time elation at being rescued." He had never, he said, seen anyone so appreciative of a Maersk T-shirt.

But still, he says, sitting in his comfortable cabin on F deck on *Kendal*, looking at a picture of the rescue crew, he is not at peace with *Pailin*. Nineteen saved and one lost, but four never found. "What still bothers me to this day is the thought that when we picked up those two small heads in the water, what if there were four more heads further off who could see us because we had our lights on. They could see our ship and they would see us leave. That still bothers me."

Briefly, Captain Glenn was a hero. The Shipwrecked Mariners Society presented him with a Lady Swaythling Trophy for outstanding seamanship. He made headlines in papers in the north of England. LOCAL SKIPPER LEADS DRAMATIC RESCUE. TYNESIDE CAPTAIN LEADS RESCUE MISSION ON THE HIGH SEAS. The *North West Evening Mail*, based in Cumbria, was inspired to publish an article apparently only because *Kendal* was named after a Cumbrian town. That the rescue made only small ripples is not surprising. You don't read much about merchant navy heroism anymore, although it is common enough. The last time the merchant navy was thought heroic was seventy years ago, and its limelight was brief, like the sun breaking through clouds, then gone again.

On the first floor of Liverpool's Merseyside Maritime Museum, there is a small section on the merchant navy. It is not crowded: most people are crammed into the *Titanic* area nearer the entrance. There, the crowds at the glass displays of disaster are three deep. But here among merchant navy history there is space formed by uninterest. I watch an old P&O recruitment video—"Run away to Sea!"—for a while. A young boy comes and stands beside me for a few minutes, also watching, but glancing sideways at me now and then with puzzlement. He watches long enough to be told that if he runs away to sea to work with P&O his accommodation will be excellent and he will eat well, before he finds the courage to speak his mind. "Isn't this about the *Titanic*?" Then he leaves, because it is not.

This is baffling. The *Titanic* attracts an audience for its combination of glamour and tragedy. But so should the stories of the merchant seamen who fought in World War II, although they were classed as neither veterans nor fighters, despite losing more men, proportionately, than any branch of the armed services, and despite enduring extreme danger and the constant chance of being torpedoed, of facing a death from drowning or burning by flaming oil, or countless days in an open lifeboat. Down the corridor from the *Titanic* crowds, I notice a newspaper cutting pinned to the wall. It is dated 1942, comes from the *Daily Mail*, and in headline and content is brief. "GIRL TENDED 51 MEN IN BOAT OF DEATH. A 21-year-old English girl, a bride of a few months, played Florence Nightingale to 51 men and two women drifting in an open boat after their ship had been torpedoed in the South."

This Florence Nightingale was Diana Jarman. Actually, she had been married a few years, not months, and her husband was dead. So she was a twenty-one-year-old widow, traveling as a passenger in 1942 on *City of Cairo*, a small liner heading from India to England, empire-backward. That year was the deadliest of the war for ships at sea. Enemy battleships and U-boats had been active since four hours after war was declared on September 3, 1939, when *Athenia*, a passenger vessel, was torpedoed two hundred miles from Ireland on her way west. One hundred and eighteen of her passengers—which included evacuating children, Jewish refugees, and Americans heading home—were killed. The attack was a mistake on two counts: the submarine captain thought he was targeting an auxiliary liner on military business. It also contravened the Second London Naval Treaty of 1936, an international protocol signed by Germany that required attackers to give ships fair warning and sink civilian ships only if passengers had been first delivered to safety. That was the beginning and so it went on. Warships, passenger ships, merchant ships: they were all targets. Merchant ships came off worst.

There was never any question that Britain would use its merchant seamen in war. How else do you stock an army? In 1939, Britain was the most important maritime power in the world. It had a third of the global deep-sea fleet and exported multimillions of iron, steel, chemicals, textiles, and coal. Its "merchant navy" was three thousand deep-sea ships and one thousand coastal vessels. No one was in merchant seafaring for the luxury of it: the master of a tramp steamer was paid thirty-six dollars a month and had to supply his own soap, uniform, sextant, and charts. Even the best shipping companies, wrote historian Richard Woodman, like Alfred Holt's Blue Funnel line, "thought that ten days of leave after six months' voyage without a weekend in port was enough to keep an officer happy." Lady Astor, the first female member of Parliament, reported to Parliament in 1938 that "a colleague who had taken a look at the conditions in which seamen lived had said he would not expect ferrets to live in such conditions." (She also thought—apparently after her daughter had an affair with one—that seamen should wear yellow armbands to signify that they might carry venereal disease.)

Britain was also a politically and geographically isolated island. It had to be stocked by sea, then as now. It had to export its coal and chemicals to earn currency to buy imports. War does not change the economic necessity of trade, but adds to it: every war is fought on a foundation of supply, which is why logistics corps are the largest sector of most modern armies. The United States at war still sends more than 90 percent of its supplies by sea. The tail of an army is long and it is afloat. Modern fighting methods have not changed this: television pictures during the Gulf Wars showed soldiers trooping down the bellies of giant cargo planes, but the tanks and jeeps do not fly. Heavy weapons and matériel have to come by sealift, the same way they always have. Arms trade researchers can calculate illicit heavy weapons flows by monitoring ships and shipments.

When Republican candidate Mitt Romney chided President Obama for the small size of the U.S. Navy during a presidential debate, the president responded with condescending humor. Military styles have changed, he said. We don't use longbows either, and we don't need a huge navy when we have aircraft carriers. This was disingenuous: the United States needs ships as much as ever, including merchant vessels to supply its military. The 1904 Military Cargo Preference Act requires 100 percent of items owned, procured, or used by military departments or defense agencies to be carried on U.S.-flagged vessels—probably the only reason some U.S. shipowners still fly the Stars and Stripes—while the 1996 Maritime Security Act provides financial incentives for shipowners to make their vessels available in wartime or during a disaster. (Even so, American commentators were shocked after the Deepwater Horizon oil spill in 2010: not only were most oil rigs off the U.S. coast foreign-flagged, but so was most of the rescue and cleanup fleet.)

Newly at war in early September 1939, Britain had enough merchant ships to do its shopping and selling: oil from the Gulf, the usual commodities from India. In the words of seaman Frank Laskier, who became Britain's most famous merchant navy star in the war years, "they got the ship to Calcutta with munitions, and back to England with tea." Across the Atlantic, from a still-pacific United States, flowed precious timber, pit props to shore up blitzed houses, pig iron for all sorts of uses. America became Britain's corner store. No sailor liked a cargo of pig iron, although it carried the blessing that a torpedoed ship loaded with iron will sink fast and clean, with no time for him to burn to death from ignited oil or to be strafed by German guns. Nor were pit props popular: as the crew of *Pailin* discovered, timber does not float serenely but is launched at you by the force of the waves. The currents that a sinking ship create are even more murderous.

The ships were a mishmash of identities and interests. Some had been co-opted by the Royal Navy, but most were privately owned, grouped together artificially in convoys as they were grouped together artificially, metaphorically, into something called "the merchant navy." King George V was the first to sanction this phrase, after fifteen thousand merchant sailors died during the First World War carrying supplies. But by 1939, merchant seamen still had no standard uniform, no badge, no identifying features. When about ninety-five merchant ships were sunk during the first few months of the Second World War, their surviving sailors were required to pay bus fare, even if they were traveling home from a torpedoed ship, although uniformed men were not. They had to endure scorn and spit for seeming to be noncombatants in their unofficial sailors' clothes. In Canada, merchant seamen were called zombies. They were a national service that was not considered one. In *My Name Is Frank*, a collection of his radio broadcasts, Frank Laskier tells of a sailor back from a seven-month trip at war. "He's been dive-bombed, he's been shelled, he's been raided, he's been mined; he's done everything, and he's walking down the street with a deep-sea roll and his best civvies on, and an old lady comes along to him and pins a white feather on to him."

Angry old ladies and Nazis: they were all confused about the status of these fighting civilians. For the first couple of years, enemy treatment of merchant seamen was inconsistent. Sometimes they shot at survivors in the water, sometimes they took them prisoner. Although merchant ships were sailing alongside navy ships in convoys, until 1941 a merchant seaman's pay was stopped as soon as his ship sunk. Widows received no compensation or pension. Exposure in a lifeboat, wrote the historian Richard Woodman, "was an unpaid excursion." And seamen continued to be disdained. Having survived an explosion when SS *Ashby* was torpedoed, then several days in a lifeboat, a merchant seafarer named Bill Linskey took a train home to Newcastle. Then, "soon I became aware of sideways glances from uniformed gigglers and realized how I must

look to them. I was young, tanned, fit. Why wasn't I in uniform? . . .
I looked at their complacent little faces and wondered how they
thought the food arrived to fill their bellies, not to mention ammunition for their guns, petrol for the tanks and tinned food for their
Mum's rations."

After Germany invaded France, the U-boats became more
lethal. They were based in French ports and could go farther and
stay out longer. Then someone at the Admiralty realized that seamen could be helpful propaganda. Finally the propagandists realized that it is hard to mobilize public opinion around something as
amorphous as "trade." It is easier to stir people up about a battle, so
there was a Battle of the Atlantic, and plucky merchant seamen
fighting it mostly without weapons. Winston Churchill called the
Battle of the Atlantic decisive to the war effort. Now merchant
seafarers became useful heroes, too, not just loaded with cargo on
their ships but freighted with a rousing message for a besieged
island population. There were posters of housewives and business-
men thanking the merchant navy for bringing their dinner. Wartime Britons were urged to shop carefully—"Let your shopping
save our shipping"—and eat homegrown food, to ease the pressure
on the merchant service.

Once the United States entered the war, Franklin Roosevelt
followed suit rhetorically. In a 1941 letter to Admiral Emory S.
Land, he wrote that "if we are going to keep away from our shores
the forces that have convulsed the Old World and now menace the
New, the job will be done in large measure by the ships and sailors
of the Merchant Marine and by the working men who build the
ships and supply them. If they fail, the whole effort fails." If only
sensible practice had accompanied his rhetoric: even by the spring
of 1942, defenses on the U.S. East Coast caused U-boat commander
Peter Cremer to think the Americans "asleep, to put it mildly."
Europe was blacked-out for war, but the U.S. coast was ablaze as if
in peacetime, guiding friend and foe alike. Of course, the watching
U-boats took advantage of the helpful illumination and American

and Allied merchant seamen were killed before even leaving territorial waters. On one evening alone, Cremer destroyed the *Ama-
zone* and the tanker *Halsey* with hardly any effort. "None of us had
imagined it would be so easy," he wrote, "and it could not and
would not continue."

He was right, though not immediately. The lights stayed blaz-
ing for another three months. Then the United States began speed-
building Liberty ships to add to the cargo-carrying fleet, but 1942
was the worst time to be at sea. Their attacks were so ferocious and
so successful, Germans called this period "The Happy Time."
Casualty statistics vary but by the end of 1942 more than a thousand ships had been sunk, and ten thousand British merchant
seamen were killed. Survivors arrived at missions in the United
States, Canada, and Britain, often after days at sea in open boats.
Staff at the Seamen's Church Institute in New York City distributed shoes, socks and underwear to shipwrecked crews from its
Sloppe Chest. British arrivals were given a new suit through a deal
with the British consulate and a local department store. The institute didn't just cater to grown men: British child evacuees also
passed through and were "particularly delighted with the showers,"
having to be dissuaded from taking two or three before breakfast.

The horror was routine and the calmness of the men submitted
to it astonishing. In December 1941, four men arrived in New York
after thirteen days drifting in freezing seas off Iceland. They had
suffered gangrene and exposure. Among the four, wrote Homer
Strickler in the *New York Sun*, there was but one leg. Another journalist in the *New York Herald Tribune* told the story of the "mad
Russian," Waldemar Semenov, a U.S. merchant mariner serving on
SS *Alcoa Guide* when it was hit. While shells were crashing all
about, "Semenov went to his cabin to brush his teeth and put on his
best clothes." (He even took the time to choose between two neck-
ties.) In the galley, he stuffed his pockets with loaves of bread, and
from the library he picked out a book to while away the hours in a
lifeboat. Then he borrowed two dollars from a shipmate against

the day he would again be set ashore. "With his mind, body, and finances accounted for, he announced himself ready to quit the ship." Semenov survived long enough to donate his compass from that day to the National Museum of American History in 2005.

In 1942, the *New York Times* tried to educate its readers in the discrepancy between the merchant marine's slaughter and its status.

> Many come through three or four sinkings, yet do not hesitate when new ships are ready. No one turns in the street to admire their uniforms. They wear no uniform. No one steps up to the bar to buy them drinks. No moist-eyed old ladies turn to them in the subway to murmur, "God bless you." The cop on the beat, gentle with the tipsy soldier or the unsteady gob, is apt to put his nightstick to the breeches of a merchant sailor who has tippled heavily in the town's bar to celebrate his rescue from the sea.

After years of abuse from civilians and police alike, a silver merchant navy badge was finally given to British mariners, and a lapel pin to Americans. (Seafarers liked to turn the MN upside down and say it stood for "Not Wanted.")

I watch a British Pathé film called *Saved from the Sea*, about the rescue of yet another boatload of torpedoed men. The war had some famous boat dramas, such as that of Poon Lim, a Chinese sailor who survived 133 days at sea. But the boat in *Saved from the Sea* is not famous. Just another sinking. "A handful of survivors," says the narrator, "picked out of the sea after an experience which in peacetime would have made headlines in every newspaper in the world." The camera shows men who are bearded and thin and spent. They come onto the rescue ship and sink down rather than sit. They smoke. "This is how men look after a month in an open boat," the narrator continues. I see how they look as survivors, but how did they live while they were surviving?

*　*　*

Diana Jarman has left barely any trace and exists largely in the accounts of other survivors from *City of Cairo*, who remember her as a jolly blonde, as indefatigable, as a good egg who talked of liking tennis and living somewhere in Hertfordshire. She was an ordinary survivor of an extreme journey on an open boat.

Diana did not keep records of her thirty-seven days in lifeboat number 1. Others did, including Jack Edmead, third steward and "ship's writer," who in his official survivor's report to the Admiralty testified that *City of Cairo* carried 136 passengers, including nine officers of the navy, army, and merchant navy, and eighteen children. The crew numbered 197, including seven naval and four military gunners. They were also carrying ten thousand tons of what Edmead describes as "General Stores."

Many passengers were women and children leaving India for personal reasons, for greater safety. It took four weeks to reach Cape Town, which they left on October 31. They had now been traveling for six days. The liner was no *Titanic* or *Athenia*, but scrappier and slower. It would not have been your first choice of transport, had you a choice. The route was dangerous, but not as dangerous as other routes farther north. A U-boat wolf pack was known to be hanging around Cape Town, but *City of Cairo* was not powerless: she was armed with guns that included one 12-pounder, two Twin Marlins, two Twin Hotchkiss, and two Oerlikons. There were four PAC rockets. She sailed alone because there were no convoys to join.

On November 6 at 8:30 p.m., the Indian stewards, dressed in native clothes, were clearing away food and tableware. The British merchant navy, despite King George V's blessing of it as such, was only half British. The other half consisted of Arabs and Somalis and lascars in the engine rooms, where they stoked the coal-fired engines that ships were still being using, though they could do only 7 knots at best. Chinese and Indians were stewards and sailors. The engine-room men were the black gangs, for the color of coal, not of their skin, and they died in greater numbers than deck sailors. It was more difficult for them to escape the ship, to begin with, but also they were dressed more scantily to cope with the heat of coal-fired engines, putting them at a disadvantage if suddenly ejected into the cold water or an open boat.

On *City of Cairo* the liqueurs had not yet been served when there was a terrific bang (said Joan Redl), or a sickening crack (said Dr. Douglas Quantrill), or a heavy dull explosion (said Jack Edmead), or a BOOM! (said Marjorie Miller). The ship shuddered, glass broke, and then there was the silence of shock. I read survivors' accounts gathered on a website by Hugh Maclean, whose father, Calum, was a seaman gunner on *City of Cairo*, and they converge on one thing: there was no panic. People who had their life belts at their feet, as they were advised to do, took them and made their way to their life boat station. People who didn't have their life belts nearby headed for their cabins to fetch them. The ship carried nine lifeboats. Lifeboats, life belts, life rafts: as if naming an object with life gives it more power to save one.

Diana Jarman ended up in boat number 1 along with quarter-master Angus MacDonald. The boat was full with lascars and women and children and male crew and passengers. When Mac-Donald said that some people needed to go overboard for a few minutes so they could better bail out the water, it was the women who immediately responded. They jumped into the water, even Lady Almond, who had three small children with her, and swam to a water tank floating nearby. While they were bailing, *City of Cairo* was sinking. "There she goes," said someone, and there she went, and then there was only quiet. "There was no show of emotion," wrote MacDonald. "I expect the others, like myself, were wondering what would happen to us."

The captain—a forty-six-year-old Liverpudlian named William Rogerson—survived the sinking, perhaps because he made sure to keep fit while on board. Perhaps just because of good luck. That did not always happen. The captain often went down with his ship because he was delayed by duties on the bridge. The ship's confidential books had to be thrown overboard in the weighted bag provided for such a purpose. Radio operators also died more frequently, as they would stay in their radio rooms sending out urgent messages and often didn't make it out.

Although he was propelled far below the water, Captain Rogerson came to the surface and survived. He called for all lifeboats to tie up together and to use their sea anchors, a canvas contraption that was trailed in the sea to slow a boat, to create some safety in numbers. There was colossal danger around them, in the form of an open ocean. But there was also the U-68, the submarine that had sunk them. It was likely to be around because U-boat captains often hung around after the violence, hunting for information and senior officers to take as prisoners of war. Many captains spent uncomfortable and frightening weeks on U-boats. The commander of U-68, Karl-Friedrich Merten, asked the survivors for the captain, gave him directions and distances for land—Brazil, two thousand miles, Africa, one thousand miles, Saint Helena, only five hundred—then left. According to Ralph Barker, who wrote a book about *City of Cairo*, the U-boat did not leave before its captain told the dazed passengers in number 6 boat, "Good night, sorry for sinking you."

Boat number 1 was open and wooden. It had nothing in common with *Kendal*'s enclosed orange capsules except that it floated. It was little more than a jollyboat, a small wooden craft that is used for going from ship to shore, not for survival. Half the boat's drinking water had been lost in the confusion and bailing, but there were thirty gallons left, along with enough food to last for three months. That meant one tablespoonful of water—four ounces—for each person, morning and night. Also there was pemmican, a compressed meat and fat substance invented by Native Americans and popular with polar explorers and lifeboat equippers. There were some tablets of Horlicks, a malt extract. There was no fishing tackle: this was not thought vital until after the war. Nor were there barley sugar sweets, which were later understood to provide energy but also saliva. Countless lifeboat survivors found it impossible to masticate hard biscuits when their mouths had been dry for weeks.

Captain Rogerson advised a course of north by northeast and all the boats set off. Diana Jarman was one of three women on board, and the youngest. There was not enough room for everyone to sit, so people sat and stood in shifts. The boat carried a medical doctor named Tasker, but his mind seemed to have been damaged in the sinking, so Diana took on most of the first aid. "She could never do enough," wrote MacDonald, "either in attending to the sick and injured, boat work, or even actually handling the craft. She showed up some of the men in the boat, who seemed to lose heart in the beginning."

What else were they losing? Hydration, obviously. Energy. Weight. *Kendal* may carry fancy closed lifeboats, but if her crew ended up in a life raft, they would be as exposed to as much physiological threat as Diana Jarman in 1942. The open sea does not suit human physiology. We are not made for so much salt and air and wet. There are other things to consider: seasickness is inevitable once the protection of a high-sided ship is removed. "A singular disadvantage of the sea," wrote Stephen Crane in "The Open Boat," "lies in the fact that after successfully surmounting one wave you discover that there is another behind it just as important and just as nervously anxious to do something effective in the way of swamping boats." Sunstroke is another deadly threat. And all these privations are intensified by sleeplessness. Diana's boat was crowded. Legs had to stay in the same position for hours. Movement around the boat involved somehow stepping over twenty-six Indians who had congregated in its amidships. There was elbowing and kicking and little chance of rest. When Wilbert Widdicombe and Robert Tapscott spent forty-seven days in an open boat after SS *Anglo-Saxon* was sunk in August 1940, their diagnosis when they were rescued was pellagra, deranged nervous systems, and insomnia.

Somehow a difficult night passed, and before lunchtime on the first day in open sea sharks appeared. They were not afraid and kept approaching the boat. At least the boat was more sturdy than other life-saving craft: when *Cingalese Prince* chief engineer R. H. Wilson was sunk in 1941 in the southern Atlantic Ocean, he spent twelve days on an open life raft. "The whole time we were on the raft, day and night, we were constantly surrounded by sharks of different species . . . Very often they would come tearing towards the raft, then just before reaching it would turn over and scrub their belly on the side, no doubt to try to get rid of the parasites which grew on them." But Diana's boat was making good speed, and the sharks were kept away. However, it was leaking. The chief officer in charge of number 1 boat decided then to set off for Saint Helena without the others, in a race against time and leaks. It made sense, the captain agreed, and that was that.

I wonder about details. How do you go to the toilet in a lifeboat? The women rigged up some privacy with clothing and fabric, but after a while they didn't care. Nearly everyone was soon consti-pated, anyway. In Bill Linskey's lifeboat—after his first torpedoing, for there were two more—"a man had to hang his bum over the side to crap. The first mate said, 'It would be appreciated if all the shitting and peeing could go on well before we have our meager meal.' 'And don't forget to wash your hands,' someone shouted, 'it can be quite dangerous.'"

The first to die was Dr. Tasker, whose mind had gone. After four days he was calling for beer, and then he was dead. It depressed everyone. The lascars were pleading for water: *Pani, sahib, pani.* MacDonald doesn't sound sympathetic to them in his account, and he never gives them names. Jack Edmead dismisses them as lazy natives who did not do the work they could have done, so that the Europeans had to do twice as much. Even in Richard Woodman's forensically researched account of the Battle of the Atlantic, *The Real Cruel Sea*, these foreigners are usually blank "Chinamen" or a mass of "lascars." They seem to die faster; they seem to fear that they are of a lower priority. When *Calchas* sank and its second offi-cer jumped over the side of the lifeboat, "this triggered fractious behavior among the Chinese, 'but after they been threatened with an axe,' reported Second Steward Curtis, 'we managed to restore some kind of order [although] our position was none too secure.'"

In the second week the deaths began in earnest. Macdonald remembers that Tasker died on day 6; Edmead thinks it was day 10. Time slipped. Some Indians died, and they were pushed overboard "as the lascars never would help bury their dead." Then it was the Europeans' turn. Curiously, the people who did not help others died first. Then it was death by domino: Miss Taggart and Mr. Watkins-Ball entwined together one morning, both dead. A few more lascars. A young engineer who tried to heed MacDonald's instructions to be more like Diana, always cheerful, but he "dropped back and died." The ship's stewardess, Annie Crouch, died in the bottom of the boat, with swollen legs and a mind swollen by exposure. Then Tiny Watts, a large and good man; and Frank Stobbart, the ship's storekeeper. Some more lascars. A fireman—one of the black gang from the engine room, a coal shoveler—jumped overboard, but he had forgotten to remove his life jacket so he floated helplessly until the sharks got him.

There was still food in the boat—under Board of Trade regulations a lifeboat was required to carry dry biscuits—but with barely any water it was impossible to chew. For this reason, anyone setting out to sea should take a button to suck on, to create saliva and sweep the food down. Merchant seaman Norman Watts, sunk three times in two seas, described his lifeboat experience with scorn. What use was a shiny merchant navy badge when all they were given to survive was biscuits and brackish water in a foul tank? "Even though the ship was new, the tanks hadn't been sterilized. It was good enough for seamen. Nobody gave a damn if seamen survived or not, really."

By now most of the passengers were burned: the sun assaulted them every day, all day, and there was nowhere to hide from it. Everyone had sore throats. Everyone was desiccated. Most had salt-water boils and ulcers caused by chafing where salt crystals had collected on the joints. Everyone in the open at sea gets ulcers, because the circulation is poor from lack of nutrients and water and inactivity; muscle has wasted, so there is less cushioning between the skin and bones; the lack of protein makes healing difficult. But there was still bailing to be done, and it was heavy work even for someone with strength.

On the seventeenth night, there was sabotage: a young European man kept removing the plug, flooding the boat with water. He said, if we are all to die we may as well die together, but he was stopped and died the next day with "seven or eight lascars and a banker from Edinburgh." On the jollyboat of the *Anglo-Saxon*, sunk by a German raider in 1940, the rudder detached on the thirteenth day, by either accident or design. For Chief Officer C. B. Denny, in charge of the survivors until then, it was enough. He was going overboard and asked if anyone would come with him. Third Engineer Hawkes said yes. I don't know what is more extraordinary about this: that they carefully shook hands and jumped into the sea, where Hawkes's blond head could be seen above water for an uncomfortably long time after; or that they first took a short sleep. What can that sleep have been like? What did they dream? Wilbert Widdicombe, one of two *Anglo-Saxon* crew who survived, took over the recording of the boat log, written on sailcloth. He didn't waste time with unnecessary words. "Chief engineer and third mate go overboard. No water."

No water but the sea. Everyone on boat number 1 had begun gargling with seawater. They were careful: they knew drinking seawater was deadly. In a lecture to the Royal College of Physicians in 1942, MacDonald Critchley, a physician who had studied survival at sea, said that "seawater poisoning must be accounted, after cold, the commonest cause of death in shipwrecked sailors." At first, it wouldn't seem so: seawater is liquid and it quenches. The relief would be immediate. But seawater has an average salt content of 3 percent. This increases thirst dramatically so that more seawater is drunk, and more, and salt levels go ever more haywire, until the body tries to regulate it by urination, and you expel a quart of urine for every quart of seawater drunk, making matters worse.

There are also complicated and intricate effects of seawater on cells, blood, and tissue, but in essence, too much seawater can fry your brain. Then this happens, in the words of Critchley: "The victim becomes silent and apathetic, with a peculiar fixed and glassy expression in the eyes. The condition of the lips, mouth, and tongue worsens, and a peculiarly offensive odor has been described in the breath. Within an hour or two, delirium sets in, quiet at first but later violent and unrestrained; consciousness is gradually lost; the color of the face changes and froth appears at the corners of the lips. Death may take place quietly: more often it is a noisy termination, and not infrequently the victim goes over the side in his delirium and is lost."

In some lifeboats, a powerful disincentive to drink seawater was developed. "Whenever a seaman threatens to drink seawater," a sailor explained to *The Lookout*, "an officer knocks him out."

Diana Jarman didn't drink seawater. She was too sensible. She was waiting for time to pass. Survivors have not recorded their methods for doing this. The excruciating slowness of the minutes must be best forgotten. MacDonald writes that by now, "a good few people sat all day with their heads on their chests doing and saying nothing." This was dangerous: there was work to be done. The boat had to be steered. People had to keep watch for a ship, for anything. Sharks had to be batted off. By the third week, it still hadn't rained and the water had run out. They tried to eat a dogfish and drink its blood, but it was too disgusting for them to swallow. When Jack Oakie, Jack Litte, and a Zanzibar fireman died, it took the others a whole day to find the strength to lift the three bodies into the ocean.

I wonder where they were by now. There are names on nautical charts: Orange Fan, the Angola Basic, the Discovery Seamounts, the Pernambuco Abyssal Plain. But to them it must have been an awful blank. Even Diana must have quietened, because she had the sickness that everyone had, which gave her a sore throat and yellow phlegm oozing from her mouth, probably from the constant dampness. Joe Green was next. He placed himself carefully, the night before he died, at the after end of the boat, so it would be easier to throw him off. Now they were three. Jack, Angus, and Diana, lying in the bottom of the boat, drifting, "thinking about water in all sorts of ways." A stream. A hose spraying water around thoughtlessly. A simple glassful.

Diana sickened, but she could still talk about horses and tennis and how much she liked them, and that Jack and Andrew should visit her in England when they were rescued. There was a rain shower and freshwater, then three days later, a German ship. Diana said it didn't matter that it was German, as long as it was a ship. They were taken aboard *Rhakotis* and treated well, but Diana's throat was too swollen and she couldn't swallow. For five days the men were kept in a cabin, and Diana stayed in the captain's quarters, fed by injections. The first night, MacDonald wet the bed, and for a year his bladder, strained by disuse, could not hold water for more than an hour. The inflammation of Diana's throat persisted, and the ship's doctor decided to operate. The men saw her in the captain's quarters. Her hair had been washed and set, that lovely hair that got her the nickname Blondie, and she was thin but in good spirits. By seven o'clock that evening, she was dead. "The doctor spoke," writes MacDonald, "and said in broken English that the operation was a success, but the girl's heart was not strong enough to stand the anesthetic. I couldn't speak, and turned away broken-hearted." The men went back to their bunks, these strong men who kept a boat afloat for thirty-seven days with hardly any navigational equipment and watched their friends die: they cried in their bunks like babies, all night, for the loss of that young bride who was actually a widow, who had not only ministered to fifty-one men in a boat of death but steered its tiller, bailed its water, kept it going. She was buried at sea. It sounds like kindness to me: the enemy crew, lined up in uniform on deck, showing the greatest respect to an enemy girl, covering her coffin with a Union flag. They cried as well. Everyone had liked Diana. "It was a gallant end," wrote MacDonald, "to a brave and noble girl."

The end? Of course not. Even if their ship had been torpedoed, they had to return home by sea, no matter how terrifying. The *Rhakotis* was shelled by an English ship on New Year's Day, and MacDonald was set to sea again in an open boat. Edmead was in another and reached Spain. MacDonald ended up on a U-boat, where the young captain took pity on his bladder—movement was restricted, as well as noise, when making noise on a submarine can betray you to listening enemy ships—and let him pee into bottles. On January 4, 1943, the U-boat reached St. Nazaire, and MacDonald went into Milag Nord as a prisoner until the end of the war. Then he went back to sea.

Such men as MacDonald and his American counterparts did their service, then were treated shoddily by peace. American merchant mariners weren't given veteran status until 1988, although at least five thousand of them had died supplying and fueling the war effort. Now they are at least entitled to use veterans' hospitals and be buried in a national cemetery, although not to financial compensation for their service. The Britons who sailed on Arctic convoys, in weather so cold that tears froze, were finally awarded medals in 2013.

The merchant seaman Frank Laskier had his leg blown off by a German torpedo. He did not swallow his anger but spat it out in his radio broadcasts and books, addressing the enemy who had taken his leg and who had destroyed the passenger ship *Laconia* and two thousand of its passengers; he had found one of *Laconia*'s open boats drifting in the Atlantic with sixteen dead children in it. In one broadcast, Laskier addressed the captain of the *Von Scheer*, the German battleship that torpedoed his ship, then fired at the survivors in the water. "You saw us, you watched our ship sink. And you machine-gunned us. But you didn't do the job properly. Because out of that ship's company ten men are alive, and those ten men know what you did. Three of us were wounded. Seven of us were not. Those seven are back at sea."

A mass of dots, and each one a ship
(ROSE GEORGE)

11

DISEMBARK

It's raining. Warm rain. Water on deck, oily and shiny. Flat gray sea. My mood is low and not shifted by running. I must be in predeparture mourning. We are in the Malacca Straits now, which Derek calls the M4 (the New Jersey Turnpike) of shipping. I call them my final stretch, to be reluctantly traveled.

The straits are five hundred miles long, join the Indian and Pacific Oceans, and are surrounded by places of spice and treasure. They are also a captain's nightmare, because they are busy and narrow and overcrowded. They are less crowded than before, because there are fewer pirates now. This used to be the shipping channel most feared by seafarers, with reason. The pirates here were robbers rather than hijackers, but still brutal and often lethal. In the nineteenth century they drowned the young son of a captain while he watched, then cut off the captain's fingers joint by joint. In the twentieth century there was murder and beheadings. In the same way that Somali pirates have a division of labor, the

Indonesians were the foot soldiers—they are the poorest in the region—and Malaysians and Chinese the managers.

It is a terrible task to police these areas, with their thousands of islands, inlets, and rivers, and thousands of coastal supporters and suppliers of piracy. Once I met a merchant seaman who had been on a ship here when a small boat approached. "They said, 'Fish? You want fish?'" No, thank you, said the crew; then the men showed their guns. They took everything they could, then turned to leave. "Then they signaled by light and all the palm trees lit up with signals back. All along the shore." From 2004, the littoral governments of the straits—Malaysia, Singapore, Indonesia, Thailand—began mounting serious piracy patrols, using air, sea, and intelligence. Attacks dropped from seventy-five in 2000 to ten in 2005. By 2006, the Joint War Committee of *Lloyd's* had removed the straits from its Hull, War, Strikes, Terrorism and Related Perils Listed Areas. Pirate experts desperate to solve Somalia look at the straits for answers, but there is no like to compare with like. There is nowhere as disintegrated as Somalia, spitting out its youngsters to the sea. Anyway, here there have again been reports of attacks, and a shift in pirate behavior. Less robbery, more kidnapping and ransom, along the Somali model. The latest judgment of war risks by *Lloyd*'s finds some of Sumatra to be dangerous but "only the north eastern coast between 5° 40' N and 0° 48' N, excluding transit."

This is the first time I've been allowed on deck for days. Farther north in the Lakshadweep Sea, the weather had been too bad for excursions. Beaufort wind scale 7, sea -state 6–7, sea description "rough/very rough." The captain sent me a message through the internal e-mail: "Flippers are out—Glenn." *Kendal*'s stabilizing fins had emerged from the hull like wings, to make the ride smoother. But they were soon withdrawn, because they use too much fuel. Anyway the ship never much rolled or pitched. We had it better than a small tanker that Julius watched from the bridge as it was tossed all ways, and water covered the deck with each wave. "Poor guys," he said. "They must be so seasick they're not even driving the ship." *Kendal* was smoother, but my stomach was tuned to the waves still and rolled enough for the captain to give me the medical definition for seasickness. "It's when you ask for death." At mealtimes seasickness was a welcome change of topic. By now most conversations were echoes. People competed with tales of hundred-foot waves and pitching through sea spray for weeks. The captain once saw seas so high that he thought he saw moonlight shining through a break in the clouds, but it was the crest of a wave.

Marius has done midwinter passages through the Pacific. He says that given a choice between Pacific winter weather and pirates, he would choose pirates. Of course he jokes. You must make a joke of everything at sea, wrote Richard Henry Dana in *Two Years Before the Mast*. "If you were to fall from aloft and be caught in the belly of a sail, and thus saved from instant death, it would not do to look at all disturbed or to make a serious matter of it." Behind the cross talk and swaggering is a serious point. When crews are so small, there is rarely anyone to spare to stand in for someone crippled by nausea. A ship's cook once told me that in rough seas he was so sick he had one foot in the grave and one hanging on. He kept cooking.

By now the weather has subsided enough for me to go out. The captain accompanies me, in hard hat and jeans. He worries that he could lose his passenger and says, "You are only as good as your last mistake." We set off to the fo'c'sle, starboard route. The captain peers down the passageway. "Sometimes you can see her flex. It's quite alarming to see." On the fo'c'sle, which I have only just learned to pronounce to his satisfaction (long "o" like "folk," not short like "fork"), he introduces me to local clouds. Nimbus are different here. They are flatter-shaped than back home. He knows his clouds and enjoys them. "We had to do meteorology as part of our training. I can plan when I'm going to hit fog from the temperature. I bet none of these foreign officers can."

This is the first time in over a month he has come on deck. I have questioned him often about his refusal to emerge. He says,

"But I go out on the bridge wings." Or, "The sea? It's cold and wet." Sometimes he indulges me, following me out to the bridge wing just to watch the water. Then he says, "I love the sea and she loves me. We have this relationship. She's looked after me for forty-two years." It is a private relationship that is nobody's business.

He will retire soon after four decades, one rescue, and no napkins, and I wonder how he will like it. He says that he can switch swiftly between his worlds, that sometimes he can be at home and someone will ask something straightforward about the ship and he'll have to think about it because he has his land head on. "I definitely have two heads." Once his land head won, and he went ashore for six months. He had just married, his wife was pregnant, and he wanted to be at home. That is the reason most men leave the sea: marriages stressed by so much absence last only with difficulty and need preservation. He got a job selling insurance and hated it. His charm meant he had no trouble getting the appointments, but he couldn't get his head around selling an intangible thing like risk. All through those six months, he would drive to the coast to look out to the ocean. He watched the ships pass for comfort. Eventually, his doctor told him he needed to go back to sea.

There is time to go ashore in Port Klang, our port call in Malaysia. The captain could go, too, but declines. He is too nervous about Singapore, our next stop, where I will disembark. Singapore will be busy and dangerous, because it always is. "Maybe on the way back." On the way back he will find another excuse. He went ashore recently at Laem Chabang and realized how much he used to enjoy it. Then he got back on board and forgot. Port Klang is a small port attached to a small town with nothing to recommend it except fish restaurants that sit on stilts over a lagoon and dentists. Both Dilbert and Archie need their teeth seeing to. Fleeting medical attention is normal for seafarers when there is none aboard beyond the second officer, who is responsible for first aid. The captain has done his share of assisting and ministering on his way up the ranks: the most memorable involved a case of gonorrhea and a pencil inserted into a penis. He has seen syphilis, nonspecific urethritis, all sorts. HIV became a concern, so he talks to cadets when he can, rather laconically. "If I were them, I'd give it a miss altogether."

The ship's agent arrives at the gangway with diamond studs in his ears and flowers for me. It is a kind gesture but embarrassing: the crew on gangway watch find it hilarious. The agent offers to have me driven to Kuala Lumpur, an hour away. There is time. It would be no trouble. He proposes skyscrapers and shopping. But the thought of a city leaves me indifferent. I have only one day left on the ship and already I don't want to leave it. I go into Port Klang to change money and eat rice, but I hurry back. As we pass through the port gates I see the big blue ship in the docks and she looks like home. Briefly I think of changing my plans, of staying until the final port of Laem Chabang, then staying for the loop back to Europe, too.

Briefly, my plans may be changed for me. All that zooming through pirate waters has left us first with too much time and then too little. We arrived outside Port Klang at 2:00 p.m. to pick up the pilot as expected, and for no good reason he still hasn't turned up, hours later. The captain tells me we may not stop in Singapore after all and that Singapore-bound cargo can be discharged when *Kendal* calls again on the way back from Laem Chabang. I'll have to jump into a launch, he says, as we steam past. But I have often watched launch boats zooming up to the ship like Starfighters approaching a Deathstar. I have seen pilots climb up the rope ladders, up several sheer stories, and I know they sometimes get smashed against the side or miss their footing. To the captain, I translate all this anxiety as, "But I'll have a laptop." He actually says, "Pish!" The crew drop into launch boats, all the time. There's nothing to it.

The drama lasts an hour or two and then the schedule changes again. Singapore it is.

* * *

At their narrowest point, the Malacca Straits are 1.7 miles wide. This is the oil highway from the Gulf to the east, and each year sixty thousand ships must pass through that 1.7-mile chokepoint. The wheelhouse radars show a mass of dots, and each one is a ship. Alarms are going off in the wheelhouse because the system overloads if there are more than two hundred ships in a 2-mile radius. There are more people than usual on the bridge, an air of concentration, and no time for tea or Skyflakes. The captain is on the bridge constantly these days, partly because Vinton has stacked the boxes too high outside the cabin and blocked his ability to check from his dayroom for fools and delinquents driving other ships. But really it is stress that pushes him up the stairs. Singapore always puts his stomach in knots. He exudes anxiety and I don't dare distract him with questions. Another reason for caution: we are near the spot where *Kendal* once ran aground under the control of a previous captain, who decided that going at 21 knots in the Malacca Straits was a good idea. It was as good an idea as driving at 100 miles an hour around a playground. Derek was on board at the time. He was in his engine room and remembers no thud or grinding, just a sudden removal of movement. Even so, he knew what that meant, but he won't say what word came out of his mouth first. The damage cost millions and *Kendal* was in drydock for months for repairs. The captain responsible was investigated and fired, possibly because the bridge's black box—the Vessel Data Recorder—mysteriously didn't save its data as it was meant to. He is still skippering ships, for Germans. The captain's views on this are unprintable. His beautiful ship, crippled.

We wait for a gap in the sea traffic to cross into port. It is the captain's responsibility to decide when to cross. Overseers working for Singapore's Vessel Traffic Information Service office will tell him what is coming, but not when to go. He says aloud but to himself, "If only we could get to those barges, we'll be all right." He gets to the barges and we are all right and we safely berth again, as *Kendal* does dozens of times a month with no drama. We have sailed through an ocean infested by pirates; we have avoided ships, wooden boats, families of fishermen, fast ferries, and reefs. We have transported what needs to be transported, traveled 9,288 nautical miles through the wildest place on the planet, and done it all safely and efficiently. All that accomplishment is hailed by a man coming to check our immigration status and another one selling SIM cards. I find him in the mess room displaying his wares in a briefcase, and nearly buy one before I remember that his prices are inflated for seafarers. More visitors begin to come up the gangway, the usual stream of port busybodies, and really by now I should have gone down it, but I dawdle. I don't want to leave the bridge and its windows, the boxes, the quiet nights at sea, the depth beneath. I don't want what Singapore has to offer: shops filled with choice and stuff, everything that we have been removed from on *Kendal*, while carrying it.

I find ways to put off departure. I show the crew a Malaysian ten-ringgit note that I got in Port Klang, because it has a picture of a container ship on it. Isn't it pleasing to see your work recognized on a banknote? They say, "So what? We're only here for the money." Vinton has found me a blue Maersk boilersuit and asks if I want workboots, too. He has piles of boots that are of no use. Not even the Filipinos are size 6 but the office sent dozens of them. He doesn't know why.

Marius asks, "Will I be in your book?"

Maybe.

He thinks. "Is it revenge for beating you at backgammon?"

Pinky is also paying off, as are a handful of other crew. They may meet again, they may not. Friendship, say seafarers, ends at the gangway. Francis is staying, so I give him my Botlek-bought coffeemaker and packets of Rotterdam coffee. I leave a box of sea-themed books in the captain's cabin to be shipped back and for him to read, if he can be persuaded to read "about facts." Then to B deck, down to the gangway to sign out, to leave the sea. The cadets are leaning on the rail. There is no shore leave for them in this port, no need for parental advice from the captain. The Scottish lad, stuck with boring boxes for at least another two months, watches me go. "Take me with you?"

I asked the captain once whether *Kendal* was a happy ship. He said, "Well, no one's happy to be here." Then he checked himself. I am a positive person, he says. Sunny by nature. But the last years have brought such dramatic changes, such cuts and slashes, such a diminishment, that he can't help the gloom. He knows he is training his replacements and recognizes that that is the way of things in a globalized world. "I just wish they would be honest about it." He wishes that he would be sent officers who knew their knots and sextant, whose levels of English, maritime or otherwise, were safer. They don't have to be British or American, they just have to be good. In 2012, the Philippines was almost blacklisted by the European Union for its poor quality of maritime training.

At a nautical seminar in Liverpool I met two cadets back from sea-based training who sounded shocked. Their "sea-phases" had been served on ships where they didn't share a language with the crew. They had served under captains who had autocratic views on knowledge and power, and who kept hold of theirs ferociously. The shipowners admitted that some cadets did their three years of training and never went back to sea. They talked constantly, as people talk in conferences and committee rooms, of the shortage of skilled sea people, of the worry of it. A parliamentary committee, in a report on the state of British shipping, wondered what would happen if Britain needed merchant ships to go to war again, as it did in the Falklands. It's all very well having foreign seafarers, they wrote, but what if they refuse to work for British military aims? During the recent Gulf War, Japanese seafarers refused to crew supply ships. American politicians sometimes get excited about the same thing. A truer measure of the value given to the maritime industry is that a 2004 maritime security bill, the Safe Port Act, passed in 2006 only when a provision about Internet gambling was tacked onto it.

What would keep those two cadets at sea? An industry that learns to stop calling its most valuable asset the "human element" and calls them humans instead. International conventions that can actually be enforced and flag states that can be compelled into good behavior. Oversight, governance, fair play. All the things expected on land that dissolve twelve miles out, in open seas.

Disembarked, I wander around Singapore, dispirited. It is half docks, this port city, but the dock area is high security and closely guarded. Singapore's port authority is always expecting terrorist attacks from Indonesia's Muslim terrorists, and even official visitors have to sign a nondisclosure agreement to visit. The cranes, though, are tall enough to tower over the highway and I look at them with wistful affection. I imagine them loading and unloading *Kendal*, swarming over her as she sits passively at the dock, having things done to her. The empty boxes will be exchanged for filled ones, sinking her farther in the water with paint and Valium and chemicals and airbags. Thousands of moves, boxes taken and boxes put back, and at the end of it *Kendal* will look exactly the same.

Then Julius and Marius will head for the fo'c'sle to haul in the ropes, rat guards too. They will switch on the machinery that hauls up the anchor chain, which will return to its casing reluctantly, spitting rust and dust, requiring all the humans nearby to wear safety goggles but not face masks, adding to their respiratory infections and damaged hearing. My cabin will have been cleaned by Francis and empty, probably, and my note removed from the bridge. No more obligations for watchkeepers to record dolphin sightings, no need for Pinky's portly replacement to learn that there are people who voluntarily don't eat meat. The pilot will signal verbally for departure, the captain will echo him, the engine room will spark to work, the wheel will turn. *Kendal* will set off with six thousand boxes, back to business.

During her return trip, the captain e-mails. He wants to know whether my transition to land has gone well, whether he has safely delivered his supernumerary along with the cargo. Of course he didn't go ashore in Laem Chabang, not even with Derek's best efforts of persuasion. He has decided to read one of the sea books I left, and it has inspired indignation. He once gave me a few pages of his autobiography, full of the color of his first three decades at sea, of exotic ports, friendly maidens, unfriendly stevedores, and reliable sextants. Captain Glenn concluded the autobiography by writing to an imaginary cadet, wondering if he will have as good an experience as he did. He thinks so, because:

he will be in awe at the sight of his first vessel, looming so much larger before him than it was for me.

He, a deck cadet, will be mesmerized by the technology on the bridge, more reminiscent of a jet aircraft cockpit.

He, an engineer cadet, will be shocked at the jaw-dropping huge main engine, probably larger than his house.

He may find that every day could be an adventure.

He may not have so much time in port, but he will see the world, and he will get past the dockside areas of my day.

He will face the same high seas as I, and may even feel the romance of the oceans.

He will behold sea-borne wild life such as dolphins, whales, and lost souls of the albatross, all in their natural state.

He will meet peoples of so many different cultures and creeds, to become truly international in outlook.

He will meet captains who will have time for him, not like in my day, as they rarely spoke to lowly cadets.

It is a lovely, compelling picture of a life at sea. Who wouldn't sign up if it was like that? A job that is vital. A career that will never disappear, for we will always need ships, as the captain's mother said. He must be feeling differently when he writes his e-mail. Perhaps he has his other head on. "You can see how we are really thought of," he writes. "Riffraff that no one really cares about, no matter the lip service paid to our safety and welfare by the likes of owners, flag state, IMO." I picture him in his F deck office, pinioned at his computer by paperwork, kept from the ship handling and navigation that he loves, his job now to cut spending and speed at all costs, his industry transformed, his fury rising as he steams toward retirement. "We are mere chattels, a human resource, dispensable nonentities. We are the front line troops who dance forward into the breach at point-blank range to whatever tune is played. Whining over. I am right though."

NOTES

PAGE

ix   Maurice Oliver, quoted in Tony Parker, *Lighthouse*, (London: Eland, 2006), p. 110.

Introduction

2   "pensioners, servants, thieves": Henry Mayhew, Letter III, *Morning Chronicle*, October 26, 1849. There were also sailors of the kind described in 1968 by anthropologist Jesse Lemisch: "His bowed legs bracing before him as if the very Broadway beneath his feet might begin to pitch and roll. In his dress he is in the words of a superior 'very nasty and negligent,' his black stockings ragged, his long, baggy trousers tarred to make them waterproof. Bred in that 'very shambles of language,' the merchant-marine, he is foul-mouthed, his talk alien and suspect." Lemisch quoted in David James Stewart, "'Rocks and Storms I'll Fear No More': Anglo-American Maritime Memorialization, 1700–1940," PhD dissertation, Texas A&M University, May 2004.

3   Trade carried by sea: International Maritime Organization, International Shipping, Carrier of World Trade, background paper, 2005.

3   In 2011: American Association of Port Authorities, U.S. Public Port Facts, http://www.aapa-ports.org, accessed February 2013.

3   we need to live: United Nations Conference on Trade and Development (UNCTAD), *Review of Maritime Transport 2011*, p. 36.

3   If they were stacked: Maersk Line company facts and information, http://www.maerskline.com, accessed February 2013.

4   half of its gas: Gas supplies are changeable. In the last three months of 2012,

LNG imports, mostly from Qatar, were only 18 percent of all supplies, and Norwegian imports by pipeline had risen. Even so, the UK is widely expected to be mostly reliant on gas imports by 2016. UK Government Department of Energy and Climate Change, *Energy Trends*, December 2012, p. 95.

4   of its oil supplies: *Lloyd's List Intelligence*, "Paradox in U.S. Seaborne Crude Oil Imports," August 16, 2012.

4   Every day: Michelle Wiese Bockman, "Oil Tanker Surplus Seen by Clarkson Persisting for a Third Year," *Bloomberg Business Week*, January 30, 2013.

4   The chief of the British: "Ministers Accused of 'Sea Blindness' by Britain's Most Senior Royal Navy Figure," Jasper Gerard, *Telegraph*, June 12, 2009.

5   with respect: Funeral of Sir Winston Churchill, BBC Archive, http://www.bbc.co.uk/archive/churchill/11026.shtml, accessed February 2013.

6   Denmark's GDP: Martin Adeney, Mærsk Mc-Kinney Møller obituary, *Guardian*, April 22, 2012, http://www.guardian.co.uk/world/2012/apr/22/maersk-mckinney-moller-obituary.

6   carry his briefcase: Robert Wright, "Møller on Course to Step Back from Helm," *Financial Times*, June 6, 2008.

6   Order of the Elephant: Maersk Media Center, http://www.mmm.maersk.com/en/Practicalities/Media-Center, accessed February 2013.

6   "transportation sector": Reuters, AP Moeller-Maersk A/S, Profile, http://www.reuters.com/finance/stocks/companyProfile?symbol=MAERSKa.CO, accessed January 2013.

7   less than Microsoft's: Maersk press release, February 27, 2012. Microsoft's 2011 revenues were $69.943 billion, http://www.microsoft.com/investor/reports/ar11/financial_highlights/index.html, accessed January 2013.

7   if they care to: The expected twenty-strong fleet will also be able to carry 3.64 billion iPads, enough for half the world's population, and one ship's worth of containers, stacked end to end vertically, would break through the earth's stratosphere. Allianz Global Corporate and Specialty, "Safety and Shipping 1912–2012," p. 48.

7   became SS *Santa*: Some other items carried by SS *Santa* included two thousand martini glasses, four thousand pairs of women's underwear, three thousand poker tables, and 19,500 pairs of men's and boys' socks. Tim Spanton and Charles Rae, "One Hull of a Christmas," *Sun*, August 3, 2007.

7   the construction industry: *Oxford Economics*, "The Economic Impact of the UK Maritime Services Sector," December 2012, pp. 2–3.

8   there were 63: International Chamber of Shipping, *Annual Review, 2012*, p.17.

8   For the International Chamber: "Pejorative terms such as 'flags of convenience' have more to do with industrial relations issues of the 1980s than the situation which pertains to 2012." Ibid., p. 45.

8   "managed anarchy": "Brassed Off: How the War on Terrorism Could Change the Shape of Shipping," *Economist*, May 16, 2002.

8   In 1961: The Merchant Navy Welfare Board, "Almonising Working Group Report," April 2005.

8   The United States: U.S. Department of Transportation, Maritime Administration, "Comparison of U.S. and Foreign-Flag Operating Costs," September 2011, p. 7.

8   Now British seafarers: There was a 10 percent decrease in UK seafarers between 2011 and 2012, due to a drop in ratings and uncertified officers.

Eight percent of officers are women. Seafarer Statistics 2012, Department for Transport, January 2013.

8   U.S.-flagged ships: According to the U.S. Maritime Administration, there are ninety-two foreign-going U.S. ships and ninety-eight operating under the Jones Act. Properly called the Merchant Marine Act of 1920, but named for Senator Wesley Jones, the Jones Act's main aim was to protect U.S. shipping and ensure that the country had enough U.S.-flagged ships to call on in an emergency. To protect domestic interests, the act banned foreign-flagged ships from carrying freight between U.S. ports. It is not popular and is expensive. A 1999 study by the U.S. International Trade Commission found that ending it would save more than $1.3 billion a year. But there are nearly forty thousand ships with some American ownership, just not American flags. U.S. Department of Transportation, Maritime Administration, "U.S. Water Transportation Statistical Snapshot," February 2011; "How the Jones Act Blocks Natural Disaster Relief," *Bloomberg*, editorial, January 1, 2013.

8   Only 1 percent: U.S. Department of Transportation, Maritime Administration, "Comparison of U.S. and Foreign-Flag Operating Costs," p. 26.

9   Its 320 articles: United Nations Convention on the Law of the Sea, Preamble, p. 25.

10   "consensual but rough": Baroness Jane Campbell has called for an inquiry into Akhona's death on the grounds that *Safmarine Kariba* was a UK-flagged ship. As she said in the House of Lords in 2011, "For women, living and working on board ship requires great dedication, tolerance, and self-belief. Often they will be the only female on board, with a group of men used to a male-only environment. At sea it is impossible to walk away, to change one's surroundings, or one's ship-mates." Julian Bray, "Safmarine Death Probe Call," *Tradewinds*, sourced from http://safewaters.wordpress.com/2011/03/07/maritime-safmarine-death-probe-call.

10   could be demanded: Adam Corbett, "Latest Probe Casts Doubt over Death," *Tradewinds*, July 7, 2011.

11   "stays at sea": Mzilikazi wa Afrika, "SA Teen's Horror on the High Seas," *Sunday Times*, July 18, 2010.

11   no access at all: The research was done by questionnaire and 1,533 questionnaires were returned. Thirty-nine percent of respondents were from the Philippines, 32 percent were Chinese, 15 percent were Indian, 12 percent were UK nationals, and 3 percent were of other nationalities. N. Ellis, H. Sampson, I. Acejo, L. Tang, N. Turgo, and Z. Zhao, The Lloyd's Register Educational Trust Research Unit/Seafarers International Research Centre (SIRC), Cardiff University, "Accommodation on Contemporary Cargo Ships," December 2012, p. 3.

11   "Seafarers and fishers": International Transport Workers' Federation, "Out of Sight, out of Mind: Seafarers, Fishers, and Human Rights," June 2006, p. 5.

11   was the same: Personal communication with ITF.

12   "I've always been": Furuseth when threatened with jail also said, in a thick Norwegian accent, "I put my inyunction in my pocket and to go yail." Leah Robinson Rousmaniere and Peter Larom, *Anchored Within the Vail: A Pictorial History of the Seamen's Church Institute* (New York: The Seamen's Church Institute of New York and New Jersey, 1995), p. 27.

12 "the provision of leisure": Erol Kahveci, *Port Based Welfare for Seafarers* (Cardiff, Wales: Seafarers International Research Centre, Cardiff University), p. 51.

12 by Somali pirates: ICC International Maritime Bureau, "Piracy and Armed Robbery Against Ships," Report for the Period 1 January–30 June 2010, p. 20.

12 its conclusion: Cesar Illiano and Terry Wade, "Chilean Miners Rescued after 69 Days Underground," Reuters, October 13, 2010.

1: Embarkation

16 Samuel Johnson wrote: Johnson, wrote James Boswell, was trying to get his servant Francis Barber, who had gone to sea, back to shore. Barber's master "kindly interested himself in procuring his release from a state of life of which Johnson always expressed the utmost abhorrence. He said, 'No man will be a sailor who has contrivance enough to get himself into a jail; for being in a ship is being in a jail, with the chance of being drowned.' And at another time, 'A man in a jail has more room, better food, and commonly better company.'" *Life of Johnson*, Project Gutenberg, http://www.gutenberg .org/files/1564/1564-h/1564-h.htm, accessed February 2013.

18 it's just shipping: The fish is caught, frozen, unfrozen for filleting, then refrozen for the return journey. "The joke that 'a fish travels more dead than alive,' said an official from the Scottish Fishermen's Federation, 'has become a reality.'" Mike Merritt and Rob Edwards, "The Madness of Filleting Scottish Fish in China," *Sunday Herald*, August 23, 2009.

21 In 2010: Rupert Saunders, Jason Downer, and James Meaby were all experienced sailors. They were wearing life jackets when they were found. James Meaby was forty miles from the others, and probably survived for up to a dozen hours in the water. Nothing was ever found of *Ouzo*. Marine Accident Investigation Branch, "Report on the investigation of the loss of the sailing yacht *Ouzo* and her three crew, south of the Isle of Wight, during the night of 20/21 August 2006," Report no. 7/2007, April 2007.

22 are at sea: The International Labor Organization puts the global total of seafarers at 1.2 million. The Commission on Filipinos Overseas calculates that there are 369,104 "seabased workers." Stock Estimate of Filipinos Overseas, December 2011.

23 The rush to seafaring: UNCTAD, *Review of Maritime Transport 2011*, p. 159.

23 in remittances: Department of Foreign Affairs press release, "President Aquino Conducts Historic Trilateral Meeting with EU leaders at ASEM9," November 6, 2012.

24 A senior government: International Chamber of Shipping, *Annual Review, 2012*, p. 30

25 weeks to move: Marc Levinson, *The Box: How the Shipping Container Made the World Smaller and the World Economy Bigger* (Princeton, NJ: Princeton University Press, 2006), p. 33.

2: Aboard

33 "a mess of coal-dust": Joseph Conrad, *The Mirror of the Sea* (London: Folio Society, 2005), p. 64.

34 his night vision: Marine Accident Investigation Branch, "Report on the investigation into the loss of the sailing yacht *Ouzo*," p. 22.

35. "less serene brow": Conrad, *Mirror of the Sea*, p. 30.

39   its own system: Confusion reigns about how many containers exist, as
      different bodies use different calculations. There are various figures and
      estimates: UNCTAD calculates that as of January 2011, the global number of
      TEUs traveling worldwide was twenty-nine million. The United Nations
      Office on Drugs and Crime (UNODC) meanwhile uses a figure provided by
      the Bureau International des Containers (BIC), which estimates twenty to
      twenty-five million actual containers (not every container is a TEU). As for
      container movements, UNODC uses the figure of five hundred million, an
      up-to-date figure based on a calculation made by the World Customs
      Organization. On the online search engine Yahoo, the most popular answer
      to the question "How many containers are there?" is "a lot." Frédéric Carluer,
      *Global Logistic Chain Security: Economic Impacts of the U.S. 100% Container
      Scanning Law* (Le Havre: Le Havre Université/World Customs Organization,
      June 2008), p. 6. UNCTAD, *Review of Maritime Transport 2011*, p. 39.

39   using twist-locks: "In 1958, *The New York Times* described the new technology
      this way: 'A trailer is loaded, for example, in Springfield, Mo. It travels by
      road to New York or San Francisco, sealed, virtually damage-proof and
      theft-proof. By ship it goes to France or to Japan, eliminating warehousing,
      stacking and sorting. Each ship takes on her cargo with a few hundred lifts,
      compared to 5,000 individual lifts by the old method.'" Margalit Fox, "Keith
      Tantlinger, Builder of Cargo Container, Dies at 92," *New York Times*,
      September 6, 2011.

39   dockers came twenty-ninth: Levinson, *The Box*, p. 26.

39   more supply than demand: The nature of shipping means that prices can
      fluctuate wildly. "Economies of Scale Made Steel," *Economist*, November 12,
      2011.

41   2 and 10 percent: The United Nations Office on Drugs and Crime uses the
      lower figure. UNODC, "Executive Director Lauds Container Control
      Programme in Tackling the Smuggling of Drugs and Cultural Artefacts,"
      press release, May 11, 2011.

41   5 percent of them: The U.S. Army Corps of Engineers calculated an inbound
      total of 17,083,057 TEUs in 2011. Nearly twelve million more foreign-going
      TEUs left U.S. ports. U.S. Army Corps of Engineers, Waterborne Commerce
      Statistics Center, http://www.ndc.iwr.usace.army.mil/wcsc/by_porttons11
      .html, accessed February 2013. The Government Accountability Office,
      however, calculates that "about 10.7 million" ocean-borne containers arrived
      in U.S. ports in 2011. Stephen L. Caldwell, director, Homeland Security and
      Justice, United States Government Accountability Office, Testimony before
      the Subcommittee on Border and Maritime Security, Committee on
      Homeland Security, House of Representatives, GAO-12-422T, February 7,
      2012.

41   Counterfeiters: Hugh Griffiths and Michael Jenks, "Maritime Transport and
      Destabilizing Commodity Flows," Stockholm International Peace Research
      Institute Policy Paper 32, January 2012, p. 1.

41   Some had paid: The women working in the brothels were citizens of China,
      Korea, Thailand, Vietnam, Malaysia, Singapore, Hong Kong, Japan, Taiwan,
      and Laos. A twenty-one-month investigation discovered that the criminals
      "attempted to avoid law enforcement scrutiny by using code words when
      talking on the phone. They referred to the women as ethnic foods, makes of

cars or as ships." The United States Attorney's Office, Western District of Washington, press release, February 23, 2007.

42   the GAO was blunt: Government Accountability Office, "Drug Control: Cooperation with Many Major Drug Transit Countries Has Improved, but Better Performance Reporting and Sustainability Plans Are Needed," July 2008, p. 5.

42   This showed that: Griffiths and Jenks, "Maritime Transport," p. 23.

42   "A single bomb": Letter from Albert Einstein to F. D. Roosevelt, August 2, 1939, accessed February 2013 from the President Roosevelt Presidential Library and Museum, www.fdrlibrary.marist.edu/archives/pdfs/docsworldwar.pdf.

42   "every available means": Toby Harnden, "US Casts Doubt on Bin Laden's Latest Message," *Daily Telegraph*, December 28, 2001.

42   "to create catastrophe": Stephen Cohen, "Boom Boxes: Containers and Terrorism," in *Protecting the Nation's Seaports: Balancing Security and Cost*, eds. Jon D. Haveman and Howard J. Shatz (San Francisco: Public Policy Institute of California, 2006), p. 116.

43   no one checked: Howard Kurtz, "ABC Says It Shipped Uranium as Safety Test," *Boston Globe*, September 12, 2003.

43   signals jammer: *Lloyd's List*, February 11, 2011.

43   When the UK's: Ibid.

43   "phony papers": Quoted in Michael Richardson, *A Time Bomb for Global Trade: Maritime-Related Terrorism in an Age of Weapons of Mass Destruction* (Singapore: Institute of South East Asian Studies, 2004), p. 10.

44   nothing wrong: Griffiths and Jenks, "Maritime Transport," p. 8.

44   In response: Caldwell, Testimony before the Subcommittee on Border and Maritime Security.

44   The box is shipped: Government Accountability Office, "Supply Chain Security," GAO-08-187, January 2008, p. 2.

45   The process was: Caldwell, Testimony before the Subcommittee on Border and Maritime Security, p.16.

45   In reality: Ibid.

45   It is more outlandish: In fact, research into honeybees (*Apis mellifera*) has shown that their odor detection is as good as that of dogs. "It is quite remarkable," writes Ivan Hoo, chief executive officer of Inscentinel, "to know that our single automatic training unit can produce 500 trained sniffer bees in just five hours; training a single sniffer dog takes up to six months." The bees would be inserted in special "bee holders," trained to detect explosives, then used in a handheld detector. The company is still looking for funding. Ivan Hoo, "Using Sniffer Bees for Bulk Screening of Cargo," *Port Technology International*, May 2012, pp. 146–47.

45   The new scanning: "Secure Trade and 100% Scanning of Containers," European Commission Staff Working Paper, February 2010, p. 5.

45   In 2012: Caldwell, Testimony before the Subcommittee on Border and Maritime Security, p. 2.

46   "the fault of the bridge": Theodora Fitzgibbon's book compiles examples of nautical cookery that include hamburgers, invented, she claims, by Jewish emigrants traveling on ships. "Jewish emigrants were able to bring large quantities of their own kosher dried beef with them which they scraped off, or chopped finely and made into little cakes, sometimes with chopped onion or

even soaked bread to make it go further. When they settled in the United States, they continued to make Hamburg steaks, as the patties were then called, and as the popularity of these meat cakes spread, they became known as 'hamburgers.'" *A Taste of the Sea* (Vancouver: A. S. Barnes and Company, 1977), p. 13.

47 "in suspense before them": John Flavel, *Navigation Spiritualized. Or, A New Compass for Seamen Consisting of 32 Points Of Pleasant Observations Profitable Applications And Serious Reflections, All Concluded With so Many Spiritual Poems* (Newburyport, MA: Edmund M. Blunt, 1770), pp. 3–4, accessed February 2013 via openlibrary.org http://archive.org/stream/navigationspirit00flav#page/n5/mode/2up.

47 The men had all: Interview with Father Colum Kelly, Immingham Seafarers Centre; Marine Accident Investigation Branch, "Report on the investigation of work undertaken in a dangerous enclosed/confined space and the consequent attempted rescue on board ERRV *Viking Islay* resulting in the loss of three lives at the Amethyst gas field, 25 miles off the East Yorkshire coast, UK," September 23, 2007.

48 "Two miles away": Richard Woodman, *The Real Cruel Sea: The Merchant Navy in the Battle of the Atlantic, 1939–1943* (London: John Murray, 2005), p. 562.

3: Harbor

52 "The flies were": Frank Laskier, *Log Book* (London: George Allen & Unwin Ltd, 1942), pp. 32–33.

53 sex-starved sailor: Dunton's technique of offering printed advice in the *Athenian Gazette* was later copied by Daniel Defoe, who set up the *Review* in 1704 and employed himself as its "agony uncle." Lucy Mangan, "A Brief History of Agony Aunts," *Guardian*, November 13, 2009.

54 "and a headwind": Dickens unsurprisingly suffered great nausea. "I lay there, all the day long, quite coolly and contentedly; with no sense of weariness, with no desire to get up, or get better, or take the air." The nausea overtook him so comprehensively that "if Neptune himself had walked in, with a toasted shark on his trident, I should have looked upon the event as one of the very commonest everyday occurrences." Charles Dickens, *On Travel*, ed. Pete Orford (London: Hesperus Press, 2009), pp. 18–19.

57 a British celebrity: Simon's initial career wasn't promising. His siblings were taken on ships as rat catchers, but his black color made him unlucky to sailors, so he was stuck scrounging in the docks for two years. But he charmed Captain Griffiths of HMS *Amethyst*, and once on board always accompanied the captain on his evening patrols through the ship. When the ship was attacked in the Yangtze River, twenty-five crew were killed and Simon was hit by shrapnel. He slowly recovered and gained his rank of Able Seaman Simon for killing a huge rat, named Mao Tse-Tung by the crew. Val Lewis, *Ships' Cats in War and Peace* (Shepperton, UK: Nauticalia, 2001), pp. 21–39.

57 A mongrel puppy: United States Coast Guard, Frequently Asked Questions, accessed January 2013, http://www.uscg.mil/history/faqs/Sinbad.asp.

58 A survey of: International Transport Workers' Federation, "Out of Sight, Out of Mind," June 8, 2006, London, p. 33.

58 A survey by: Ibid.

58 "After all": Tony Lane, "Study Looks at Mixed Nationality Crews," *The Sea*, March–April 2001, p. 4.

59 "save the whale": *Lloyd's List*, "Piracy as a Business," December 1, 2009.

60 Even then, a study by: House of Commons Select Committee on Transport, Eighth Report, July 2006, p. 68.

60 A 2006 study: The International Union of Maritime Insurance (IUMI) reported that in the fifteen-year period up to 2008, 60 percent of accidents involving the serious or total loss of vessels over five hundred gross tons were due to human error. That works out at two serious incidents a day. Maritime and Coastguard Agency, *The Human Element: A Guide to Human Behaviour in the Shipping Industry*, April 2010.

60 When the *Exxon Valdez*: Maritime and Coastguard Agency, *Human Element*, p. 47.

61 I shot the cook: Seamen's Church Institute of New York, *Lookout*, May 1942, vol. 33, no. 5.

64 They were soon sold: Levinson, *The Box*, pp. 229–30.

66 The crew had to: Burial at sea is permitted in the United States under the Ocean Dumping Act. According to the EPA's frequently asked questions on ocean burials, the requirements for whole body burials are that "all plastic and fabric materials be removed from the casket before burial at sea. EPA recommends that a minimum of six 3-inch holes be drilled into the casket to facilitate rapid flooding and venting of air. To further aid in rapid sinking, EPA recommends that additional weight be added to the casket based upon a four to one ratio of the body weight. For example, a whole body that weighs 150 pounds would need an additional 600 pounds to offset the buoyancy of both the body and the casket. Finally, the casket should be wrapped with stainless steel chain along both axes. EPA does not recommend the use of shipping straps due to the rapid deterioration of such materials in the marine environment."

66 "With heads bowed": Curtis Ebbesmeyer and Eric Scigliano, *Flotsametrics and the Floating World: How One Man's Obsession with Runaway Sneakers and Rubber Ducks Revolutionized Ocean Science* (New York: Harper Collins, 2009), pp. 183–85.

67 a paper entitled: Gunnar M. Lamvik, "The Filipino Seafarer: A Life between Sacrifice and Shopping," PhD thesis, Dept. of Social Anthropology, Norwegian University of Science and Technology, 2002.

4: Open Sea

69 at sea every year: All death rates for seafarers, given the complicated disparate nature of the industry, are estimates. ITF uses the two thousand figure. The IMO puts the annual fatality rate at one thousand a year, of which one hundred were "lives lost in the fishing sector, 400 in domestic operations, and around 500 in other categories, including international shipping." However, maritime safety expert Detlef Nielsen, in an investigation into how casualty statistics are gathered, concluded that there was severe underreporting, by up to nine times. IMO, "Lives Lost at Sea Halved and Piracy Eradicated Should Be Targets, Says Sekimizu," press release, January 8, 2013. Detlef Nielsen, "Safety and Working Conditions in International Merchant Shipping," PowerPoint presentation, accessed February 2013 from www.cepal.org/usi/perfil/iame _papers/ proceedings/nielsen.ppt.

69 The next year: Maritime and Coastguard Agency, *Human Element*.

69 Even now: One hundred and six vessels were recorded as losses in the twelve months prior to November 25, 2012, or nine per month on average. Busy shipping lanes around South China, Indochina, Indonesia, and the

Philippines contributed twice as many losses as any other region. Allianz Global Corporate and Specialty, "Safety and Shipping Review 2013," p. 3.

72 those died, too: RSPCA, "Livestock Deaths Just the Tip of the Iceberg," media release, December 21, 2009.

72 "What these loony lefties": Animal rights activists, the author continued while writing about the deaths of men and beasts, "live by the three B's: beans, brown rice, and bullshit." *Meat Trade News Daily*, December 20, 2009.

74 Shocked, trapped: Ahmad Harb interview, accessed December 2012 via http://www.youtube.com/watch?v=cfZ7hm7amJo.

76 They had to cut: Owen Milloy, video, "Captain John Milloy Rest in Peace Dad," accessed January 2013 via http://www.youtube.com/watch ?v=yagysu7tmF4&noredirect=1.

77 Not only had he: Tom Kington, "Costa Concordia Captain Claims He Tripped and Fell into a Lifeboat," *Guardian*, January 18, 2012.

77 "If some people want": After the *Oceanos* sank, it was discovered that it was the third ship owned by Epirotiki Lines to have sunk in three years. Avranas was found negligent by a Greek board of inquiry but never jailed, and later worked on a Greek ferry. *New York Times*, "Headliners: Career Overboard?" August 11, 1991.

77 When Moss Hills: Moss Hills, "My Story of the Sinking," accessed February 2013 via www.oceanossinking.com/MYSTORYOFTHESINKING.htm.

78 Ninety passengers: BBC News, "Ethiopian Airlines Jet Crashes into Sea off Beirut," January 25, 2010.

79 Now 68 percent: UNCTAD, *Review of Maritime Transport 2011*, p. xv.

80 5.3 times higher: U.S. Department of Transportation, Maritime Administration, "Comparison of U.S. and Foreign-Flag Operating Costs," pp. 1, 6.

80 The UN Law: Article 94 of the Convention on Nationality of Ships requires that "every State shall fix the conditions for the grant of its nationality to ships, for the registration of ships in its territory, and for the right to fly its flag. Ships have the nationality of the State whose flag they are entitled to fly. There must exist a genuine link between the State and the ship."

80 Liberia may have: The embassy of Liberia in London offers a figure of $18 million on its website for the revenues provided by the Liberian International Ship and Corporate Register (LISCR) to the Government of Liberia, but that dates from 2000. Cables captured by Wikileaks talk of gross revenues to LISCR in 2007 as $38 million, with revenues then disbursed to the Liberian government of $13 million, or 6 percent of the country's GDP. The latest figures on LISCR's website put the number of ships flying the Liberian flag at 3,750; www.liscr.com, cable reference 09MONROVIA70 accessed via http:// www.cablegatesearch.net/cable.php?id=09MONROVIA70, February 2013, cable dated January 21, 2009.

80 Kiribati: In another cable captured by Wikileaks, a local maritime official describes Sovereign Ventures as "pretty cunning," and mentions an all-expenses-paid trip to Singapore made by the transport minister of Tuvalu, a small Pacific island nation also approached by Sovereign Ventures. Sovereign Ventures has no obvious web presence, but the mailing addresses for both Kiribati and Tuvalu—in the same building on Anson Road in Singapore— are strangely similar. Cable 07SUVA169 accessed December 2013 via http:// www.cablegatesearch.net/cable.php?id=07SUVA169&q=cook-islands.

81 Liberia's general counsel: Brad Berman's paper "Does the UNCTAD Convention on the Registration of Ships Need Amending?" is available on the ITF website at www.itfglobal.org/seafarers/icons-site/images/120 _BERMAN.PDF.

81 Liberia is certainly: According to an investigation by Global Witness, a group that investigates resource exploitation, after Charles Taylor came to power in Liberia in 1997, he launched a court action against IRI, the company that had run Liberia's shipping registry for forty years. The new company, the LISCR, was linked to Taylor's lawyers. When IRI then sued the government of Liberia for breach of contract, its lawyers claimed that Taylor was pocketing a third of the shipping revenues. Not only that. One container, which Taylor claimed contained presents for his wife, contained armaments, according to a witness present at its unloading. A UN expert panel on Sierra Leone condemned the Taylor government for "the improper use of its maritime registry." When I searched the website of LISCR for "Charles Taylor," I found no results. Global Witness/ITF, *Taylor-Made: The Pivotal Role of Liberia's Forests and Flag of Convenience in Regional Conflict*, September 2001.

81 The *Economist*: "Brassed Off," *Economist*.

82 By the end: Cour d'Appel de Paris, pôle 4 chambre 11E, n° RG 08/02278, arrêt rendu le 30 mars 2010.

82 "That is normal": Tom Mangold, *From Our Own Correspondent*, accessed February 2013 from http://news.bbc.co.uk/hi/english/static/audio_video /programmes/correspondent/transcripts/883110.txt.

82 A report by: Organization for Economic Cooperation and Development, Directorate for Science, Technology and Industry, "Ownership and Control of Ships," March 2003, appendix B, p. 23.

83 All this amounts to: The OECD report is reproduced in a Report of the Secretary-General, Oceans and the Law of the Sea, Consultative Group on Flag State Implementation, March 5, 2004.

83 Total has already: Cour d'Appel de Paris, p. 173 (Lambion), p. 461 (Courmier).

83 Now Lloyd's has: Terry Macalister, "Lloyd's Register and the Art of Staying Afloat in Troubled Waters," *Guardian*, June 5, 2012.

84 Matters had slightly: Michael Richardson, "Crimes Under Flags of Convenience," Yale Global Online, May 19, 2003, accessed January 2013 from http://yaleglobal.yale.edu/content/crimes-under-flags-convenience.

84 The top four: Personal communication with ITF.

5: Sea and Suez

89 UNESCO estimates: UNESCO, http://www.unesco.org/new/en/culture /themes/underwater-cultural-heritage/the-underwater-heritage/wrecks/.

90 Its salvage rights: R (oao Rosemary Fogg and Valerie Ledgard) v Secretary of State for Defence & John Short, Case No: CO/132/2005, High Court of Justice, London, transcript accessed February 2013 via http://www .richardbuxton.co.uk/v3.0/node/196#_jmp0_.

90 "The helicopter did not": Tom Kington, "Priest Appeals for Justice for African Migrants 'Left to Die' on Boat," *Guardian*, September 7, 2011.

90 UN commissioner: Office of the High Commissioner for Human Rights, press release, September 15, 2006.

92 On the overseas: Natural Resources Defense Council, "Clean by Design:

Transportation," accessed December 2012 from http://www.nrdc.org/international/cleanbydesign/transportation.asp.

92 "atmospheric emissions": International Maritime Organization, *International Shipping Facts and Figures—Information Resources on Trade, Safety, Security, Environment*, March 2012, no page numbers given.

92 In 2009: John Vidal, "Health Risks of Shipping Pollution Have Been 'Underestimated,'" *Guardian*, April 9, 2009.

92 The tug leaves: "She resembled an enormous and aquatic black beetle, surprised by the light, overwhelmed by the sunshine, trying to escape with ineffectual effort into the distant gloom of the land. She left a lingering smudge of smoke on the sky, and two vanishing trails of foam on the water. On the place where she had stopped a round black patch of soot remained, undulating on the swell—an unclean mark of the creature's rest." Joseph Conrad, *Narcissus*, Project Gutenberg e-book, accessed February 2012 via http://www.gutenberg.org/files/17731/17731-h/17731-h.htm.

93 In 2003: Robert D. Diaz and Rutger Rosenberg, "Spreading Dead Zones and Consequences for Marine Ecosystems," *Science*, vol. 321, no. 5891, August 15, 2008, pp. 926–29; United Nations Environment Program, GEO Year Book, 2003.

94 Concern at the: Even when seafarers report environmental crimes, they can be detained for months as material witnesses. Most cases in the United States involve a "magic pipe," an illegal hose discharging oily water overboard in contravention of MARPOL laws, which require oil to be separated and incinerated. Under a 1987 whistle-blowing law, seafarers who report crimes can earn a fortune. In 2012, Salvador Lopez, a crew member on Malta-flagged *Aquarosa*, was awarded $462,500 by a U.S. court for reporting that *Aquarosa* had discharged oily water and sludge into Baltimore waters using a magic pipe. Candus Thompson, "Judge Awards Whistle-Blower $462,500 in High-Seas Pollution Case," *Baltimore Sun*, April 18, 2012.

95 "It was the worst": *The Peninsula*, "Tanker Skipper Blames Spain at Oil Disaster Trial," November 14, 2012.

96 cancer deaths annually: J. J. Corbett, J. J. Winebrake, E. H. Green, Prasad Kasibhatla, V. Eyring, and A. Lauer, "Mortality from Ship Emissions: A Global Assessment," *Environmental Science and Technology*, vol. 4, no. 24, 2007, pp. 8512–18.

96 Corbett's predictions: In correspondence with James Corbett, he wrote that given the shipping recession and efforts to instill cleaner fuels, this may not have come to pass, but he had not reviewed the current global data.

96 Bunker fuel can: J. J. Winebrake, J. J. Corbett, E. H. Green, A. Lauer, and V. Eyring, "Mitigating the Health Impacts of Pollution from Oceangoing Shipping: An Assessment of Low-Sulfur Fuel Mandates," *Environmental Science and Technology*, vol. 43, no. 13 (July1, 2009), p. 4776.

97 The IMO, they noted: In 2011 the IMO did pass strong measures to cut sulfur content in fuel, both in ECAs and in general. Bunkers will have to cut sulfur content from 3.5 to 0.5 percent by 2020, as long as low-sulfur fuel supplies allow it. If they don't, the deadline will be 2024. House of Commons Environmental Audit Committee, *Reducing CO_2 and Other Emissions from Shipping*, fourth report of session 2008–2009, printed May 12, 2009, p. 3.

100 "Who knows": Andrew Scutro and David Brown, "Filipino Monkey behind threats?" *Navy Times*, January 11, 2008.

101 It was built by: http://www.suezcanal.gov.eg.

105 The European Union: EU weblog, "EU Must Act on Containers Lost at Sea," February 14, 2013.

106 The settlement was: Monterey Bay Aquarium Research Institute news release, "MBARI teams with Monterey Bay National Marine Sanctuary to Study Effects of Shipping Containers Lost at Sea," March 7, 2011.

106 "They were arguing": Maggie Koerth-Baker, "Under the Sea: Life on a Lost Shipping Container," *BoingBoing.net*, July 7, 2011, accessed February 2013 via http://boingboing.net/2011/07/07/under-the-sea-life-o.html.

107 Antares Shipping: Office of the Commissioner for Federal Judicial Affairs Canada, citation Ford Aquitaine Industries SAS v. Canmar Pride (The) (F.C.), 2005 FC 431, [2005] 4 F.C.R. 441, 31 March, 2005 Docket:T-1291-03.

6: High-Risk Area

112 The IRTC is: Congressional Research Service, *Piracy off the Horn of Africa*, April 27, 2011, p. 25.

112 It includes the IRTC: The Indian Ocean includes two major oil "chokepoints," in the Strait of Hormuz and the Suez Canal. Robert D. Kaplan, "Center Stage for the 21st Century: Power Plays in the Indian Ocean," *Foreign Affairs*, March/April 2009.

116 I tell him the latest: ICC International Maritime Bureau, Piracy and Armed Robbery Against Ships, Report for the Period 1 January–30 June 2010, p. 20.

117 Forty-two thousand: Nick Hopkins, "Outgunned Somali Pirates Can Hardly Believe Their Luck," *Guardian*, May 8, 2012.

117 If it has a helicopter: House of Commons Foreign Affairs Committee, *Piracy Off the Coast of Somalia*, Tenth Report of Session 2010–12, December 20, 2011, Ev. 13.

117 The pirates "did not": Ibid., Ev. 57.

119 On MV *Arillah*: Oceans Beyond Piracy, "The Human Cost of Somali Piracy," June 6, 2011, p. 15.

120 "saviors of the sea": Jay Bahadur, *Deadly Waters: Inside the Hidden World of Somalia's Pirates* (London: Profile Books, 2011), p. 15.

121 The U.S. Congress: Congressional Research Service, p. 19.

121 I find this smug: Marcus Rediker, *Villains of All Nations: Atlantic Pirates in the Golden Age* (Boston, MA: Beacon Press, 2004), p. 174.

121 Once his ransom: Plutarch does not specify that the talents were silver, but as a Greek writing for a Greek readership, where talents generally were silver, perhaps he didn't need to. Plutarch, *The Parallel Lives*, vol. 7, p. 443, accessed February 2013 from http://penelope.uchicago.edu/thayer/e/roman/texts /plutarch/lives/caesar*.html.

121 Colonel Frederick Philipse: Michael Scott Moore, "We Were Pirates Once, and Young: An American Way to Understand Somali Pirates," *New Republic*, October 22, 2011.

123 They then targeted: President of Puntland press release, October 22, 2011.

123 "in about a day": Robert Young Pelton, "Somali Pirates' Rich Returns," *Bloomberg Businessweek*, May 12, 2011.

123 against fishing vessels: Ibid.

123 In the words of: House of Commons Foreign Affairs Committee, *Piracy Off the Coast of Somalia*, Ev. 17.

125 Four years later: Matthias Gebauer and Dietmar Hipp, "Passengers Fought Pirates with Tables and Deck Chairs," *Spiegelonline*, April 28, 2009.

129 The same group: U.S. embassy cable captured by Wikileaks, accessed via www.cablegatesearch.net, cable reference 09PORTLOUISE146.

130 and intelligence gathering: Captain Alexander Martin, U.S. Marine Corps, "Pirates Beware: Force Recon Has Your Number," published on U.S. Naval Institute http://www.usni.org, July 24, 2010.

132 The United States has: "US Sentences Somali Pirates to Life," *Al Jazeera*, March 15, 2011.

132 The following year: Tom Hays, "Somali Pirate Sentenced in NYC to Over 33 Years in Prison," NBC, February 16, 2011.

133 "There was a stampede": Justin Penrose, "Prison Officers Swap Isle of Wight for the Seychelles . . . To Guard Somali Pirates," *Mirror*, February 12, 2012.

133 model prisoners: U.S. embassy cable via Wikileaks, accessed at http://www.cablegatesearch.net/cable.php?id=10PORTLOUIS44&q=high-seas-affairs.

136 paying his fees: The EU also provided computers, which swiftly went missing.

7: No-Man's-Land

139 none of these are piracy: Hugh Williamson, "Piracy at Sea: The Humanitarian Impact," presentation given at International Conference on Piracy at Sea, October 16–18, 2011, Malmo, Sweden.

140 "Yo-Ho-Toe": David Willetts, "Yo-Ho-Toe: Navy Nab Pirate with 24 Digits," *Sun*, February 6, 2012.

140 thin Somali in a yellow jumpsuit: *Indian Ocean with Simon Reeve, Kenya and the Horn of Africa*, BBC Two, released May 13, 2012.

140 "profit-maximising entrepreneurs": "The Economics of Piracy: Pirate Ransoms and Livelihoods Off the Coast of Somalia," *Geopolicity*, May 2011, p. ii.

140 $300,000 to kit out a pirate attack: Pelton, "Somali Pirates' Rich Returns."

141 one hundred most important people in shipping: *Lloyd's List*, "4. Garaad Mohammed, Pirate, Somalia Inc.," December 14, 2010, http://www.lloydslist.com/ll/incoming/article351642.ece.

141 hostages killed in 2011: "A Moment for Victims of Piracy At Sea," OceanusLive.org, January 1, 2012, http://www.oceanuslive.org/Main/ViewNews.aspx?uid=00000389.

141 violent assaults in South Africa: Oceans Beyond Piracy, "The Human Cost of Somali Piracy," p. 4.

141 amputated the hand of its captain: "Pirates Copy Al-Shabaab's Amputation Tactic," Somalia Report, January 24, 2012.

142 "detestable activity": House of Commons Transport Committee, Eighth Report, printed June 26, 2006, accessed http://www.publications.parliament.uk/pa/cm200506/cmselect/cmtran/1026/102604.htm#_jmp0_.

147 They hoped to "sneak through": Nancy Knudsen, "Released Hostage Sailors' Regrets—First Interview," Sail-World.com, October 28, 2011, http://www.sail-world.com/Asia/Released-hostage-sailors-regrets—first-interview/90054.

147 a gleeful article: "Somali Pirate Offers to Release Danish Family in Exchange for Hand of Daughter, 13," *Daily Mail*, March 28, 2011.

147 "it's like sailing out of Falmouth": Decca Aitkenhead, "Paul and Rachel Chandler: How We Survived Being Kidnapped by Somali Pirates," *Guardian*, October 30, 2011.

147 a 0.26 percent risk: George Kiourktsoglu, "Somali Piracy vs Flag of Attacked Vessel," University of Greenwich, 2010, supplied by author, available from http://uk.linkedin.com/pub/george-kiourktsoglou/13/bb6/a7.

148 fifty die each month: House of Commons Foreign Affairs Committee, *Piracy Off the Coast of Somalia*, Ev. 18.

149 250 days: Stephen Askins, a maritime lawyer at the London firm Ince & Co, has kept a rolling average of detention times for years: 250 days was among the highest averages. House of Commons Foreign Affairs Committee, *Piracy Off the Coast of Somalia*, Ev.7. Tanker figures from Stephen Askins.

154 When pirates came: Somalia Report, "Into the Heart of the Pirate Lair," May 13, 2011.

154 Being a pirate town: Anja Shortland, "Treasure Mapped: Using Satellite Imagery to Track the Developmental Effects of Somali Piracy," Chatham House Africa Program Paper, January 2012.

155 "this is a business": Pelton, "Somali Pirates' Rich Returns."

156 it was Budiga: Chirag's crewmate Sandeep Dangwal, who was also trussed and tortured, called Budiga "the nastiest pirate devil ever." Colin Freeman, "Somali Pirates Raise Ransom Stakes," *Telegraph*, May 4, 2011.

158 "the infinity of the sea": Allan Sekula, *Fish Story* (Frankfurt: Richter Verlag, 1995), p. 116.

160 This procedure: James Kraska, "Freakonomics of Maritime Piracy," *Brown Journal of World Affairs*, vol. 16, no. 2, Spring/Summer 2010, p. 114.

161 Harvard economists: The translator involved in the *Marida Marguerite* hijacking, Mohammed Saaili Shibin, also known as Khalif Ahmed Shibin or just Shibin, was convicted in a U.S. court in April 2012 for his part in the hijacking of the U.S. yacht *Quest*, in which four Americans were killed. He was also indicted for being the negotiator for the pirates holding *Marida Marguerite*. The Virginia court sentenced him to "to 10 concurrent life sentences for piracy, two consecutive life sentences for the use of a rocket-propelled grenade/automatic weapons during crimes of violence, 10 years consecutive on six counts charging discharge of a firearm during a crime of violence, and two 20-year sentences for the remaining counts of discharge of a firearm during a crime of violence." He also had to pay $5,408,000 in restitution. FBI Norfolk Division, press release, August 13, 2012.

162 Armed security: Michelle Wiese Bockman, "Armed Guards Can Help Cut Insurance Costs for Shipping Companies," *Bloomberg*, May 11, 2012.

162 India, meanwhile: Some 2.3 million fishermen work in the Indian Ocean and many carry weapons. Italy has objected to India's prosecution on the grounds that the fishermen were killed in international waters and because the marines are active-duty personnel. "Such a view," P. S. Gopinathan, a Kerala High Court judge, wrote in a May 29 judgment allowing the case to go forward, "will not merely be a bad precedent, but a grossly unjust one." Alan Katz, "Fighting Pirates Goes Awry with the Killings of Fishermen," *Bloomberg*, September 17, 2012.

8: Sanctuary

166   Overseas Filipinos: Lamvik, "The Filipino Seafarer," p.128.

167   "As a result": E. Kahveci, T. Lane, H. Sampson, "Transnational Seafarer Communities," SIRC, Cardiff University, March 2002, p. 9.

167   When the English king: A Commander, R.N., "Religion on Board Ship," *The Churchman*, vol. 19, no. 7, April 1905, p. 355.

168   opened a sailors' home: Royal Museums Greenwich, Port Cities, accessed January 2013 from http://www.portcities.org.uk/london/index-2.html.

168   In his history: L. A. G. Strong, *Flying Angel: The Story of the Mission to Seamen* (London: Methuen & Co., 1956).

168   Flogging was banned on: U.S. Navy, The Navy Department Library, accessed February 2013 from http://www.history.navy.mil/library/online/flogging.htm.

168   Until then, captains could: Greg Marquis, "Review of Brutality on Trial: 'Hellfire' Pedersen, 'Fighting' Hansen and the Seamen's Act of 1915, by E. Kay Gibson," *Law and Politics Book Review*, vol. 17, no. 1, January 2007, pp. 1–4.

169   It was a stunning example: Rousmaniere and Larom, *Anchored Within the Vail*.

170   "Boys who are sailing": "Port of Missing Men," *Lookout*, vol. 25, no. 5, Seamen's Church Institute of New York, May 1934.

171   "that effective friendliness": Royal Museums Greenwich, Port Cities.

171   first ever time ashore: Ng Sing, *Flying Angel, Port of London*, The Missions to Seamen, 1965.

171   Nearly two-thirds: E. Kahveci, "Port Based Welfare for Seafarers," SIRC, Cardiff University, 2007.

172   "A family reunion": Graham Cardwell, "Reggie Perrin Father Escapes Punishment," BBC News, June 8, 1999.

174   In 1942: *Lookout*, vol. 33, no. 7, July 1942.

174   The Port of London: Ng Sing, *Flying Angel, Port of London*.

178   "They can really help us": Kahveci, "Port Based Welfare for Seafarers," p. 22.

178   "It is nice to hear": Ibid., p. 25.

179   "gates more tightly": Arsham Mazaheri, "How the ISPS Code Affects Port and Port Activities," University College of Borås School of Engineering MSc thesis, 2008.

182   "under duress": "*Philipp* Crew 'Robbed' by Crewing Agent in Manila," ITF media release, October 25, 2011.

183   "We were just too hungry": Yevgenia Borisova, "Abandoned Crew Starves in City Port," *St. Petersburg Press*, 1995.

9: Animals Beneath

188   "'Shed tears'": Conrad, *Mirror on the Sea*, p. 79.

189   A crowd gathered: Bob Welch, "It's Still Whale of a Tale for Blubber Victim," *Eugene Register Guard*, January 14, 2008. For a video of the explosion and other background, http: www.theexplodingwhale.com.

190   ten thousand spectators: D. W. Laist, A. R. Knowlton, J. G. Mead, A. S. Collet, and M. Podesta, "Collisions Between Ships and Whales," *Marine Mammal Science*, vol. 17, no.1, 2006, pp. 35–75.

190   In June 2012: Port of Rotterdam Authority, press release, June 6, 2012.

191   policeman's clubs: Mr. Sevey also listed busks, back supporters, and forearm bones. List of items accessed December 2012 via http://www.scran.ac.uk /packs/exhibitions/learning_materials/webs/40/articles.htm.

195 Whales get entangled: Scott D. Kraus and Rosalind M. Rolland, eds, *The Urban Whale: North Atlantic Right Whales at the Crossroads* (Cambridge, MA: Harvard University Press, 2007), p. 382.

196 "the size of fleas": Ibid., p. 140.

197 "to sail it back": Euan Ferguson, "After a Day of Struggles, the London Whale Dies a Lonely Death," *Observer*, January 22, 2006.

197 Between 1970 and 2007: Kraus and Rolland, *Urban Whale*, p. 410.

201 three hours later: Michael Jasny, *Sounding the Depths II, The Rising Toll of Sonar, Shipping, and Industrial Ocean Noise on Marine Mammals*, Natural Resources Defense Council, November 2005, p. 3.

202 fish use hearing: "In 1962," Slabbekoorn writes, "Rachel Carson wrote about a 'silent spring' in the context of the detrimental impact of the use of pesticides on singing birds. Here we call attention to a 'noisy spring', and the possible detrimental impact of increasing levels of anthropogenic noise on fishes." H. Slabbekoorn et al, "A Noisy Spring: The Impact of Globally Rising Underwater Sound Levels on Fish," *Trends in Ecology and Evolution*, vol. 25, no.7, July 2010, pp. 419–27.

202 The movement of propellers: R. Leaper and M. R. Renilson, "A Review of Practical Methods for Reducing Underwater Noise Pollution from Large Commercial Vessels," *International Journal of Maritime Engineering*, vol. 227, April–June 2012.

203 3 decibels every decade: Andrew J. Wright and Lauren Highfill, eds., "Considerations of the Effects of Noise on Marine Mammals and Other Animals," *International Journal of Comparative Psychology*, vol. 20, no. 2–3, 2007, p. 127.

203 Every ten years: A. J. Wright, ed., "International Workshop on Shipping Noise and Marine Mammals," Okeanos–Foundation for the Sea, Hamburg, Germany, April 21–24, 2008.

203 a single seismic survey: Jasny, *Sounding the Depths II*, p. 29.

203 Shipping noise: Kraus and Rolland, *Urban Whale*, p. 326.

204 "For biologists": Ibid., pp. 235–36.

206 During the week: Rosalind M. Rolland et al., "Evidence that Ship Noise Increases Stress in Right Whales," *Proceedings of the Royal Society, Biological Sciences*, vol. 279, no. 1737, June 2012, pp. 2363–68.

10: Rescue

211 Ian McIntosh: Vice Admiral Ian Stewart McIntosh, oral interview, Imperial War Museum, recorded April 15, 1991, catalogue number 11950.

212 "peril on the sea": Marine Accident Investigation Branch, "Safety Digest 1," 2010, p. 7.

215 extremely difficult: Frank Laskier writes of convoy duty, "We wore our eyelids out, looking for submarines; we did watch and watch and watch and watch." Frank Laskier, *My Name Is Frank: A Merchant Seaman Talks* (London: Allen & Unwin, 1941), p. 48.

215 three hundred feet away: Of a crew of eighty-six, only six survived. In one lifeboat, two died from exposure in the first twenty-four hours, and two others drank seawater, went mad, and jumped overboard. Frank Golden and Michael Tipton, *Essentials of Sea Survival* (Champaign, IL: Human Kinetics, 2002), p.189.

217 When rescue arrived: The ship had delivered the world's first operational atom bomb to the island of Tinian on July 26, 1945. She was hit by two torpedoes fired by a Japanese submarine and sank in twelve minutes. It was the worst disaster in U.S. naval history. Survivors' stories are gathered on www.ussindianapolis.org.

218 a Cumbrian town: "Kendal's Ship in Dramatic Rescue," *North West Evening Mail*, August 16, 2007.

220 Even the best: Woodman, *Real Cruel Sea*, p. 43.

220 venereal disease: Ibid., p. 44.

220 supplies by sea: This is as true today as in 1941, when Winston Churchill wrote that "The whole power of the United States, to manifest itself, depends on the power to move ships and aircraft across the sea. Their mighty power is restricted; it is restricted by the very oceans which have protected them; the oceans which were their shield, have now become both threatening and a bar, a prison house through which they must struggle to bring armies, fleets, and air forces to bear upon the common problems we have to face." Quoted in Pierre Bélanger and Alexander Scott Arroyo, "Logistics Islands: The Global Supply Archipelago and the Topologics of Defense," *Prism*, vol. 3, no. 4, September 2012, p. 57.

220 Heavy weapons: The last time the UK military conscripted merchant ships was in the 1982 Falklands conflict, where more than fifty merchant vessels became STUFT, or Ships Taken Up From Trade. The most famous were the passenger lines *Canberra* and *QEII*, converted into troop carriers, but there were also tugs, ferries, and fishing trawlers.

221 rescue and cleanup fleet: Offshore oil rigs are treated as oceangoing ships in legal terms. *Deepwater* was flagged to the Marshall Islands, along with thirty-four other rigs owned by Transocean. Andrew Clark, "BP Oil Registration Raised in Congress over Safety Concerns," *Guardian*, May 30, 2010. Tom Hamburger and Kim Geiger, "Foreign Flagging of Offshore Rigs Skirts U.S. Safety Rules," *Los Angeles Times*, June 14, 2010.

221 "to England with tea": Frank Laskier, *Log Book* (London: Allen & Unwin, 1942), p. 56.

222 uniformed men were not: Terry Hughes and John Costello, *The Battle of the Atlantic* (New York: Dial Press, 1977), quoted in *American Merchant Marine at War*, accessed February 2013 at http://www.usmm.org/battleatlantic.html.

222 In Canada: Woodman, *Real Cruel Sea*, p. 62.

222 "He's been dive-bombed": Laskier, *My Name Is Frank*, p. 28.

223 "food for their Mum's rations": Bill Linskey, *No Longer Required: My War in the Merchant Marine* (London: Pisces Press, 1999), p. 111.

223 "the whole effort fails": President Franklin D. Roosevelt, letter to Admiral Emory S. Land, May 22, 1941.

224 "None of us": Peter Cremer, *U333: The Story of a U-boat Ace* (London: Triad Grafton, 1986), p. 75

224 before breakfast: Rousmaniere and Larom, *Anchored Within the Vail*, pp. 74–75.

224 Among the four: Homer Strickler, *New York Sun*, December 2, 1941, quoted in Seamen's Church Institute, *Lookout*, vol. 33, no.1, January 1942.

225 "With his mind": Seamen's Church Institute, *Lookout*, "Sea Heroes," vol. 33, no. 6, June 1942.

225 Semenov survived: Owen Edwards, "A Compass Saves the Crew," *Smithsonian*, September 2009.

225 "rescue from the sea": Editorial, *New York Times*, June 22, 1942.

226 "General Stores": Jack Edmead's account to the Admiralty, ADM199/2143, is reproduced on http://www.sscityofcairo.co.uk along with accounts from survivors Dr. Douglas Quantrill, Gladys Usher, Angus MacDonald, Joan Redl, Marjorie and Donald Miller, Eileen Sims, Dulcie Kendall, and Robert Faulds.

228 "sorry for sinking you": Ralph Barker, *Goodnight, Sorry for Sinking You: The Story of the SS City of Cairo* (London: Collins, 1984), p. 72.

229 "swamping boats": Stephen Crane, "The Open Boat: A Tale Intended to Be after the Fact. Being the Experience of Four Men Sunk from the Steamer Commodore," *Scribner's Magazine* 21 (May 1894), p. 728.

229 insomnia: Woodman, *Real Cruel Sea*, p. 169.

230 "grew on them": Ibid., p. 376.

230 "'quite dangerous'": Linskey, *No Longer Required*, p. 98.

230 When *Calchas* sank: Woodman, *Real Cruel Sea*, p. 300.

231 "Nobody gave a damn": Norman Watts, oral interview, Imperial War Museum sound archive.

232 "No water": Woodman, *Real Cruel Sea*, p.167.

232 In a lecture: William H. Allen, "Thirst. Can Shipwrecked Men Survive if They Drink Seawater?," *Natural History*, December 1956.

233 "Whenever a seaman": Seamen's Church Institute, *Lookout*, vol. 33, no. 3, March 1942.

235 Now they are at least: Casualty statistics vary because of the disparate nature of the merchant wartime fleet. *New York Times*, "Wartime Merchant Seamen to Get Veterans' Status," January 21, 1988.

235 who sailed on Arctic convoys: Three thousand men died in the Arctic convoys. Winston Churchill called the convoy route "the worst journey in the world." The first medals, a newly created award named the Arctic Star, were handed out by Prime Minister David Cameron in March 2013, seventy years after the convoys ended. BBC News, "Convoy Veterans Given First Arctic Star Medals," March 19, 2013, http://www.bbc.co.uk/news/uk-england-hampshire-21845753.

235 "back at sea": Laskier, *My Name Is Frank*, p. 65.

11: Disembark

237 joint by joint: Peter Gwin, "Dark Passage," *National Geographic*, October 2007.

238 "excluding transit": Lloyd's Market Association Joint War Committee, "Hull War, Piracy, Terrorism and Related Perils Listed Areas," JWLA/020, March 28, 2012, accessed February 2013 from http://www.lmalloyds.com/Web /market_places/marine/JWC/Joint_War.aspx.

239 "If you were to fall": Richard Henry Dana, *Two Years Before the Mast*, Project Gutenberg e-book, accessed January 2013 from http://www.gutenberg.org /cache/epub/4277/pg4277.html.

242 1.7-mile chokepoint: U.S. Energy Information Administration, "World Oil Transit Chokepoints," August 22, 2012.

244 maritime training: Philip C. Tubeza, "EU May Ban PH Seamen Over Training Deficiencies," *Philippine Daily Inquirer*, March 8, 2012.

244 a provision about Internet gambling: The Unlawful Internet Gambling Enforcement Act appears as Title VIII in the Security and Accountability of Every Port Act of 2006, accessed from http://www.gpo.gov/fdsys/pkg/PLAW -109publ347/html/PLAW-109publ1347.htm.

FURTHER READING

Auden, W. H. *The Enchafed Flood or the Romantic Iconography of the Sea*. London: Faber & Faber, 1951.

Baboulene, David. *Jumping Ships: The Global Misadventures of a Cargo Ship Apprentice*. Chichester, UK: Summersdale, 2009.

Bahadur, Jay. *Deadly Waters: Inside the Hidden World of Somalis' Pirates*. London: Profile Books, 2011.

Barker, Ralph. *Goodnight, Sorry for Sinking You: The Story of the S.S. City of Cairo*. Glasgow: William Collins & Sons, 1984.

Buckley, Christopher. *Steaming to Bamboola*. London: Flamingo, 1983.

Bullen, Frank Thomas. *The Men of the Merchant Service, Being the Polity of the Mercantile Marine for 'Longshore Readers*. London: John Murray, 1900.

Crane, Stephen. "The Open Boat." E-book, Electronic Text Centre, University of Virginia Library, 1995.

Cremer, Peter. *U333: The Story of a U-boat Ace*. London: Triad Grafton, 1986.

De Botton, Alain. *The Pleasures and Sorrows of Work*. London: Hamish Hamilton, 2009.

Dickens, Charles. *On Travel*. Ed. Pete Orford. London: Hesperus Press, 2009.

Ebbesmeyer, Curtis, and Eric Scigliano. *Flotsametrics and the Floating World: How One Man's Obsession with Runaway Sneakers and Rubber Ducks Revolutionized Ocean Science*. New York: Harper Collins, 2009.

Ekin, Des. *The Stolen Village: Baltimore and the Barbary Pirates*. Dublin: The O'Brien Press, 2008.

Evans, Bob. *A Dog Collar in the Docks*. Birkenhead, UK: Countryvise, 2002.

———. *Mersey Mariners*. Birkenhead, UK: Countryvise, 2002.

Fitzgibbon, Theodora. *A Taste of the Sea in Food and Pictures*. Vancouver: David & Charles, 1977.

George, Bill (the Bosun). *On the Bridge: A Story of King Billy and the Derby Grange*. Self-published, no date.

Golden, Frank, and Michael Tipton. *Essentials of Sea Survival*. Champaign, IL: Human Kinetics, 2002.

Hanson, Neil. *The Custom of the Sea: The Shocking True Tale of Shipwreck and Cannibalism on the High Seas*. London: Corgi Books, 1999.

Hardberger, Max. *Seized: A Sea Captain's Adventures Battling Pirates and Recovering Stolen Ships in the World's Most Troubled Waters*. London: Nicholas Brealey Publishing, 2010.

Heaton Vorse, Mary. *Time and the Town: A Provincetown Chronicle*. New Brunswick, NJ: Rutgers University Press, 1991.

Hohn, Donovan. *Moby-Duck: The True Story of 28,800 Bath Toys Lost at Sea and of the Beachcombers, Oceanographers, Environmentalists and Fools, Including the Author, Who Went in Search of Them*. New York: Farrar, Straus and Giroux, 1990.

Johnson, Captain Charles. *A General History of the Robberies and Murders of the Most Notorious Pirates*. London: Conway Maritime Press, 1998.

Kemp, Peter, ed. *The Oxford Companion to Ships and the Sea*. Oxford: Oxford University Press, 1988.

Koeppel, Dan. *Banana: The Fate of the Fruit that Changed the World*. London: Plume, 2009.

Kraus, Scott D., and Rosalind M. Rolland. *The Urban Whale: North Atlantic Right Whales at a Crossroads*. Cambridge, MA: Harvard University Press, 2007.

Langewiesche, William. *The Outlaw Sea: Chaos and Crime on the World's Oceans*. London: Granta, 2005.

Laskier, Frank. *Log Book*. Aberdeen: Aberdeen University Press, 1949.

———. *My Name Is Frank: A Merchant Seaman Talks*. London: Allen & Unwin, 1941.

Levinson, Marc. *The Box: How the Shipping Container Made the World Smaller and the World Economy Bigger*. Princeton: Princeton University Press, 2006.

Lewis, Val. *Ship's Cats in War and Peace*. Shepperton, UK: Nauticalia, 2001.

Linskey, Bill. *No Longer Required: My War in the Merchant Marine*. London: Pisces Press, 1999.

Macdonald, Kenneth. *Three Dark Days*. Isle of Lewis, Scotland: Acair, 1999.

McPhee, John. *Looking for a Ship*. New York: Farrar, Straus and Giroux, 1990.

Melville, Herman. *Moby Dick: or, the White Whale*. Kindle edition [1851].

Missions to Seamen, The. *Convoy X.K.234 Arrives: The War-time Story of the "Flying Angel."* London: The Missions to Seamen, 1947.

Parker, Matthew. *Hell's Gorge: The Battle to Build the Panama Canal*. London: Arrow Books, 2008.

Parker, Tony. *Lighthouse*. London: Eland, 2006.

Phillips, Richard. *A Captain's Duty: Somali Pirates, Navy SEALs, and Dangerous Days at Sea*. New York: Hyperion, 2010.

Raban, Jonathan. *The Oxford Book of the Sea*. Oxford: Oxford University Press, 1992.

Rediker, Marcus. *Villains of All Nations: Atlantic Pirates in the Golden Age*. Boston, MA: Beacon Press, 2004.

Roberts, Calum. *Ocean of Life: How Our Seas Are Changing*. London: Allen Lane, 2012.

Roland, Alex, W. Jeffrey Bolster, and Alexander Keyssar. *The Way of the Ship: America's Maritime History Reenvisioned, 1600–2000*. Hoboken, NJ: John Wiley & Sons, 2008.

Rousmaniere, Leah Robinson, and Peter Larom. *Anchored Within the Vail: A Pictorial History of the Seamen's Church Institute*. New York: The Seamen's Church Institute of New York and New Jersey, 1995.

Sekula, Allan. *Fish Story*. Düsseldorf: Richter Verlag, 1995.

Sekulich, Daniel. *Ocean Titans: Journeys in Search of the Soul of a Ship*. Guildford CT: The Lyons Press, 2007.

———. *Terror on the Seas: True Tales of Modern-Day Pirates*. New York: Thomas Dunne Books, 2009.

Sharpsteen, Bill. *The Docks*. Berkeley: University of California Press, 2011.

Smith, Angela (ed). *Gender and Warfare in the Twentieth Century: Textual Representations*. Manchester: Manchester University Press, 2004.

Stopford, Martin. *Maritime Economics*, 3rd edition. London: Routledge, 2009.

Trotter, Henry. *Sugar Girls and Seamen: A Journey into the World of Dockside Prostitution in South Africa*. Athens: Ohio University Press, 2011.

Winchester, Simon. *The Atlantic: A Vast Ocean of a Million Stories*. London: HarperPress, 2010.

Woodman, Richard. *The Real Cruel Sea: The Merchant Navy in the Battle of the Atlantic, 1939–1943*. London: John Murray, 2004.

ACKNOWLEDGMENTS

First, my thanks to Captain Glenn Wostenholme and the officers and crew of *Maersk Kendal*, who were kind and impeccable hosts for more than nine thousand nautical miles. Kate Sanderson, publicist for Maersk Line at the time, arranged my trip, and Claire Sneddon, Kate's successor, answered countless follow-up questions. Thank you. June Thomas, then my editor at *Slate*, published a four-part series from my trip on *Kendal*. From the shipping industry, I have had countless helpers and advisers, principally Alastair Evitt, Grant Hunter of BIMCO, Clay Maitland, Janet Porter, Gavin van Marle, and Captain Kuba Szymanski. Michelle Wiese Bockman, Bloomberg's highly capable shipping correspondent, has been remarkably and consistently generous with her knowledge. My online friends Glen Forbes and David Rider, of OCEANUS-Live and Neptune Maritime Security, respectively, have been illuminating and expansive with their insights into piracy, security, and shipping in general. Captain Quentin Oates of EU-NAVFOR arranged my trip on *Vasco da Gama*, and the men and women of the *Marinha*

Portugesa were kind enough to tolerate both me and my odd dietary requirements. (Apologies to the flight crew of Bacardi that I never bought them the crate of beer they requested.)

Father Colum Kelly has welcomed me several times to Immingham, and I thank him for introducing me to the fascinating world of a port that I would otherwise have driven past without a backward look. The Mission to Seafarers has provided knowledge and archives and also trustingly lent me books; the Seamen's Church Institute of New York generously sent me a copy of its official history. Thank you to the International Transport Workers' Federation staff, including Roy Paul, Tom Holmer, Sam Dawson, and others, who have patiently put up with my questions and interview requests for the last few years. I spent a fascinating day with the tug company McAllister in New York City, which never made it into the book. But my thanks nonetheless to Buckley McAllister and his father, Brian, as well as to the tug crew who took me out to see New York City from a new and beautiful angle, from its working waters. (Especially memorable: the tug engineer with a hinge tattooed on the crook of his elbow. Why? "Well have you ever seen one? No? That's why.") Apologies to anyone who has helped me and here gone unthanked: it is not deliberate but still delinquent on my part.

These have been a difficult few years, and this was a difficult book to write. Not because of the subject matter, but because the research and writing were being done while my stepfather was suffering with Alzheimer's, and while my family were seeing him through a rapid deterioration into violence, sectioning, and then death. Consequently I am deeply grateful to my wonderful agents Erin Malone and Cathryn Summerhayes of William Morris Endeavor Entertainment, who throughout the hard times have been supportive, patient, and never not kind. My editors, Riva Hocherman of Metropolitan Books and Philip Gwyn Jones of Portobello Books, have endured delays and more delays with forbearance and compassion. Thank you. I thank all my friends who have had to share the load, notably Richard, Georgia, and Jodi Stanley, who had to live at close quarters to it, and also Cathy and Shaun Faulkner, Elliot Elam, Ruth Metzstein, Robert Sam Anson, Tom Ridgway, and many, many more. A team of readers found errors and vastly improved the manuscript: Michelle Wiese Bockman, Simon Winchester, Robert Sam Anson, Glen Ford, Sheila Wainwright, Molly Mackey, Ruth Metzstein, and reader-copyeditor Tom Ridgway. My family, Sheila Wainwright, Simon George, Nicholas, Julie, James, and Alice Wainwright, Allison Bramall, and Patrice and Amelia Green: thank you. John Michael Wainwright, 1938–2011: Rest in peace.

INDEX

Page numbers in *italics* refer to illustrations.